Greg And Doc,
TWO SOULS
Surrounded By
BADLANDS

GREG AND DOC, TWO SOULS SURROUNDED BY BADLANDS

A Memoir of Adventure, Discovery, Anguish And Triumph

GREGORY HAGENSTON

CITI OF
BOOKS

CITIOFBOOKS, INC.
3736 Eubank NE Suite A1
Albuquerque, NM 87111-3579
www.citiofbooks.com
Hotline: 1 (877) 389-2759
Fax: 1 (505) 930-7244

Ordering Information:

Quantity sales. Special discounts are available on quantity purchases by corporations, associations, and others. For details, contact the publisher at the address above.

Printed in the United States of America.

ISBN-13:   Softcover   979-8-89391-515-0
               eBook   979-8-89391-516-7

Library of Congress Control Number: 2025901373

TABLE OF CONTENTS

PREFACE

Out of the blue, Dr. Hiatt's wife (Lois) called me one day and asked if I could take over for Doc. She said he just can't handle the public speaking, field trips and slide shows anymore. He has been doing this public service for years and is all worn out. Somebody else needs to assume the mantle. I was saddened, as we all know no one can carry on forever, all good things must come to an end. As flattering as it was to be considered, the reality is that no one can replace Dr. Hiatt, he is one of a kind. That's just the way it is. Glendive and Makoshika have been blessed by him unselfishly sharing his interests and talents with us. I knew there was no way I could help the situation, and it was painful to tell Lois I was not a candidate for Doc's replacement.

In about the year 2016 I was talking with my friend Jeff Nesset and he wanted an explanation about a "Hiatt" event. I hesitated while I thought about how to respond, and then stated; "You know, this will take too long to explain." and then jokingly said, "You'll have to read the book."

In another instance I was commenting to my wife Evelyn about a "Hiatt something" and she bluntly stated, "Well, nobody really cares about that." And she was right, nobody will know what it is all about, so of course no one will care about something they don't know anything about. It was at that time I decided I needed to figure out how to tell the story of Greg and Doc. At first I was thinking about a historical sign board of some kind, but that won't work, there is too much to tell.

So in honor of Lois Hiatt, who asked me to somehow preserve Dr. Hiatt's legacy, I humbly vowed to myself to record what I can of his contributions to Makoshika. And when their daughter Bette Payton so generously offered to give me his tote boxes full of Makoshika history, a book project was born.

I admit, with no writing background I cannot lay claim to be a writer. Much of what you read is correspondence to and from Dr. Hiatt, and along with his meticulous notes; the history of Makoshika takes shape in his own words. What you read from me is delivered to the pages of print solely through my heart. My only hope is that the reader enjoys this journey as much as I have.

AUTHOR'S NOTE

Spelling and punctuation differs only slightly from the original text of Dr. Hiatt's correspondence.

Here and there corrections were made for clarity and smooth reading, otherwise the text is "as is" in the original letters. In some cases, to capture authenticity, words are misspelled and notated as so. The words Maco Sica are spelled differently depending on the era and the party doing the spelling. At times I have summarized correspondence; however I find it best to print out the letters as written.

ACKNOWLEDGEMENTS:

There are no words that can fully express my appreciation to Bette Payton for her contributions to this project. Without her having saved Dr. Hiatt's work, none of this would have been possible. From the bottom of my heart, thank you Bette!

I appreciate the input and clarification of events that some of the "characters" in my writing helped me with. Special thanks to my wife, Evelyn, who has been much help along the way. My brother Dennis has been one of the recipients of my chapters as they developed, and I appreciate his input. Pat Norton, Jeff Nesset, Mike McCrate, Herb Meland, Wes Aardahl, John Harmala, my sister Audre Thom, along with our daughters Angie McKenzie and Sarah Olson, have all contributed as being part of the story or contributing their thoughts, and are much appreciated.

The two writers I sent chapters to as they developed were my "Auntie" Juliana Howard and locally Avis Anderson. I greatly appreciate their encouragement.

I would like to thank the Swanson family, Jim and Carol, for reading my first chapter and letting me know I had something there. I thank Scott and Lisa Swanson for sharing the history of the Glendive Greenhouse.

The Glendive Ranger-Review and Glendive Broadcasting have had a huge impact on Makoshika and Dr. Hiatt clipped many related articles from the newspaper and mentions the radio station as the "Voice of Makoshika". The Billings Gazette is another newspaper that earned many a clipping over the years.

And last but not least, my publishing consultant Jamie Belt set me on the right course and guided me along the way during the daunting process of putting a book together.

DEDICATION

This book is dedicated to Dr. R. W. Hiatt. A true renaissance man, he cradled Makoshika from its fragile beginning to its maturity as a State Park. Without his meticulous record keeping the rich historical details of Makoshika Park would be long lost.

A special mention goes to Clifford Harsh, who was one of the early pioneers of the park, and most importantly, he first introduced Dr. Hiatt to the badlands.

PROLOGUE

August 25, 2013 (midmorning)

The small group of mourners, after a difficult and hazardous ascent to the summit of the badlands ridge, began to disband their group in search of a safe route to descend, when suddenly, all stopped in their tracks to the shrill sound of a referee's whistle. On the skyline above and southwest of the group, I stand. Dangling from a lanyard around my neck, the orange dog whistle, having just given several staccato blasts, comes to rest on my chest. Right arm outstretched, I wave happily, hoping to call attention to my specific location. Lily, a yellow Lab and trusted hiking companion, gives me a puzzled look.

Doc Hiatt's ashes are scattered from a small plastic container—a film canister. With bowed head I utter a short prayer. The mourners, from where I stand, appear as little plastic soldiers stuck in the dirt beneath my feet. Momentarily having their undivided attention, they begin moving again, gradually scattering in different directions. Oh no, they don't know the best return route. Scrambling down from the top to guide the group, I'm too late —some had already hiked over the edge of the ridge. A young family with dad hoisting a small child about neck and shoulders, having departed from sight, are on their own for the climb down. Catching up to the small remaining group, I take the lead.

French fur trappers had a phrase they used for the badlands, which when interpreted says "bad lands to travel across." Native Americans had a shorter way of describing this land. "Maco Sica" was their way of saying "land bad." These lands are eroded canyons, cliffs, and buttes with colored layers of strata, shades of gray, tan and brown, mostly of sandstone and clay which are blistering hot in the summer and bitterly cold in the winter.[1] Coal seams, iron pyrite, gypsum, sulfur pockets, red baked clay the locals will tell you is scoria, leaf imprints, Late Cretaceous fossils, and the infamous Cretaceous/Tertiary boundary which is easily discernible as the highest continuous coal seam, make this area a dreamland for the geologist and paleontologist.

Doc Hiatt first showed this fossil boundary to me, where below the coal seam dinosaur fossils are found, and above the coal seam only fossils like fish, crocodile, and turtle are present.

Having hiked in Makoshika regularly for 50-plus years, I have my badlands sea legs; however, the guests here today do not have that luxury. There is no such thing as a trail to follow for our hike down, and we certainly don't want to go down the way we came up, as hair-raising and exhausting as it was. Everyone started out with a bottle of water for the hike, and by now the refreshing glugs are long gone and seem only a distant memory. The heat of the day is becoming intense, and worse yet we are on the sunny side of the hills with not a breath of breeze to cool the sweat. The age of the group ranges from an infant, to us pushing elderly—me being in my early sixties. There is no way a Jeep or a horse could get up to where we are— this terrain fit for a mountain goat. The surefooted Audubon bighorn sheep that used to roam these badlands would feel at home on our trail.[2] One thing is certain: there is always a preferred route up and down these hills. A pressing problem is not having scouted out the best way to go; it will have to be a trial-and-error descent. As I peer along the edge trying to find the way down without getting caught on a cliff, and always wary of the rattlesnakes which love this habitat, I try to remember how far to the south to travel along the ridge top to find the area that has sloughed off some cliffs making an easier climb. Unknown to my small group, the others accidentally find the best route and are well on their way to the base of the hills. Lily is tugging on her retractable leash, sniffing, panting, and leading the way with vigor. Having already warned everyone about rattlesnakes when we first began our trek, pointing out the snakebite scar above Lily's right eye and describing how her head swelled like a basketball from the venom, we trod carefully. Fortunately for the dog, a precautionary snakebite vaccine and annual booster shot probably saved her life. I imagine my guests giving a thought if there would be enough time to get down and to the hospital for the anti-venom to save them. As we drop over the ridge the immediate concern is staying afoot. The small rocks and the crumbly clay give a sensation of trying to navigate over marbles on glass. The footing is precarious. I have the right idea, but don't quite go far enough south along the ridge, so as we start down, the terrain becomes steeper and steeper until, to my dismay, we are navigating ourselves along a series of small cliffs and ledges with ten to twenty-foot drops in between. The rock hammers and walking sticks I passed out earlier are earning their keep. My favorite stick is a diamond willow rod about five and a half feet long. It has a short rawhide strap attached to the top and has been beautifully sandblasted and varnished. A gift from my brother-in-law, I added one more accessory to the willow by embedding a strong magnet to the top end of the handle. Eyeing a suspect stone, I twirl the handle and check the rock for magnetic effects. Is it a meteorite?

The skinned and bleeding knees of at least one mourner attest to the fact that long pants are always a good idea when hiking in the badlands. I stand on a precarious ledge, and with my palms pushed against tennis shoe soles above me to save the poor soul from falling below me, we gradually make it past the drop-off without disaster. I point out the buzzard circling overhead. My guests by now are in no mood for morbid comedy. Now here's another peril. To keep from sliding down out of control, the safest-looking handhold appears as harmless sagebrush. Actually this shrub has prickly leaves, ready to pierce palms with thorny stems. Eventually all are down safely, however, done in by the heat, little-used muscles, and lack of adequate hydration. Like the African wildebeest stampeding to the scent of a waterhole, the mourners lunge across the short grass prairie, up and down the gullies and to the side of my house, instinctively finding the hydrant and hose. As I bring up the rear with the stragglers, the scene in front of us is one of cool well water bursting from the hose end and splashing across the head and necks of the first arrivals. Soon we are sitting around the front porch glugging ice water and iced tea to our heart's content. We reminisce about Doc and Makoshika. Our hike is described by Frank, our elder hiker, as a death march. Life is great! Still tired but refreshed, all feel accomplished. Not much is said about my purpose for dragging them up the ridge.

The wooden pole is there, at the base of the badlands; several in the group saw it. It measures eighteen feet long and rests on three and four-foot sections of three-inch plastic sewer pipe. My plans are explained when we briefly meet on top of the ridge, before Lily and I take off on the double, with dog whistle and film canister for the final ascent, having invited others to follow, to no avail.

1.	https://www.legendsofamerica.com/sd-badlands/ (online publication)

2.	P.A. Norton – Audubon sheep skull found in Makoshika

CHAPTER 1

Maco Sica

Where the wild coyotte[sic] howls out his woes

To the northern lights and the frozen snows.

The <u>*Authoritative*</u>*,* <u>*Definitive*</u> *and Chronological Rise and Fall of Maco Sica*

Maco Sica

THE SAGA OF THE BADLANDS

By G. W. Copping (1954)

There are strange things to see where the cedars grow
In the Badlands of the West.
Where Glendive stands in the shadow
Of the butte called Hungry Joe.

Where Old Sitting Bull was monarch
In the days of long ago.
Where never again will the war hoop ring
While the Warriors circle the wagon train.

Where the wild coyotte[sic] howls out his woes
To the northern lights and the frozen snows.
Where the artifact of ancient men is scattered hereabout
And the fosseled[sic] remains of the dinasour[sic] slowly weathering out.

Where the silhouette of the Badlands in the early morning dawn
With the morning sun a shining 'neath the rim:
'Tis a picture you'll remember though you've been a long time gone
From the Valley of the Scenic Yellowstone.

Where a tender foot would soon get lost
In a maze of deep ravines.
With the Yellowstone River flowing by
Like a silent hopeless dream.

Now this is the end of my story
Of a weird, fantastic land.
The Maco Sica of old Montana
In the great Historic West.

The Lakota Sioux moved into the western plains during the late 18th century. The rough and difficult-to-traverse terrain they referred to as Maco Sica has been translated as "land bad" or "eroded land."

1930

Many years ago Glendive pioneer Andrew Larson is credited with naming Maco Sica Park.

Late in the 1930s, the Work Projects Administration (WPA) built the main roads and the tributary car trails in the badlands located southeast of Glendive.

2013

In a rental car, as my wife and I are on a special one-day vacation to visit a Civil War battlefield prior to a weekend of meetings in Memphis, the highway dips into and out of Mississippi. My first time in the state of Mississippi, it feels special. We stop at a small restaurant and enjoy several tall glasses of sweet tea from a bottomless glass pitcher. Today I learned the sad news: Dr. R. W. Hiatt has passed away.

As the car skirts the border of Mississippi and Tennessee and rolls on toward the Shiloh battlefield, my mind is whirring in reminiscences. I remember taking the long hollow-sounding steps up to Doc Hiatt's optometry office. I remember sitting in his office looking at the large black- and-white aerial photograph of the Makoshika badlands, the familiar scent of warm plastic as he stirs the temple frames of my glasses in the heated sand, meticulously adjusting for a perfect fit. The signature red socks he wore earned a ribbing he enjoyed—"Red Socks Doc"—however, through the work he did to help establish first Maco Sica and then Makoshika Park, and the subsequent years of promotion and educational contributions, he acquired the well-deserved nickname "Mr. Makoshika." No one that ever met him will forget the boisterous laugh that triggered a bent torso, arms stretched until his fingers brushed his shoes.

Born in Kansas in 1922, Robert W. Hiatt had an older sister and no brothers. At the age of eight his family moved to Dickinson, North Dakota.[1] He was a talented basketball player, a trombonist and lover of the outdoors. Curiosity and nature, combined with his intellect, molded hobbies into a passion of enthusiastic botanical, geological, ornithological, and paleontological endeavors. Bob inherits his college professor father's intellect, attending college for optometry in Chicago. He marries Lois in 1943 and soon after is enlisted in the army. After a stint in the service he returns to Dickinson with intentions of setting up his optometry practice in Bismarck.

1. Obituary

———— ∞◦C/∾◦∞ ————

1945

After teaching in Sidney for 13 ½ years, Clifford Harsh moves to Glendive and runs a Studebaker garage.

———— ∞◦C/∾◦∞ ————

1947

At the age of 25, after as Doc says, "a 45-minute exploratory visit to Glendive," the family decides Glendive will be their new home.[2] Doc is first introduced to Maco Sica, Glendive's badlands park, by local businessman Cliff Harsh, who was the most active Glendive Chamber of Commerce member in promoting the park and its development. One of Doc's favorite people, Cliff loves the park's rare beauty. Hiatt's first car, a Studebaker Champion, is purchased from Cliff, and his only house in Glendive is also bought through Cliff, a real-estate agent.

2. Book: *Our Times, Our Lives*

1949

The Studebaker garage operated by Clifford Harsh is destroyed by fire.

July 1, 1953

By an act of the 1953 Montana Legislature, the State Park Commission was dissolved and its powers, duties, and activities were transferred, effective July 1, to the State Highway Commission. The purpose of the Highway Commission for Park Division Affairs is to conserve the scenic, historic, archaeological, and recreational resources of this state, and to provide for their use and enjoyment and contribute to the cultural, recreational, and economic life of the people and their health. With an extremely limited Park Division budget, the State Highway Commission reports to the Governor they have directed their efforts to accomplishing these objectives, pleading that with a more adequate budget they could build up the park system to be a real credit to the state.

July 20, 1953

As chairman of the Chamber of Commerce Maco Sica Park Committee, Cliff Harsh can take credit for encouraging Mr. and Mrs. A. J. McCarty to donate land through the county, suitable for campsites, to the state for a park. Of the reported 56,000 acres of badlands south of Glendive, the State Park Division will have title to 160 acres, which includes most of the switchbacks and a general area suitable for picnic tables. The well-known McCarty cabin lies on adjoining land.

Vernon Samuelson, Chairman of the Board of County Commissioners in Dawson County, signed, sealed, and delivered the indenture deed between the county and the state of Montana for the land to establish the state park, subject to all established public road easements. This deed numbered 246552 to be filed by County Clerk L. C. Elliot is a monumental act to forever put the eastern Montana badlands near Glendive on the map as a tourist destination.

Ashley C. Roberts is the Deputy State Park Director in Helena.

August 19, 1953

All weather roads for Montana's newest state park are one of the first priorities. Maintaining, improving, and replacing roads face one major simple obstacle. Money! Funds that are raised for gravel on the Maco Sica lower road and the excavation of the red baked clay from some of the hillsides on top sufficed in transforming the dirt roads from impassable in wet weather to passable. The locals warmly refer to the pinkish red clay as scoria. There is nothing more pleasant than a leisurely drive on the way to a picnic, a hike, or simply a sightseeing tour over the red scoria trails to the lookouts in the park.

In the *Glendive Daily Ranger*, a short article is titled "Maco Sica Road in Top Condition." Reported by Cliff Harsh, he explains the road is now passable in all weather after spreading gravel over the gumbo patches on the two big hills, and more gravel work will be done this summer. Minutes from a Chamber of Commerce meeting summarize the efforts of the Maco Sica Park Committee. A thousand dollars in cash and labor donations were solicited for road improvements. New signs were erected, making it easier for tourists to find their way to the park. Chairman Harsh reports that the State Park Commission assured that everything possible would be done to make this new state park one of Montana's major attractions. State Park Director Ashley Roberts has visited the park and is most enthusiastic over the possibilities it offers.

The Committee recommends every effort to follow up the good work of the past year and promote Maco Sica Park at every opportunity.

The Maco Sica Park Committee takes on a project of conducting a feasibility study to determine whether a loop road through the park entering from Highway 10 east of Glendive to meet with the present park road would be possible.

⋙⋘

January 1954

The new State Park Director, Ashley Roberts, apologizes for being unable to use the correct pronunciation of Maco Sica at the annual Chamber of Commerce banquet.

The Maco Sica Park Committee decides to establish an authoritative pronunciation. The only local source of authority is a Chamber of Commerce brochure describing the Glendive area. The publication says Maco Sica is the Sioux Indians' name for badlands and is pronounced "Mah-ko Shee-ka." By word of mouth, publicly and privately the Committee begins to emphasize that pronunciation and KXGN uses the same pronunciation on the radio, which helps immeasurably.

⋙⋘

April 26, 1954

Doc Hiatt writes a letter to Art Selke, Ph.D., a geologist at Dickinson State Teachers College.

⋙⋘

April 29, 1954

A letter signed by Ashley Roberts, the State of Montana Highway Commission Park Division Director, to Bill Vondrashek, the Glendive Chamber of Commerce Manager, formally authorizes representatives of the Glendive Chamber of Commerce to pick up six picnic tables at the Bozeman yard of the State Highway Commission. He went on to comment how he enjoyed his brief visit to Glendive and the trip over to the park area. He stated, "While our progress at the park will be rather slow I feel that eventually we will have a park that we can all be proud of."

On his next trip to Glendive he hopes to be able to spend more time working out plans for the development of the park.

The seeds of conflict, power struggle, and an un-surfaced victim triangle between the State Highway Commission, the State Fish and Game Commission, and Dr. Hiatt have been planted. The germination of this fracas won't show its head until many years later on what Doc Hiatt describes as "Black Tuesday."

May 4, 1954

A friend of Irene Krug Hanrahan sends her a clipping from a San Francisco newspaper showing a Montana Highway Department photo of Maco Sica "Hell Cooled Over." She is impressed with the publicity generated by Dr. Hiatt's efforts and asks to perhaps pass this clipping on to Cliff Harsh. Signed, "In haste, Irene Krug Hanrahan."

May 8, 1954

With a truck borrowed from Jack Milne, Doc Hiatt and Dan Palen along with Ken Haag make the trip to Bozeman to pick up 6 rustic split-log treated picnic tables, weighing up to 400 pounds each, from the State Highway Commission yard in Bozeman. Dan returns home on the train with the Montana Toastmasters 1954 speech contest championship trophy under his arm. Doc and Ken return with the truck and tables. It takes 98.9 gallons of gas and 3 quarts of oil to make the trip up and back. With gas running at 32 or 33 cents per gallon and oil 45 cents per quart of fuel, costs totaled $33.71. The big old truck burned a little oil—two quarts on the way up and a quart on the way back. Just imagine the gears grinding as the novice truckers attempt to double-clutch their way up and down, first the Hysham Hills and then a steep climb up and down the Bozeman Pass between Livingston to Bozeman.

Dr. Hiatt brainstorms; he is fully armed on this trip with a recipe card for notating, a full page and a scrap quarter page of thin translucent paper, a torn optometry application form, and an ink pen. The thin paper sheet, first folded in half, and then again in thirds, fits nicely in a shirt pocket. Bouncing down the road while attempting to write a note, Hiatt scribbles in a nearly illegible scrawl, "Band of wild horses, stallion." Understanding the impossibility of drafting notes while in motion, thoughts are registered in memory and legibly written when the truck is either not in motion or Doc is seated outside of the cab. Hiatt makes fractured notes that say the following: *Ashley Roberts State Park Director. 13 in system including Maco site. Sinclair for tourists, trails, etc. Bumper stickers (scotch lite) 4 X 11 /500. Hiatt chairman - publicity. McCone - Bd. Haag - golf course. Dempewolf - signs - directions & descriptions. Wagesser - roads. Copping - exhibits museum. Kolstad - flora identification, photographs, brochure. Ewing - water - Seismograph & drilling company. Harsh - History.* Scribbled out is *Cross - state road information. Palen - Road(s). KXGN -* (arrow sign to :) *The Voice of Maco Sica* (and a line back up the page to: *Hiatt chairman - publicity*). The notes above are scrawled on a folded one- sixth section of the thin paper.

On the next sixth section, written larger and horizontally, Hiatt notes the following: *Ask Carrico about nailing 12" X 8" Maco Sica Park directional sign on light pole at Barry and Sargent. Signs for specific painting after Dempewolf rides. With Dempewolf through Park for directional signs. Sam Selman, President of Mako Sica Riders Club. Publicity (radio and Ranger).*

On a scrap piece of thin paper, Hiatt notes the following bullet points below the heading "Maco Sica":

On top of "old Smokey" (scoria butte) More land acquisition (Haag)
More picnic tables below switchbacks (Haag)
Starr or Wagesser grade roads? Ted Johnson 104 S Rosser
Haag - with Pierce stakeout 160-acre boundary.
Visit Copping display (fossils)

Sketch out rough outline of copy of brochure.
Have Palen's sketch proposed off highway #10
Kolstad

On the index card, more notes: *Picnic tables at Bozeman (Highway Department building) (George Barrett). We may pick up sign lumber too. Benches and bolts for attachment. Maco Sica Park Dedication. Travel editors around the 12th of July. Art Selke, Dickinson State Teachers College, PH.D. Geologist. Otis Waters, State Highway Commissioner (invite for tour through park and lodge dinner). Get permission to gather up 24 old street signs. (Mako Sica signs.) Park commission will defray some materials expense. Telephone company (when loop is installed). Install emergency phone on radio hill. Search for water (springs/Maco Sica Riders Selman). Barnay - M.D.U. Post hole diggers - Carrico.*

Next, on the blank side of the optometry application form, Hiatt lists the locals and their tasks assigned to making Maco Sica into a real park: *May 18 - Johnson. May 10 - dismantle old city street signs. P.M. Milne truck, Holas Boom truck, Lars and I unload and place 6 tables in the Park. Holm Construction Company - match and drill and bolt benches to picnic tables. 19 May chairman of Commission report. Dempewolf - post signs. Ever (City) old sign markers. Milne - truck for tables - Haag, Hiatt. Highway department grade road - 13 May. Davis and Engle -gravel $35. Selke - DSTC PH.D. - 10 May. Roberts, Palen, Haag, Harsh, Soare - road. Kolstad - Flora identification. Copping - Fossil information. Haag, Larson - recreation and geology. Palen - Sounding board. Maco Sica Riders - hunt for water (spring). Harsh - history.*

Kodachrome slides - speech. Marge Grinde will paint some signs. Bluebirds, 8 does, crocuses. Police area.

⊷∘⟡∘⊶

May 10, 1954

Arthur Selke from the State Teachers College in Dickinson, North Dakota, writes a return letter to Hiatt. He comments, "it's a small world!" He taught George Urbanec, knows his wife and other relatives, and mentions Mr. Harsh and other mutual acquaintances. After small talk, the subject matter switches to the scenery and geology of the

North Dakota and Montana badlands: *The well-traveled Mr. Selke, having visited twenty European and five Latin American countries, has not seen anything like our Badlands, except in Mexico. He feels we don't yet know how to utilize our type of impressive topography, and this type of scenery has not been appreciated as it should be.* In an earlier letter to Selke, Hiatt inquired about the area geology. Selke's reply in this letter soaked into Hiatt like a sponge. The formations he referred to—Fort Union, Tongue River, the Lance, Fox Hills, Colgate, and the Cedar Creek Anticline—are terms that Doc Hiatt filed in memory for future use in his slide shows and field trip presentations. Mr. Selke in his letter impressed that a park must be multiple use. Scientific value and scenery are only two aspects. "Tourists must be educated, advertising must be effective. Sincerely, Arthur Selke."

Hiatt scribbles notes on the right-hand margin of the letter.

Picnicking, outdoor performances, and game refuges that create a center of attraction are suggestions Selke includes in his letter to Hiatt.

[This letter, written in 1954, was written five years after the dedication of Theodore Roosevelt National Memorial Park, which in their brochure introduces "The Pageant" as the beauty of the badlands unfolding in "moving scenes" as you drive your automobile along the red scoria highway on your tour through the badlands.

[By 1958 The Burning Hills Amphitheater was built and performances to celebrate Theodore Roosevelt's 100th birthday are sold out; Great Plains wildlife, including bison and bighorn sheep, become the centers of attraction in the North Dakota National Park.]

The letter from Arthur Selke is one of the first cogs to take hold as Doc Hiatt's mental gears begin turning. The turkey vultures, which seem to take pleasure in riding the thermal currents over the badlands, become one of Hiatt's favorite subjects. Bison and bighorn sheep, even though skulls of both have been found in the park, were never thought practical to reintroduce, even though, in an early Maco Sica Park brochure with a paragraph on the mule deer and "plumb wild" horses, the State Fish and Game Commission was considering plans to restock the area with bighorn sheep. Doc's buzzards, which are not year-round residents and usually show up in April, will become the park's wildlife centerpiece and also the centerpiece for a future Buzzard Day spring celebration. The natural centerpiece will eventually be Hiatt Amphitheater, named after its discoverer.

May 18, 1954

Doc receives a letter from Highway Commission State Park Director Ashley Roberts confirming receipt of request for reimbursement of travel expenses to pick up picnic tables in Bozeman. Instructed to sign the claim blank, have the signature notarized, and return it to Ashley's office, they will be glad to handle the expense.

Ashley comments, "If the Legislature next year is kind perhaps we will be able to step in and make some more improvements. Yours very truly, Ashley C. Roberts."

May 29, 1954

Not waiting for the state to make a plan of action, Hiatt takes the reins. Written in pencil on the brown cardboard side of a 5-by-8-inch section of a six-pack Schlitz beer carton are fourteen numbered vista point and state park signage sketches.

On two sheets of thin translucent paper, meticulously hand drawn in pencil, are maps of sections surrounding the 160 acres of Maco Sica State Park and a map of signage plans to lead travelers into Glendive Merrill Avenue, first uptown and then downtown to the underpass and then through the streets on the south side, leading travelers to emerge on the park road.

June 16, 1954

A member of the Maco Sica Riders challenges a committee member on the validity of "Mah-ko Shee-ka." To standardize once and for all the pronunciation of Maco Sica, the Committee hopes to find agreement from at least two recognized authorities.

Although Hiatt does not include a reference number for a Reference Library Service Certificate when he wrote to The World Book Encyclopedia Reference Library in Chicago, probably because he doesn't have one, nonetheless he receives a letter in reply to his request for an authoritative pronunciation of Maco Sica. The library refers the question to the librarian of the Edward E. Ayer Collection, which includes "purely Indian material, archaeology, ethnology and linguistics" in the Newberry Library of Chicago. In the 1852 publication *Grammar and Dictionary of Dakota Language*, the pronunciation as given there is MA KO SEE CHAH. *Mako* means land or country and *Sica*, bad or ugly. The librarian suggested Hiatt contact the Haskell Institute in Lawrence, Kansas, and the Smithsonian Institution in Washington D.C., which has experts in Indian linguistics and lore.

In closing, the letter instructs Hiatt, when writing for special information in the future, to be sure to include the reference number from his Library Service Certificate and to please follow instructions on the back of his certificate and write directly to the reference library.

"Sincerely yours, FIELD ENTERPRISES, INC., Deborah Peck, Assistant Librarian."

The gentle scolding is taken, you might say, with a grain of salt. Hiatt is now armed with enough information to pursue the proper wording and pronunciation of the park.

June 18, 1954

Dr. Robert W. Hiatt writes a thank-you letter to the Chicago librarian and writes to both the Haskell Institute and to Frank H. H. Roberts, Jr., Acting Director of the Smithsonian Institution Bureau of American Ethnology in Washington D.C.

June 25, 1954

Hiatt jots down notes on the flip side of the reference library letter. A list of to-do's and reminders include asking and following up with

Jack Thompson to see if he would build some fireplaces for picnic areas in the park. He notes that committeeman George Copping asked carpenter and "Maco Sica archeologist" Ed Lewis if he would build toilets for the park (built to WPA specs). Ed has had a twenty-year hobby of studying the geology, paleontology, and history of the area and is considered an outstanding local authority on the park. Lewis told Hiatt he would do it, but suggested they inquire around to find concrete slabs to save time, labor, and money. Doc Hiatt notes with interest the prehistoric animal tooth that Lewis has in his possession.

More notes on the back of the letter include informational and specific view signs such as:

Park Entrance, suggested turnaround point, Baked Potato, Radio Towers, and Panorama.

Where there had been a fire, a sign should say "Help Avoid This." And then some tongue-in-cheek sign sketches: Hiatt's Highest Height, Haag Hollow, Palen's Peak, Roberts Road, and Ducks on a Pond.

July 2, 1954

The Director of the Smithsonian Institution, in replying to Hiatt's letter of June 18th, refers to Dr. J. P. Harrington, linguist in the bureau, who states the scientific equivalent Sioux word for badlands is Mako'shika. "The first two syllables *mako*, are the standard combining form of *makoche*, country. The syllable *-shi-* means bad, and appears independently as *shicha*, bad. *-ka* means place. Therefore the whole word means Badlands Place. The tendency is to write the name as one word both in English and in Sioux. The pronunciation is: mak-koh-shih-kah.

Very truly yours, Frank H Roberts Jr."

The Committee likes very much the Smithsonian pronunciation "Mah-ko Shee-ka."

No reply has been received from the Haskell Institute.

———◦◦◦◦———

July 6, 1954

Hiatt goes back to the prior notes made on the back of the reference letter, and on the blank area on the left-hand side adds more below the underlined heading "Acknowledgements."

Maco Sica Park float in "best parade in Glendive history."

Large dinosaur painting - Grinde. Banners alongside truck - Billie Haag. Cedar trees, rocks, picnic table, Dr. Hiatt. Sage, cacti, etc., and driver for float - K Haag. The truck for the float was provided by Jack Milne, Milne Implement Company. Help loading the picnic table - Western Hide and Wrecking Company.

On stationery from Glendive Greenhouses is a typewritten list of plants and flowers native to Maco Sica: *Sago Lily, Yucca - Spanish bayonet, Crocus - pasque flower, Wild Daisy, Evening Primrose, Fall Asters, Cactus, white, yellow, lavender Lupine, Wild sweet peas, creeping or running cedar, Jack Pine, Ponderosa or Yellow Pine, Juniper, Rocky Mountain badlands cedar, Chokecherries, Buck Brush[sic], Wild roses, Sagebrush*, and a note at the bottom of the page, *(no state flower in the Park, Bitterroot)*. Added later were photos and a negative attached to the back side of the Greenhouse stationery showing the streets lined with parade watchers, Cliff Harsh's "Send a boy to Montana" float with boys and girls riding on top of and in the back of the truck. The Maco-Sica float is all decked out with signs, banners, picnic table and rocks, as described by the acknowledgments, and most of the plants represented on the Greenhouse list.

Hiatt makes a note to acknowledge "spring and summer - KXGN, the Voice of Maco Sica State Park, KXGN sounding board."

———◦◦◦◦———

Saturday, July 24, 1954

In a letter confirming the upcoming tour, Art Selke extends greetings to Doc Hiatt's father and comments on how Doc's son is such a growing youngster.

Arthur Selke, a leading geologist from North Dakota who has written several publications about the North Dakota badlands and given numerous talks on the subject, along with Hiatt and members of the Maco Sica Park Committee, Ed Lewis, Cliff Harsh, Ed Prevol, Al Ahlquist, Bill Ellis, and Glendive Chamber of Commerce Secretary Manager Bill Vondrashek, conduct a Travel Editors Tour which should result in some national publicity for Glendive's Maco Sica Park. After the tour Mrs. Bertha Sundling serves her usual delicious dinner at the Badlands Lodge, which she built, owns, and operates. Noel Carrico is on hand to greet the editors on behalf of the Montana Chamber of Commerce. Al Erickson, State Publicity Director, and Frank Wiley, State Aeronautics Director, also accompany the tour. The tour is a huge success and these editors are also very favorably impressed with the beautiful hotel and city parks. Glendive is indeed the "GATEWAY TO MONTANA."

Rumblings of thought to build a museum to consolidate and display Glendive's history are surfacing due to the increasing interest in the priceless collections of Indian relics and geologic specimens native to Glendive which are displayed in the Chamber Office and City Library.

Lobbying for permanent air service, Aeronautics Committee Chairman Vern Paulson and members of the Committee including Bert Hilger, who traveled to Washington D.C. on behalf of the Committee, are successful. Frontier Airlines is planning to begin flying from Billings to Bismarck through Glendive.

August 13, 1954

In a paper he titled "Ramblings" about Maco Sica State Park, Dr. R. W. Hiatt, now Chairman of the Maco Sica State Park Committee, writes about the flora and fauna, the roads, the area, the name Maco Sica, the personalities, the facilities, and comments on publications and the uniqueness of the park. Most interesting to him in the wildlife category is a permanent band of about 30 wild horses including some Mavericks from time to time that can be seen silhouetted along the long high butte about 2 miles northeast from the panoramic observation point.

He notes, "fireplaces and toilets are forthcoming in and near the picnic area."

In his ramblings about the rattlesnake Doc says, "He is a popular and aggregated dread of the average Glendive woman." In commenting that although snakes have been observed on occasion, he downplays the risk. On his rare encounter with a rattler Doc considers he is encroaching on the snake's territory, and simply backs off and takes another route.

The Advertising Office of the State Highway Commission of Montana produced a widely distributed colored picture magazine about the size of a comic book titled *Come to Montana: Land of Legend and Promise*. The booklet is illustrated and the artwork in the cartoons appears to be very similar to the work of Stan Lynde from the popular Rick O'Shay comic strip. The pages have titles such as Gold Fever … Vigilantes vs. Road Agents, The Indian War Years … Custer's Last Stand, The Vanishing Red Man … Chief Joseph Surrenders, Gold on the Hoof … Texas Trail Herds Arrive, The Ancient Lands, Montana's Land of Magic, a glossy colored two-page map of the state that forms the center of the booklet with drawings of tipi, cattle, buffalo, a rodeo, dinosaurs, wildlife, skiing, fishing, etc., and then more pages with titles of Sportsmen Paradise, The Good Old Outdoor Life, The Pictorial Playgrounds, followed up with a few more pages promoting Montana Agriculture, Business, Industry, and lastly Happy Riding to You! … Come Back Often.

This brilliant marketing publication in the hands of kids in the back seat of a station wagon on their way to a Montana vacation builds exciting anticipation! In the section titled "The Pictorial Playgrounds" the caption reads, "Perhaps the most fascinating of State Parks is 'Maco Sica,' the Badlands near Glendive on U.S. 10. You can find the bones of many a prehistoric monster among its weird rock formations, and what a spot for the camera bug! But then, what part of Montana isn't?"

August 24, 1954

As chairman of the Maco Sica Park Committee, Dr. Hiatt sends a letter to Mrs. John Grinde thanking her for the excellent job she did on the

Maco Sica Park signs and for her wonderful spirit of cooperation and beautiful job she did on the Maco Sica float in the Glendive Rodeo parade. "Sincerely yours, Dr. Hiatt."

October 13, 1954

Ashley C. Roberts, State Park Director, sends a reply to Mr. W. J. Vondrashek, Secretary Manager of the Glendive Chamber of Commerce, acknowledging his letter to Mr. Frank Connelly with reference to a representative on the State Park Advisory Committee. Bill suggests Dr. R.

W. Hiatt and Mr. Clifford Harsh represent Glendive; however, Ashley noted that only one of them can be named the actual representative. Nevertheless, both are invited to attend the next meeting at 1:30 P.M. on Wednesday, October 27th. "Yours very truly, Ashley C. Roberts."

October 14, 1954

A memo and a copy of the law that sets up the State Park system is sent by Ashley to the Advisory Committee with reference to the October 27th meeting in Helena. Also included is a copy of the budget to be presented to the Legislature for approval. Ashley said in the memo, "We would like to have your representative review this information as it will be the basis for our discussion at the Helena meeting." He also says, "We will be looking forward to meeting your representative at this meeting."

Ashley politely ends his letter with, "Yours very truly, Ashley C Roberts." Clearly, there can be only one representative for Glendive.

Today the State Park Director also writes to Mr. Vondrashek to let him know he will arrive in Glendive during the late afternoon of Wednesday, October 20th. He would like to get together Thursday morning, take a drive out to Maco Sica, and perhaps have a luncheon at noon with Bill and one or two members of the Park Committee. "Yours very truly, Ash Roberts."

On the blank side of three index cards from a Rolodex, Doc Hiatt makes 28 mileage and time-elapsed calculations with descriptions of each of 28 locations. Two of the index cards have the calculations made during the drive through Maco Sica, including all the vista points. The third card's back side is charted from right to left starting on the bottom right with descriptions of home, underpass, end of pavement, cattle guard, start switchbacks, and so on, all through the park with mileage noted between each and ending on the bottom left of the index card. The total of the 25- mile trip from home through Maco Sica Park including all vista points took a total of 75 minutes.

The three index cards sacrificed for this exercise, which appear to be rejects because of some spelling and penmanship errors, have the following names and addresses: Dr R. w. Hiatt, First National Bank Building, EDC 912-17- 54a, Mr. Herbert C. Heubl, Koch & Heubl, DG 912-17-54a, and Mr. Orion Cusker, 1509 North Meade, SEC 912-17-54a.

Assigned to represent Glendive on the State Park Advisory Committee is Dr. R. W. Hiatt.

—•∞•—

October 27, 1954

The State Park Advisory Committee meets in Helena and reviews Montana State Park law. Sections of the law include the Purpose, Powers and Duties, Fees and Charges, Rules and Regulations, Connecting Roads, Cooperation, Reports, Establishment of State Scientific and Recreational Park, State Highway Commission to Establish Rules Governing Use, State Parks and Recreational and Camping Grounds, and Penalties for Violation of State Park Regulations. Sections 62-302, 62-303, and 62-313 are repealed.

62-306 says in part, "Any person who violates any rule or regulation shall be deemed guilty of a misdemeanor and punished by a fine of not more than one hundred dollars or by imprisonment for not more than six months and be adjudged to pay all costs of the proceedings."

62-314 is somewhat redundant. "Any person who shall injure or damage any state or private property thereon or therein, or shall violate any of the regulations made by the state highway commission relating to the state parks, shall be guilty of a misdemeanor and be fined not more than five hundred dollars or be imprisoned in the county jail for no more than six months."

Also reviewed is the Park Division proposed budget request for fiscal years 1956 and 1957 (July 1, 1955 to June 30, 1957). The proposal lays out the steps and minimum funds required to accomplish the development of Montana's State Park program.

Headquarter salaries call for $6,000 per year for the Director, $4,800 per year for the Field Man, $1,200 per year for the Stenographer, and $600 each year for Attorney. Operations expenses are laid out, salaries for managers, guides, and operators for Lewis & Clark Caverns State Park are detailed. Also listed are expenses for Missouri River Headquarters State Monument, Bannack State Monument, Bridger Mountain State Park, and Maco Sica State Park. In Maco Sica the $1,250 salary is for a Caretaker (5 months at $250 per month) each year. For Maco Sica operations there are three items listed for each fiscal year. Picnic tables $300 (10 at $30 each), fireplaces $350 (10 at $35 each), and signs for $250.

Included in the budget are expenses for proposed state parks to be acquired during the biennium. They are Tiber Dam, Fresno Reservoir, Medicine Rocks, Hooper State Monument, Old Fort Owen, Smith River, Indian Caves, Pompey's Pillar, Bear's Paw Battlefield, Ruby Dam, Sun River, Lincoln-Ovando area, and Swan River area.

"Allocated for Capital - Land Purchases to acquire land for State Park purposes or for desirable adjacent land to existing State Parks is $2,500 each fiscal year of the biennium."

The grand total Montana State Parks budget for the biennium is $173,405.00.

In discussing the state park brochure, Dr. Hiatt suggests that the parks be listed as the tourists coming from the east would approach and enter them. In his report about Maco Sica, he points out that a connecting road to Highway 10 should be built. He says that since the Glendive radio station has been advertising the park, attendance has jumped remarkably.

November 16, 1954

A copy of the minutes is mailed to the Advisory Committee by Ashley's office. Commenting on the productive meeting, the letter states, "With the cooperation of all concerned we expect to achieve a good Park system in Montana."

"Yours very truly, Ashley C Roberts (by his secretary MMC)."

November 24, 1954

On Toastmasters International letterhead, Doc Hiatt sends an informal letter addressed to Ash. The letter discloses his lobbying strategy of indoctrinating optometry patients while adjusting their glasses. It was an easy sell to a past president of the local chamber as well as a director on the state chamber and now an elected representative of Dawson County. Art Hagenston Sr. doesn't need much prodding on the subject of building, advertising, and showing off Montana.

Back to the subject of a road connecting Highway 10 to Maco Sica, Hiatt has done his homework. A Monday patient was a local rancher, Jack Engle, who knows of a seismograph "road" that connects Highway 10 to an area of the Maco Sica badlands. The trail according to Jack is a scenic and practical route, and Hiatt plans to take a look around tomorrow morning. "Sincerely, Bob."

This same day a formal letter addressed to the Montana State Board of Land Commissioners and through the Director, State Park Division, Montana Highway Commission, is sent by Dr. R. W. Hiatt, Chairman of the Maco Sica Park Committee, Glendive Chamber of Commerce, and a member of the State Park Advisory Committee addressing the change in the name of Maco Sica Park.

The letter explains in detail the reasoning behind the proposed name change and steps taken to consult recognized authorities. Quoting a paragraph by Dr. J. A. Harrington, a linguist in the Bureau of American Ethnology, the pronunciation and definition of the new name for Maco Sica is spelled out as Mako'shika.

A sampling of Glendive locals, tourists, and other members of the State Park Advisory Committee found nearly unanimous approval of changing Maco Sica to Mako'shika.

"To avoid considerable confusion and expense before the park is officially dedicated and before the next edition of the Montana State Parks brochure is printed, in compliance with Montana Statute 62-312, approval is requested to change the name immediately. Sincerely, R. W. Hiatt."

November 29, 1954

Chairman of the State Park Advisory Committee Forrest Rockwood writes to Dr$. Robert Hiatt and other members of the State Committee reporting on a meeting and presentation to be put on by the Kiwanis Club in Kalispell promoting the state parks. The proposed budget will also be presented and the goal of this effort will be to engender interest in the State Park system.

The hope is to influence state representatives to support the proposed budget. "Yours Sincerely, Forrest Rockwood."

November 30, 1954

State Park Director Ashley C. Roberts sends a memo to the members of the State Park Advisory Committee along with a copy of the Park Division's report to the Governor. The report discusses the activities of the Park Division since July 1, 1953. Ashley wants the Advisory Committee to have this information for discussion of the Park Division budget with legislators. "Sincerely, Ashley C Roberts."

The report to the Governor details progress made on each state park, including state monuments. In Maco Sica most of the credit for its current development is the result of cooperation with the local Chamber of Commerce, the County, and local contractors. The State Park Division has been unable to do very much about its development. This park is attracting some 100 visitors per day during the travel season. Besides having some of the most fascinating and spectacular scenery in the entire state, Maco Sica is also of value for scientific purposes. Recommendations include orderly development as promptly as possible by adding more facilities, improving the road, and adding a caretaker during the summer months.

Another section of the report explains that the Highway Commission authorized organization of an Advisory Committee to the Parks Division composed of twelve individuals representing local civic groups adjacent to each of the parks. At the initial meeting of this committee it was gratifying to the Commission to note the interest these representatives are taking in the Parks Division program. It is to be understood that this committee is purely voluntary and the members serve without remuneration and attend meetings at their own expense.

"Concluding with recommendations to accomplish Park Division objectives the State Highway Commission urges the Park Division budget as presented to the Controller for transmission to the legislature should be adopted in its entirety. Respectfully submitted, Frank Connelly, Chairman."

———————<><>———————

December 2, 1954

Ashley Roberts composes a letter to Doctor Robert Hiatt in reference to the proposed change in name at Maco Sica State Park. Due to the amount of work in front of the Commission at their recent meeting, Ashley did not have time to present the name change; however, he is writing each member of the Commission outlining the proposal and the matter will definitely be brought up for discussion at the December meeting.

Thanking Bob for a good job getting the word out in Dawson County, he closes the letter, "Sincerely, Ashley C Roberts."

December 6, 1954

Another letter on Toastmasters International letterhead is sent to Ash from Doc Hiatt. "A downright shame," Doc says of the North Dakota Burning Coal Mine. "No signs, no road—a real attraction tourists would never forget."

Doc mentions he will be meeting with the Soil Conservation District supervisor tomorrow concerning land transfer of title from several sections of public domain to the state of Montana.In preparation of sending letters to senators and representatives from each of the 15 easternmost counties in Montana, he requests Ash send him 35 copies of "COME TO MONTANA, Land of Legend and Promise" to enclose with each letter.

December 7, 1954

On his optometrist letterhead Doc drafts a letter to the Glendive Chamber of Commerce requesting reimbursement for the previously voted allowable expense for the organizational meeting in Helena. He writes down the rail fare of $29.81 plus Pullman at $12.76 for a total of $42.57 travel expense to the State Park Advisory Committee meeting. Rather than send3 a less- interested proxy, Doc thought the meeting was too important so he attended himself. (Robert Hiatt)

December 8, 1954

Written in pencil on lined notebook paper, Hiatt drafts a letter to R. D. Nielsen in Billings, Montana, State Supervisor of the Bureau of Land Management.

Request the transfer of Federal Land (either shown on a plat or by legal description) to Maco Sica State Park for use in conjunction with adjoining

Park land as a habitat for wildlife, as a picnic area, scenic area, foot trails for hikers, saddle horse trails for saddle clubs, and a general recreation area.

Both BLM and SCS have recommended such as most suitable for this class of land.

Legal descriptions listing the range and sections of townships 15N and 14N are noted on the second page of his draft letter.

After reading newspaper clippings of the issues confronting the upcoming 1955 Legislature, Doc Hiatt formulates a letter he will send to the 30 or so representatives and senators from Sheridan, Daniels, Valley, Roosevelt, Richland, McCone, Dawson, Garfield, Wibaux, Prairie, Rosebud, Custer, Fallon, Powder River, and Carter counties.

In its entirety the letter reads:

Dear Mr. _____,

Next month you will join the other successful and responsible men whom we citizens have chosen to preserve the blessings and develop the resources of Montana. I know of no other assignment where a conscientious man must think harder, broader and "thorougher[sic]." It has appeared to me that an intelligent legislator is in a position where he must choose not which is right, but which is best.

Most of your thought is now, and will be, properly concentrated on the urgent needs of highways, education and oil-leasing. And that all means big money.

The purpose of this letter is to encourage your favorable reaction to the "drop in the bucket" appropriations request by the State Park Division of the Montana Highway Department. Believe me, it is modest, but it could give much encouragement to work by citizens locally familiar and interested in making the beauty and facilities of the parks more available to Montanans and tourists.

Take Maco Sica (Badlands), one of the newest of the present 13 State Parks and Monuments, as an example of a need for State investment. Note its description on "The Pictorial Playgrounds" page of the enclosed "Come to Montana" publication of the Montana Highway

Department. If you would but drive through the Badlands National Monument (South Dakota), the Theodore Roosevelt National Park (North Dakota Badlands) and Eastern Montana's Maco Sica State Park, you'd see the crazy paradox of the most colorful, most exciting, most interesting, most usable and most conveniently located park having the least recognition, promotion and development.

We have much to offer, but until a connecting road from U.S. Highway 10 east of Glendive to the existing Park road can be built, 90% of the tourist traffic will continue to bypass one of Montana's unforgettable scenic wonders. It's easy to get 'em out of the Park, but we have to get 'em in first.

Western Montana has the edge in overall scenic attraction, of course, but they don't have Maco Sica, so let's show it to our out-of-state visitors, the majority of whom enter the State from Highway 10 East, and give them a good first and lasting impression of Montana!

Best wishes for a successful 1955 Legislature!

Dr. R. W. Hiatt, Chairman
Maco Sica State Park Comm.
Glendive Chamber of Commerce

December 9, 1954

The Secretary Manager of Glendive Chamber of Commerce invites Dr. Hiatt by letter to an important meeting at the Chamber Offices Wednesday, December 15th, at 8 P.M. for the purposes of informing Dawson County legislators, Mr. R. L. Robins, and Mr. Art Hagenston, Sr., of his committee's recommendations for the greater development of Glendive and Dawson County. "Yours truly, W. J. Vondrashek."

———— ⋙∘C⌇∘⋘ ————

December 10, 1954

The 5-cent *Glendive Daily Ranger*, "An Independent Newspaper – Covering Eastern Montana Like The Stars," publicizes the Glendive Chamber of Commerce meeting with legislators.

Ashley Roberts confirms Doc's letter with reference to the proposed addition of public-domain lands as a part of Maco Sica State Park. He is appreciative of the efforts from all of the Advisory Committee. "Sincerely, Ash."

In reference to a request directed to BLM State Supervisor Mr. R. D. Nelson from Dr. R. W. Hiatt, Ashley Roberts states, "The Park Division is happy to endorse this request." The last paragraph of the letter includes a caveat of understanding that the proposed land transfer will be accomplished at no cost to the state and in trust that the BLM will see fit to cooperate with the State Park Division in this worthy project. "Yours very truly, Ashley C. Roberts."

Hiatt sends his composed legislative letter to Committee Chairman Forrest Rockwood and State Park Director Ashley Roberts for input.

December 13, 1954

"Dear Doctor" is how the Chairman of the State Park Advisory Committee begins his short letter to Hiatt, thanking him and offering a few suggestions for the letter Doc is sending out to legislators in Eastern Montana. "Yours very truly, Forrest C Rockwood."

Ashley Roberts replies to Doc, "The letter is excellent and will certainly help our cause when the Legislature meets in January." He suggests an additional paragraph be inserted between paragraphs five and six of the proposed letter, and it reads:

"And so it is with many of our other existing State Parks as well as proposed State Parks. Our State Park program is in its infancy and we are just now getting started on a well-planned program. The State of Montana has much to offer to our own citizens as well as the traveling public, but, these areas must be developed, provided with necessary facilities and put into operation. A progressive and aggressive State Park program will accomplish these objectives.

Yours very truly, Ash."

Hiatt agrees and circles with red pencil the proposed paragraph, writing in bold red block letters above an arrow pointing to the additional words "INSERT BEFORE LAST PARAGRAPH."

Hiatt provides a list of names and the draft letter, with notes to insert the suggested paragraph, to Mrs. Cliff Harsh, who volunteers to type individual letters to the following 1955 legislators:

Plentywood
Andy Dahl - Sheridan County Senator
L. Michaels - Sheridan County Representative

Scobey
C. Lindquist - Daniels County Senator
Neil Taylor - Daniels County Representative

Glasgow
R. Cotton - Valley County Senator
H. Clowes - Valley County Representative
L. Bernard - Valley County Representative

Wolf Point
Reid Taylor - Roosevelt County Senator
Chris Tange - Roosevelt County Representative

Sidney
Don Nutter - Richland County Senator
Floyd Sax - Richland County Representative

Vida
J. M. Hofland - McCone County Senator
Martin Beck - McCone County Representative

Glendive
R. L. Robins - Dawson County Senator
A. S. Hagenston - Dawson County Representative

Jordan
C. H. Mahoney - Garfield County Senator
J. McDonald - Garfield County Representative

Wibaux
Oscar Nesvig - Wibaux County Senator
Clem Parker - Wibaux County Representative

Terry
C. W. Grandy - Prairie County Senator
H. H. Haines - Prairie County Representative

Forsyth
R. D. Harken - Rosebud County Senator
S. O. Mysse, Jr. - Rosebud County Representative

Miles City
C. M. Hatch - Custer County Senator
Ted Nelstead - Custer County Representative
Roy Grant - Custer County Representative

Baker
Karl Wenz - Fallon County Senator
Frank Fulton - Fallon County Representative

Broadus
C. Scolfield - Powder River County Senator
L. D. Powell - Powder River County Representative

Ekalaka
Ben Brownfield - Carter County Senator
C. C. Bentz - Carter County Representative

———⊸○⟨◇◇⟩○⊸———

December 17, 1954

On a three-page letter addressed to the Glendive Chamber of Commerce President, Dr. Hiatt reports the activities of the Maco Sica State Park Committee for 1954. He thanks the President for the privilege of serving as chairman and remarks how educational and inspirational it has been to work with so many cooperative and enthusiastic Glendive citizens with regard to the park.

His committee had four well-attended committee meetings at 7:30 in the evening on the 21st day of February, April, June, and August. All the meetings adjourned before 9:00 P.M.

The third paragraph of his letter reads: "In March the switchbacks were graded and re-graveled. Committee member Dan Palen gave the Park a tremendous boost when he initiated identification of KXGN as 'The Voice of Maco Sica State Park' and devoted an entire 'Sounding Board' program to the Park."

He reported on the trip in early May to pick up six picnic tables at the State Highway Commission yard in Bozeman and how the following Saturday morning Doug Holm and Harold Nellans spent over four hours drilling and bolting benches to the tables. That same afternoon Maurice Holas donated his winch truck with an operator and they "staggered and squeezed" the picnic tables onto the 160 acres of land to which the park has title. As he wrote in his earlier "ramblings," the paragraph ends with "The well-worn car trails today are mute testimony that hundreds of picnics were enjoyed in Maco Sica this summer.

"Kudos to the City of Glendive for allowing the use of discarded street signs. Thanks to Mrs. Ken Haag and Mrs. Bob Grinde who lettered the signs and to Committee member Barney Dempewolf for helping plant the 20 directional signs leading to and through the park."

Page 2

The Jordan Coffee Shop sponsored a mileage chart for the Chamber. These were well distributed by Secretary-Manager Bill Vondrashek. Printed on the back of these mileage charts is an encouragement for tourists to see Maco Sica before traveling on.

"In July under the direction of member Haag and again with the artistic contributions of Mrs. Haag and Mrs. Grinde the Committee prepared and entered a 'Maco Sica State Park' float to help make the Glendive 1954 Fourth of July parade the biggest in history.

"Also in July travel editors from Portland and Chicago, State officials, Dr. Selke, head geologist at Dickinson State Teachers College, local authorities and Chamber officials spent an educational and enjoyable afternoon in the Park.

"Thanks to Bill (Von) and Peeny Holm for arranging several more loads of dirt which assured safer and more comfortable travel over the Park entrance road.

"Committee members Mel Kolstad contributed a list of flora found in the Park and George Copping wrote an excellent poem 'The Saga of the Badlands' both items of which will be incorporated into a new brochure describing the Park. Ed Lewis will be solicited for geological and paleontological background.

"In October the State Park Advisory Committee was conceived to advise and assist the State Park Director in developing a good State Park system. The organizational meeting was held in Helena with the Montana Highway Commission and State Park Director on October 27th. I was happy to represent Maco Sica.

"In November, after consulting with recognized ethnologists as well as the man on the street, we asked the State Board of Land Commissioners for authority to change the spelling and pronunciation of Maco Sica to Mako'shika which Smithsonian Institution says is a scientific–Sioux equivalent of Badlands. This should be determined in Helena this month."

Page 3

Floyd Ewing tipped off some members of the Committee, who then met with an official of the Federal Bureau of Land Management asking for transfer of federal land to the state of Montana for inclusion in Maco Sica State Park. Ode Cusker provided valuable assistance in the application process for nearly 11 sections of public domain. The State Park Director endorsed and forwarded the application to the State Supervisor of the BLM.

One of the greatest needs for Maco Sica Park is an upgraded road. "Thanks to Cliff Harsh's volunteering his wife's typing skill" to 32 individual letters for each of the 1955 legislators from the 15 easternmost counties. The letters will be sent to "persuade their affirmative reaction when voting on the new State Park budget appropriation, because you can't do much road building without a few bucks."

Hiatt quotes a paragraph from his letter to legislators describing the "Pictorial Playgrounds" of Maco Sica State Park and how on a drive through the badlands "you'd see the crazy paradox of the most colorful, most exciting, most interesting, most usable and most conveniently located park having the least recognition, promotion and development."

Doc closes his letter with the following sentence: "With the continued cooperation and enthusiasm of Park-minded citizens more use and enjoyment can and will be gained from Maco Sica. Respectfully submitted by R. W. Hiatt."

Eighteen of the people mentioned in the letter are also sent a copy.

December 1954

An undated letter from George Urbanec, President of Glendive Chamber of Commerce, to Dr. R. W. Hiatt gives credit for much of the Chamber progress in 1954 to Doc and his Maco Sica Park Committee. George extends a hearty "WELL DONE" and extends his sincere wishes for a happy and prosperous new year. "Signed cordially yours, George Urbanec."

December 20, 1954

Not all of the eastern Montana representatives have come on board with the State Park program.

The Chairman of the State Parks Advisory Committee writes to Al Hawkinson, Secretary of the Garfield County Commercial Club in Jordan, to acknowledge the difficulty in securing approval of his local representatives and encouraging public meetings to develop public sentiment in favor of the program.

Skeptical of Al's idea for a special tax to finance the program, Forrest lets him know this avenue was tried a couple years ago without success.

Thanking Mr. Hawkinson for his efforts on behalf of the program, the letter is closed with "I remain, Yours Sincerely, Forrest C Rockwood."

December 21, 1954

TO: Members of the State Park Advisory Committee

Chairman Forrest Rockwood reports on the recent Kiwanis Club meeting in Kalispell devoted to the State Park program. Legislators, Chamber of Commerce representatives, members of the press, and the State Park Director were present and "good publicity was thus secured."

He reports on a meeting held at Twin Bridges with Beaverhead and Madison County representatives with a good discussion on the State Park program.

"A very intelligent discussion of the State program was had by the Lake County Good Fellowship Club and their legislators.

"Also, I wish to report that Dr. R. W. Hiatt of Glendive has been doing some active work contacting their legislators and also on getting out a letter and other material to the legislators in eastern Montana."

The Chairman encourages other Advisory Committee members to arrange for similar meetings and to please report with appropriate news clippings to be passed on to Director Roberts. "Yours very truly, Forrest C. Rockwood."

December 22, 1954

Evidently Forrest Rockwood was impressed enough with Dr. Hiatt's letter for the Legislature he decided to follow suit and draft a letter of his own on behalf of the Committee for distribution. Realizing it is a busy season, on his cover letter to the Advisory Committee members he encourages them to get the letters out as soon as possible as it will soon be time for the legislators to be arriving in Helena. Since these letters are all the same, he suggests adding a personal note calling attention to specific parks or projects within their area. "Thanks for your cooperation and best wishes for the Holiday Season. Sincerely, Forrest C Rockwood."

The two-page letter to members of the Montana Legislature was somewhat impersonal but covered all the bullet points of the State Park program and has plenty of facts and figures to refer to. With encouragement for positive consideration the letter ends "Yours sincerely, Forrest C. Rockwood."

December 1954

Glendive Chamber of Commerce President George Urbanec presents his annual report to the Chamber Board of Directors and expresses his appreciation for the support of the Board and cooperation of the community in helping the Chamber experience "such a successful year."

In the little red 5 ½-inch-by-8 ¼-inch annual report booklet, the 24 Chamber committees each had a report on their activities in 1954 and which projects are planned for the future.

The longest report, taking a full page of the 11-page booklet, is the Maco Sica State Park Committee report. The members are as follows: Dr. R. W. Hiatt, Chairman, Cliff Harsh, Bernard Dempewolf, Kenneth Haag, George Copping, and Melvin Kolstad. Dr. Hiatt also served on the financial report auditing committee.

January 7, 1955

A "Dear Bob" letter is sent to Dr. R. W. Hiatt by State Park Director Ashley C. Roberts informing him of the unsuccessful efforts to have any action taken on the Maco Sica State Park suggested name change at the December Highway Commission meeting.

"Their immediate reaction was—let's not change." If a change is contemplated, suggestions include "Montana Badlands State Park, Glendive State Park, or Glendive Badlands State Park."

"At the moment, then, there is not agreement as to what should be done—if anything." Ashley suggests contacting Otis Waters prior to the January meeting which is scheduled for the 26th, 27th, and 28th. Whatever action Mr. Waters recommends will carry weight with the Commission. "Regards, Ash."

January 15, 1955

Clifford Harsh gives a speech to the Glendive and Wolf Point Toastmasters. This twelfth speech is a "masterpiece."

January 1955

Hiatt clips from the newspaper a two-column list of members of the State Senate standing committees.

Victor VanHee is the new president of the Glendive Chamber of Commerce. Dr. R. W. Hiatt remains as chairman of the Maco Sica Park Committee.

January 23, 1955

Dr. Hiatt sends a well-thought-out 8-paragraph, 2-page rebuttal letter to Otis Waters:

Paragraph 1.

It's "NOT THE NAME but the pronunciation and spelling of MACO SICA State Park" that our Committee has long-pondered to change.

Paragraph 2.

A point is made in agreement with the Highway Commission that the name is probably the best as it is now. "SO WHY WORRY ABOUT CHANGING THE NAME."

Paragraph 3.

The Maco Sica Park Committee is "not one bit interested in changing the name. Because of the many different and conflicting and frustrated pronunciations of Maco Sica we thought it high time to seek out an authoritative one and standardize it. After asking amateur and professional, local and State historians and ethnologists, we found no one who challenged Smithsonian Institution's linguist, Dr. Harrington, whose research came up with Mako'shika PRONOUNCED JUST LIKE IT'S SPELLED."

Paragraph 4.

"So long as our request is bottlenecked," the pronunciation "Mah-ko shee- ka" will continue to be used; however, for six months we tested Mako'shika with a few scholars, Sioux Indians, and local residents and their reaction was unanimous: "<u>not one</u> dissenter to the proposed change."

Paragraph 5.

A direct appeal is made to Otis, followed up with background information to help him clarify his thinking behind the request. Understanding challenges the Commission faces and the "ponderables and imponderables in the execution of its duties." Dr. Hiatt asks Otis, who is the logical proponent of the cause, to determine if the change has merit.

Paragraph 6.

If you visit and compare Theodore Roosevelt NATIONAL Park in North Dakota and South Dakota Badlands NATIONAL Monument with Maco Sica STATE Park, you will discover Maco Sica is "more colorful, more exciting, more interesting and more conveniently located."

Paragraph 7.

Making the point that since most tourists are traveling from the east and having already seen the boring badlands in North and/or South Dakota, why would they waste any time visiting Montana's badlands?

Paragraph 8.

"This is not my logic. This is tourist logic—just as yours and mine would be. It's what they think and say to Glendive people when encouraged to see our badlands. WE'VE GOT TO USE A LITTLE IMAGINATION AND APPEAL TO THE DETERMINING FACTOR OF CURIOSITY IN THE

TOURIST'S PERSONALITY. 'Maco Sica' does just this. 'Mako'shika' does it better and simpler."

Hopefully, Bob

R.W. Hiatt, O.D., Chairman Maco Sica State Park Committee Glendive Chamber of Commerce

January 25, 1954

Here we go again: another "Dear Bob" letter from the State Park Director. The problem this time is the letter arrived too late for the January Highway Commission meeting which had been moved up a week. The Commissioner from Richey, Otis Waters, had not had time to discuss the matter with folks down his way, so the proposal was passed over this meeting.

If Otis is reappointed to the Commission by the Governor, whatever he reports back to the next meeting will carry weight. If he is not reappointed, a "new man" will have to take up the matter.

Ashley lets it be known to Dr. Hiatt as far as his personal feelings are concerned, he is in agreement and will let his feelings be known to the Commission. The proposed name satisfies the requirements as being "attractive to the tourists, technically correct and is popular with the Glendive residents. Regards, Ash Roberts."

January 26, 1955

Handwritten in cursive on State of Montana Highway Commission letterhead, a one-page letter is written to Dr. Hiatt from Otis Waters.

In no uncertain terms Otis is on board with his first sentence. *"Your letter pertaining to parks received and contents studied, and according to facts set forth it would seem the present name with different spelling & pronunciation is what you want and that is what you will get."*

He suggests to pull more tourist trade, "the fossil find should be played up a little more and I have heard there is a big hole with no bottom in sight, if such us the case it should be made accessible to tourists."

He praises Dr. Hiatt for his efforts to have "Maco Sika[sic]" designated as a state park and wants "to do everything possible toward further development. Very truly yours, Otis S. Waters."

January 27, 1955

Ash writes to Hiatt, "still no word from the Legislature." He's not sure if they are interested in state park development. "In the meantime, my fingernails are taking a bad beating.

"It's wonderful to have someone like you working on the parks. We are giving authority to purchase up to $100.00 in lumber to build the toilets and we do have some timber available for rustic signs. Sincerely, Ash."

February 1955

Hiatt takes the scissors and cuts an index card to fit nicely in the palm of his hand. Written in bold ink on the 2 ¾- x 4-inch card, Hiatt makes notes for his presentations to, most likely, the Glendive Chamber of Commerce and local service organizations. Anxious to start promoting the proposed new spelling and pronunciation, in large block letters across the top of the note card he prints "MAKOSHIKA." His bullet points are as follows:

I. Brochure – Hiatt
II. Toilets – Lewis
III. Fireplaces – Lewis and/or Holm

IV. Land *Acquisition – Haag*
V. Road – Harsh
VI. Publicity – Hiatt
VII. Recreational Use – Harsh

On the flip side of the card the notes continue:
VIII. Entrance Sign – Holm
IX. Point of Interest Signs – Ha[not legible]
X. Dedication – Haag

Doc Hiatt writes an unrelated note in light pencil on the bottom of the card's flip side:[3]

Pamphlet (Library)

History of gen[sic] Gibbon's march.

There is no way to know when or if Dr. Hiatt actually took time to gather up and read the history of General Gibbon's march.

3. Handwriting verified by Robert W. Hiatt's daughter Bette Payton.

At 10:00 A.M. on the 17th of March in 1876, the "Montana Column" of 195 men and 12 officers begin their march to the Little Bighorn from Fort Shaw, the U.S. Army fort located on the Sun River. Painful snow blindness, piercing winds, and blizzard conditions along with bitter cold weather—at times thirty to forty degrees below zero—cause serious frostbite and misery among many of the men. Using the skills of Crow scouts, General John Gibbon and his men search until May for signs of the Sioux Indians only to discover the Sioux have been watching the army, waiting for an opportune time to steal horses. The Crow Indian scouts, bitter enemies of the Sioux, discover their horses have been raided. Alarmed that only one of the two soldiers who left camp to go hunting in the morning returns back, a search party sets out the next day. Fearing the missing soldier has been discovered by the Sioux horse thieves and killed, they are relieved to find the bewildered man. He had no idea of his location and spent an entire day walking in a huge circle only to find himself back at the overhanging rock where he'd slept the night before.

A couple days later, May 7, 1876, a detachment of seventeen soldiers, a few civilians, and four Crow scouts under the command of Captain Clifford prepare to depart down the river to see if they can find a band of Sioux. In his journal he writes, "Myself and men passed the day in preparation, and as soon as it was dark enough to conceal our departure, we mounted and rode forth, the greater part of the command gathered to see us off, many looking on us as doomed men." All night they march down the valley for ten miles, finding some signs of the Sioux. Just before daylight on May 8th they cross a tributary to the Yellowstone River. Arriving at the river bluffs they ascend up to the highlands and march about five miles cross-country.

They hear the low wolf cry supposedly from the scouts out front. The imitation wolf howl signals the enemy is near and sounds so authentic it would deceive anyone. (Except the old Indians and old scouts who say the human imitation of the wolf cry gives an echo, whereas the genuine cry of the coyote or the wolf has no echo.) Finding some Indian articles and lodges, they soon discover the Indians are gone. Having ridden all night they find a good place to halt, post lookouts, unsaddle, and graze the horses. They settle in for much-needed rest from 10:30 A.M. to 5 P.M. and then prepare to march again. Here they find more Sioux signs, war lodges, fresh tracks, and fresh ashes along with an elaborate arrangement of buffalo chips and skulls for "making medicine." Evidently the Sioux had been in a ceremony to Wakan Tanka (The Great Spirit). The Sioux believe "Everything the Power of the World does is done in a circle." Resuming the March at five o'clock in the afternoon, they ride down the valley a couple miles and find a large band of buffalo. Instinct kicks in and the Crow scouts race their horses full speed into the herd, firing their rifles. They kill several buffaloes and the fresh meat is appreciated; however, the position of Captain Clifford's men has probably been betrayed to the Sioux. With nothing else to be gained by advancing further, the detachment turns back. At night the men stop and camp at the same tributary to the Yellowstone they crossed earlier in the day, having made full circle. This stream is called by the Crows "They-froze-to-death," where some of their tribe once perished from the harsh weather.

Captain Clifford is homeward bound.[4]

4. Montana State University Library, *General Gibbon's March*

---

78 years and 9 months later a mournful howl echoes back.

Where the wild coyotte[sic] howls out his woes

To the northern lights and the frozen snows.

February 5, 1955

Not equipped for a Montana blizzard, a Lindsay farmer, William Schmidt, and Clifford Harsh are in Cliff's car on the way out to the Schmidt farm. About two miles from the farm the automobile, probably a Studebaker and not the best vehicle for bucking drifts, becomes firmly stuck. Without four- wheel drive and unable to dig out, the car tires just spin. The men assess the situation. Clifford, who once taught survival to Boy Scouts, is totally unprepared. It's late, cold, and dark out, the wind is picking up, and now it's a blizzard. With no hope of anyone coming by on a night like this, the men decide to abandon the car with a tank half full of gas and follow the fence line to the farmstead. The doomed two strike out for the farm only a couple miles down the road. It's going to feel good to get to the house and warm up. Inky-dark, the blizzard picks up, can't see anything, keep trudging, and stay along the fence. A jog in the fence line, it must be the lane to the house. It's like walking in a dream: Where have I been? How far have I gone? Keep moving, keep walking. How long have we been going? I can't keep up, where am I? Should I circle back? Can't think straight—not so cold now. Oh, I need to rest, sleepy............ It was a terrible blizzard at 7:30 Saturday night. A neighbor drives by the stuck car assuming the passengers have walked on to the farmhouse.

The men mistake an open gate to a field for the farmhouse lane.

February 8, 1955

"They-froze-to-death."

After three days of searching, the frozen bodies of the men are found a half mile southeast of the farmhouse at 4:30 P.M. Art Soare spots Schmidt's mostly snow-covered body from the air. His hands are covered with blood from barbed-wire cuts; he had no mittens. A half hour later and a half mile west of Schmidt's body, McCone County Sheriff Gene LaRowe discovers the frozen body of Clifford Harsh drifted over with snow; only his cap, gloves, and feet are visible.

He was 45 years old.[5]

The Corpus Christi Caller-Times. 09 Feb 1955 newspaper.

5. The *Glendive Daily Ranger* publishes winter views of Maco Sica Park.

February 10, 1955

Dr. Hiatt puts together a letter to the editor of the *Glendive Daily Ranger* on Toastmaster International letterhead to congratulate them for printing the winter scenes of Maco Sica in the paper. He types, "As a charter subscriber I thank you for this glimpse of God." And as Doc's blood boils a little bit, he adds, "such a dramatic exception to the rule of printing so much about humanity's crap and corruption." He ends the letter with a report that his fifth-grader son mentioned 15 classmates brought clippings of the 2 Maco Sica pictures to school. Doc calls it "grassroots reaction." "Thanks, R. W. Hiatt."

After a proofreading from committee member Haag, Dr. Hiatt cools off and retypes his letter to the editor on his Dr. Robert W. Hiatt optometrist letterhead, revising the "crap and corruption" paragraph to say, "The average reader of today's average newspaper finds little to feel good about or appreciate. As a charter subscriber I thank you for this pleasant glimpse of God. Thanks again,"

The Maco Sica Park Committee meets and discusses promotion and development. The Chamber agrees to pay the remaining $30.00 of the $130.00 cost for lumber to build the toilets.

February 11, 1955

Funeral services for Clifford E. Harsh, age 45, were held at 2 o'clock in the afternoon at the Methodist Church.

A letter to the editor of the *Glendive Daily Ranger* says the following:
Dear Editor:

I have never written a letter of this sort, but upon reading of Cliff Harsh's death, I was very deeply moved. As you know and see, everyday people make the headlines in papers all over the United States. Many times because of something spectacular but not always for deeds toward the betterment of our society.

It was because of Mr. Harsh's guidance, patience and interest that I feel I owe this letter. Through Scouting and as an advisor and teacher in school, he set a pattern for my life and many other friends of mine that only an unselfish man like Cliff does. Anyone associated with Cliff will know what I mean.

Cliff to me is "Truly a Great Man" if only for the things he did for the young people around him. I just couldn't let his passing go without trying to tell someone in Southeastern Montana what a loss we, myself and Glendive have suffered by his untimely and tragic death.

Yours truly,
Dr. D. C. Bundy,
Milligan Hotel Building,
Miles City, Mont.

Dr. Hiatt's February 10th letter to the editor is published below the one from Dr. D. C. Bundy.

February 14, 1955

An article in the Glendive newspaper is titled "Group Asks Maco Sica Name Change." After explaining the application process and the Chamber Committee efforts and investigations into changing the name, the article also informs of an application request for the Federal Bureau of Land Management to transfer 11 sections of federal land to the state. The State Parks Director endorses this request, which could greatly expand the current 160-acre state park.

Clifford Harsh would have been 46 years old today.

February 15, 1955

A Western Union telegram arrives for Dr. Hiatt from Ashley Roberts announcing the appropriation hearing tomorrow morning at 9:00 A.M. and encouraging attendance. "If not possible please wire or call your legislators to support appropriation."

Dr. Hiatt drives to Wolf Point to speak at their newly formed Toastmasters Club and delivers an 18-minute eulogy on Clifford Harsh.

February 16, 1955

Dr. Hiatt, who is the Toastmasters Club Area Governor, arrives back from the meeting in Wolf Point at 1:30 A.M. and sends a telegram to Senator Robins and Representative Hagenston: "please support State Park Appropriation @ 9:00 hearing today: Bob Hiatt."

A letter is sent to Dr. R. W. Hiatt from James Larpenteur Long, who is an authority on the Assiniboine Tribe and author of *LAND OF NAKODA*.

Enclosed with the letter is a clipping where James spotted an article about the name change. He stated that Maco Sika is the correct spelling for "badlands," and in the most common spoken Sioux dialect it is pronounced "Mako She-cha"; however, some Sioux Indians pronounced the word *Sica* as "Seecha." James has the opinion the name Maco Sica is very suitable for the name of the park, and to change the spelling and pronunciation may spoil the authenticity of the name. "Sincerely, James L. Long."

There is no record of Hiatt responding to the letter from James Long.

February 17, 1955

Interdepartmental memorandum from Ashley Roberts to members of the State Park Advisory Committee updates the members on his meeting with the appropriations committee. The bill allows a $6,000 increase over the present budget, which could be knocked down more once it reaches the floor of the house. "This is a far cry from the minimum budget we requested and the improvements and expansion plans we have are mostly out of the question. We will just have to hang on as best we can for another two years and then try again. Sincerely, Ashley C. Roberts." (ACR:mmc)

Dr. Hiatt removes the pages from a *Readers Digest* magazine titled "The Shocking Truth about Our National Parks." The thrust of the article states more money is not the whole answer; it's how the appropriations are used and how the parks are used. New developments and recreation are exciting and get the bulk of the funds, whereas boring operations, maintenance, and protection of the parks are given less money than necessary to maintain proper services. The article suggests we look back at the original purpose and refocus on parks as sanctuaries to flee from congestion "and learn again how to walk, relax and contemplate."

February 23, 1955

R. L. Robins takes time to acknowledge Dr. Hiatt's telegram, recommending support for state park appropriation. Senator Robins passes the telegram to the committee on finances and assures they will do all they can with the money available. "Very sincerely yours, R. L. Robins."

February 24, 1955

Ashley Roberts writes a better "Dear Bob" letter to Dr. Hiatt with positive developments.

The State Highway Commission meets this morning and receives a report from Otis Waters recommending the change in name at Maco Sica State Park to Mako'shika State Park. The Commission agrees with the suggestion and will pass this on to the Land Board for a final determination. Ashley Roberts asks Dr. Hiatt to write another letter to the Land Board, which he will attach with a letter giving the recommendation from the Highway Commission and present to the Land Board at their next meeting.

On another issue, there is a possibility to spend some highway money on park roads. If so, this will help Mako'shika considerably. "Sincerely, Ashley C. Roberts."

March 2, 1955

Dr. Hiatt writes the following one-page letter to Otis Waters:

Dear Otis,

Just a note to thank you for furthering our cause in establishing a simple, beautiful and authoritative name for our State Park.

Ed Lewis, a semi-retired carpenter and perhaps our best local authority on the geology and paleontology of this area, reported this morning that he has virtually completed one of the two W.P.A. Toilets which we'll plant this Spring. He's donating his labor, Ashley authorized us

$100 and Bill VonDrashek assured us the Chamber will go the balance of $30 or so on the cost of materials.

Our Mako'shika request now goes before the State Land Board, which Ashley believes meets next Wednesday. If you feel a note from you to one of the Board members would encourage favorable action, we will again be grateful. Sincerely,

After drafting the letter to Otis, Dr. Hiatt types out another letter, this time to Ashley Roberts.

Dear Ashley,

He starts out by telling Ashley about the letter he wrote to Otis. He gives the toilet construction report and informs him that Ed's shopping for materials saved about $33.00.

As for Ashley's request that Dr. Hiatt write a fresh letter to the Land Board, Hiatt tactfully writes the following:

The fact that you write a darn good letter and gave a rather complete background on this subject, I can see no advantage in re-dating my request to the State Land Board. If anything, I'd say the old date is better in that you may imply that our committee is anxious for State authority so we can start an ever-growing publicity program and repaint signs before tourist season. If they're a board whose conservatism likes to let such requests "cool," the original date should indicate that the request had already had its cooling period. (If I'm nuts, shoot me a wire, and I'll rewrite the request.)

Hiatt explains the predicament he was in with the speech in Wolf Point and there was no way he could have made it to the meeting in Helena. He reports that he heard back from Senator Robins, who gave his telegram to the Chairman of the Committee on Finances; however, Representative Hagenston has not replied.

On another note Hiatt said yesterday he was taught by a farmer how to witch for water with a green willow stick. With a little chuckle he continues to type "so we may organize a witch-hunt in Mako'shika this Spring. Sincerely,"

Using an ink pen at the bottom of the page, Hiatt writes:

P.S. - Ash, I think it would help a great deal in writing your endorsement of our request to the Land Board if you exclude the easy-to-overlook accent above and to the right of the letter "o" in Makòshika. B

March 7, 1955

For the last time Ashley Roberts addresses his reply letter to Dr. Hiatt as Chairman of the "Maco Sica State Park Committee."

The Land Board meeting has been postponed until the 23rd of March, which gives Ashley a little more time to get everything set, and he is confident the new name will be approved.

He is very sorry to learn of the death of Cliff Harsh who did so much for Maco Sica, and he will be sorely missed. "Regards, Ash."

March 15, 1955

Dr. Hiatt types the date on his letter to Ashley as "Ides of March 55."

Hiatt requests 50 more "Come to Montana" booklets, which he will need for park publicity planned in 1955. The Chamber has been out of stock for several months.

His fifth-grader son and a classmate are writing letters to fifth-graders in Pennsylvania and Texas and would also like to enclose a booklet with their letters.

"Many thanks, Bob."

March 16, 1955

The Keystone Automobile Club of Philadelphia sends a cover letter and a questionnaire to Maco Sica (Badlands) Park requesting the information be completed and returned in the stamped, self-addressed envelope as quickly as possible. The club distributes points of interest information to its 130,000 members and wants to bring their information up to date. "Sincerely yours, William A. Armstrong, Manager Touring Department."

March 17, 1955

This time Dr. Hiatt types the date on his letter as "St. Pat's Day." He thanks Ash for the speedy service on the "Come to Montana's."

Two committeemen and Doc hope to get out this weekend to inspect the possibilities of "borrowing" some cedar timbers from an abandoned stockade in order to build an entrance sign to Mako'shika.

March 21, 1955

Ashley Roberts sends a memo to the members of the State Park Advisory Committee along with a copy of the park's proposed budget for the year beginning July 1, 1955. He asks that the members look over the budget and write their approval or disapproval together with any suggested changes. The sooner the better, as the budget will be presented to the Commission for approval on the 30th of March.

The pared-down budget proposal for fiscal year 1956 makes the following suggested revisions. To start off, the Director lists his salary under the heading "HEADQUARTERS." The old proposal had Director at $6,000.00 salary and the new proposal $6,120.00. Completely eliminated are the Field Man and Attorney, while the Stenographer's salary is cut in half. Under "Operations" every line item is slashed and the new car is eliminated. Even though salaries were decreased for Lewis and Clark Caverns State Park, operations were increased with the net results being a slight decrease. Maco Sica went from salaries and operations of $2,150.00 to just operations of $750.00. And so on and so forth for the rest of the Parks and Monuments with Total Operations end result of $41,775.00 revised down from $86,540.00.

March 22, 1955

To start off the letter to Ash on Glendive Chamber of Commerce letterhead, Dr. Hiatt passes on the Chamber's approval of the suggested State Parks budget.

Committeeman Ed Lewis inquired with the Angeles Toilet Stool Company of Pasadena for information on their metal toilet seat covers; however, his letter was returned from the post office for insufficient address. "Since the company information was gleaned from the Montana Department of Health booklet he used for the specifications in building the two outdoor toilets, we are wondering if the Health or Sanitation Department in Helena would know of an alternate source of supply? We do have local plumbing outfit that will inquire with traveling representatives."

Interior Secretary McKay, who spoke to the Western States Council (Chamber of Commerce), states the following. "1. About one out of every four acres in the country is federally controlled, and that is too much. 2. The job assigned to us by Congress is to manage public domain, classify the land for its highest use and dispose of it to citizens who apply for it under various land laws." Committeeman Haag will use the summary of his speech in facilitating the acquisition of those 11 sections of public domain for the park.

"We had a small landslide on the switchbacks and the upper road will need re-graveling. The road is rutted just beyond the city limits and above the switchbacks needs gravel and grading. Will you please ask the Highway commission if we could use the Glendive State Highway Department to gravel the switchbacks and grade the road. Three loads of gravel and one day with a patrol should meet minimum requirements.

Thank you very much!"

March 24, 1955

It's Thursday and the Land Board meets and makes their decision.

This time the State Park Director addresses his neatly typed letter on Highway Commission letterhead to:

Dr. R. W. Hiatt, Chairman
Mako'shika State Park Committee
Glendive Chamber of Commerce
Glendive, Montana

Dear Bob,

Ash thanks Dr. Hiatt for the Glendive Chamber approval of the proposed budget. He hopes the Commission will add its approval next week.

In reference to the toilet seat covers the Board of Health provided the new name and address for the company in Pasadena:

Wickland Manufacturing Company
610 South Arroyo Parkway
Pasadena 1, California

Ash is hopeful the Department of Interior takes action to make Federal lands more available for the purposes of recreation.

At next week's Highway Commission meeting a number of State Park road improvement projects will be presented including the work at Mako'shika.

Sincerely, Ash.

March 25, 1955

It's Friday.

An article in the *Billings Gazette* states, "The State Land Board voted Thursday to change the name of Maco Sica State Park at Glendive to Makoshika Park at the request of the Glendive Chamber of Commerce."

The Land Board members voting were Governor J. Hugo Aronson, Attorney General Arnold H. Olsen, and Public Instruction Superintendent Mary M. Condon.

Tape recorded at 10:30 A.M. for inclusion in KXGN newscasts, Dr. Hiatt explains the reasoning behind the name change and urges all eastern Montanans to adopt the new official pronunciation of Mako'shika—"M-A- K-O-S-H-I-K-A," one word, pronounced just like it's spelled, Makoshika!

With an ink pen Dr. Hiatt hurriedly scrawls out a quick congratulatory letter to Ash thanking him for promoting Mako'shika: "!!!!!"

Ash is updated about the 1 ½-minute newscast for KXGN Dr. Hiatt taped this morning that was played on the 12 o'clock news. The newspaper has the news on page one today. "Thanks again, sir! Bob."

The local newspaper, *Glendive Daily Ranger*, covers the news of the new name of our newest state park, and KXGN radio immediately promotes Makoshika by identifying themselves as "KXGN, the voice of Makoshika State Park."

March 31, 1955

Dr. Hiatt mails the completed Keystone Automobile Club questionnaire and makes a note to send the club a Makoshika brochure when ready.

Clifford Harsh did not live to see the name change project come to fruition. Maco Sica is changed to Mako Sica, which is the correct spelling in the Sioux language, the Santee dialect. With the other *c* changed to a *k* and combined with the letter *h* to make one word, we can suppose the letter *H* (as in Harsh) added to form the word *Makoshika* is an appropriate coincidence.

A solo remembrance hike in the badlands—that's what Doc Hiatt would have done. His silent thoughts envision a memorial cross on a certain butte overlooking a feature in the landscape that looks like a coliseum.

Maco Sica is no more.

A faint echo returns one last time.

Where the wild coyotte^{sic} *howls out his woes*

To the northern lights and the frozen snows.

Chapter 2

Timeline to Makoshika

How often at night, when the heavens are bright
By the light of the glittering stars,
Have I stood there amazed and asked as I gazed
If their beauty exceeds this of ours.[1]

1. One stanza of the original poem ("Home on the Range") by Dr. Brewster M. Higley, an otolaryngologist who moved to Kansas in 1871 to claim land under the Homestead Act of 1862.

Indigenous peoples, the North American Indians, hold original title to the badlands they named Mako Sica.

1682

French explorer René-Robert Cavelier, Sieur de La Salle, claims the entire Mississippi River basin for France, a territory which includes the badlands named Mako Sica.

1762

In a secret agreement, the Treaty of Fontainebleau, the French ceded Louisiana to Spain, a territory which includes the badlands named Mako Sica.

August 1775

A group of treaty commissioners sent by the Continental Congress speak with the Six Nations of the Iroquois Confederacy at Albany, New York. The Iroquois enjoy Freedom of Speech, Freedom of Assembly, Freedom of Ownership, Freedom of Elected Leaders, and other fundamental freedoms that early colonists have not experienced. Iroquoian women have the right to vote and the right to caucus. Their caucus has the power to vote out a leader found to be inept and ineffective.[2]

2. Book. *Crazy Horse and Chief Red Cloud* by Ed McGaa, Eagle Man.

July 4, 1776

The Declaration of Independence is adopted by Congress.

December 15, 1791

The first ten amendments (Bill of Rights) are ratified. Amendment I: "Congress shall make no law respecting an establishment of religion, or prohibiting the free exercise thereof; or abridging the freedom of speech…"

October 1, 1800

France regains sovereignty of the western territory in the secret Third Treaty of San Ildefonso, a territory which includes the badlands named Mako Sica.

July 4, 1803

President Jefferson announces the Louisiana Purchase Treaty to the American people.

The United States acquisition of 828,000 square miles of the Louisiana Territory from France is an area which includes the badlands named Mako Sica.

July 3, 1806

Before crossing the Continental Divide, the Lewis and Clark Expedition split into two teams with Clark taking the southern route. Upon reaching the Yellowstone River, Clark builds canoes for the float downstream to the confluence of the Yellowstone and Missouri rivers.

July 25, 1806

Clark climbs a rock rising from the river valley and names it Pompy's Tower. On the top are two piles of stones placed by the Indians. Clark carves his name and date into the sandstone near where natives have etched figures of animals. After leaving Pompy's Tower, Clark and his party make good time in their wooden canoes. They stop and wait at times for great "gangs" of buffalo to cross the river, and they struggle to fight off grizzly bears attacking their boats. On this leg of the trip, Clark travels past the badlands named Mako Sica.

1814

Pompy's Tower is changed to a new name by Nicholas Biddle, the first editor of Lewis and Clark's journals. Biddle assumes the sandstone landmark was named in honor of the Roman general Pompey the Great[1]; however, Clark had given Sacagawea's son the nickname of Pomp and named the prominent sandstone rock after the boy. Pompy's Tower is now referred to by the name Pompey's Pillar.[2]

1. 07/09/06 *Billings Gazette*, Ed Kemmick

2. www.lewis-clark.org

October 20, 1818

The badlands named Mako Sica now become part of the Missouri Territory.

1834

Missouri receives statehood and the successor of the remainder of Missouri Territory is called Unorganized Territory and includes the badlands named Mako Sica.

May 12, 1846

The Donner Party begins a wagon train journey through Unorganized Territory on their way to California.

September 17, 1851

The Fort Laramie Treaty, also known as the Horse Creek Treaty, acknowledges that all land covered by the treaty is Indian Territory and the United States does not claim any part of it. This Indian Territory includes the badlands named Mako Sica.

1855–1856

Sir St. George Gore, a wealthy Irish nobleman on an extravagant hunting expedition out west with Jim Bridger as one of his guides, is estimated to have slaughtered 105 bears of which 40 are silvertip grizzly bears, deer and elk killed total 1,600, around 2,500 buffalo shot dead and wounded—who knows how many more animals *"For Sport."* The trophy heads and some hides are collected, and otherwise the animals, much to the disgust of the Sioux, are left to rot on the prairie.[1]

He brings an assortment of trade goods along with 250 gallons of whiskey as gifts for the Indians he encounters. A stockade of 100-foot by 120-foot (Fort Gore) is constructed at the confluence of the Tongue River and Pumpkin Creek.[2]

After about 10 months hunting around the Tongue River and Yellowstone Valley, he builds two flatboats, burns his fort, and loads up the buffalo robes, hides, pelts, antlers, and trophy heads to float down the Yellowstone River to Fort Union.

With Jim Bridger guiding, Sir George Gore spends about a month on horseback exploring the country all the way to Fort Union. His return trip takes him past the badlands named Mako Sica. A tributary to the Yellowstone River nearby reminds him of a similar place in Ireland and he names it Glendale Creek.

At Fort Union Gore wants to sell off all his surplus goods, livestock, and wagons and then he plans to float downstream to St. Louis with some men and his trophies. James Kipp, the 70-year-old senior trader for the American Fur Company, offers him a pittance for all of his equipment, which angers Gore greatly. After getting tanked up with fine liquor he orders his men to pile all his excess supplies near the fort's gate and he puts a match to it. Gore, an articulate man who kept meticulous journals and a logbook of the expedition, in a rage tosses all his papers into the flames.

Billings Gazette – 10/09/2002, writer Brett French, book by Dave Walter

Salt Lake Tribune – 2/16/97, Sir George the Buffalo Slayer

May 20, 1862

The Homestead Act of 1862 stipulates who is eligible to apply and the ones that qualify: "From and after the first of January 1863, be entitled to enter a one-quarter section of un-appropriated public lands." (Native Americans Excluded.)

⸺◦C∽◦⸺

June 30, 1862

Brigadier General Henry W. Slocum sends five batteries forward to engage the Confederates in a duel of artillery near Glendale, Virginia.[1]

Book, *To the Gates of Richmond* by Stephen W. Sears

⸺◦C∽◦⸺

July 1, 1862

Colonel Thomas Rosser, 5th Virginia Cavalry, while scouting on the army's right flank, spots Federal columns moving hurriedly. Richard Anderson's division of Confederates advances to the Glendale crossroads where George Meade's brigade of Yankees is posted in front of the advance.

The Seven Days Battle of Glendale is described by the men of the 14th Louisiana as "The Slaughter House." More than any other battle in the Civil War, the Battle of Glendale has more hand-to-hand, actual bayonet and butt- of-gun melee fighting.[2]

A headstone should read: *Many a brave soldier died at Glendale Virginia.*

⸺◦C∽◦⸺

Book, *To the Gates of Richmond* by Stephen W. Sears

⸺◦C∽◦⸺

July 1862

Congress passes a law requiring presidential approval of death sentences emerging from military trials and court-martials.

⸺◦C∽◦⸺

August 1862

The Dakota War is a six-week violent uprising by Dakota Sioux in response to hunger, privation, and treaty violations on the part of the United States federal government.

The death toll estimates include 77 American soldiers, 29 citizen-soldiers, 358 settlers, and 29 Dakota Sioux warriors.

September 28, 1862

Two days after the Sioux surrender, General Henry Sibley establishes a military commission to try the men accused of participating in the war.

November 9, 1862

A list of 303 condemned Sioux fighters is sent to President Lincoln for his approval of their executions. A couple days later Lincoln reviews the cases and trials. Lincoln commutes the sentences of 264 Sioux men and orders the other 39 to be executed.

December 26, 1862

One more condemned man has his death sentence commuted.

The largest mass hanging in U.S. history takes place in Mankato, Minnesota.

Thirty-eight Sioux Indians are escorted to their doom on the hanging scaffold at precisely 10 A.M.

More than 4,000 people crowd the square to watch the hangings and cheer when the third doleful drumbeat signals the sharp ax to slice the rope holding the platform.

Later it's discovered that two men were mistakenly hanged.

May 26, 1864

President Lincoln signs an act of Congress regulating Montana Territory, which includes the badlands named Mako Sica.

July 28, 1864

General Alfred Sully, having been ordered to set up forts and clear a path through Sioux territory east of the Missouri River encounters a large Indian trading village of about 1,500 lodges near Killdeer Mountain. The army is bent on punishing the Sioux for the hostilities in Minnesota. The army attacks the peaceful Indians who had nothing to do with the Sioux war. The army is successful in killing scores of warriors, scattering the village inhabitants and burning lodges along with their winter supplies of food.

With the "hostiles" cleared out of the way, the railroad is free to forge ahead to the Yellowstone.

February 2, 1865

The territorial government of Montana forms nine counties. Big Horn County includes the badlands named Mako Sica.

April 29 – November 6, 1868

The Sioux Treaty signed at Fort Laramie recognizes the Black Hills as part of the Great Sioux Reservation, set aside for exclusive use of the Sioux people.

In this treaty President Andrew Johnson said: "As long as rivers run and grass grows and trees bear leaves, Papa Sapa—the Black Hills of South Dakota—will forever be the sacred land of the Sioux Indians."[1]

The hunting grounds unceded by the Sioux include the badlands named Mako Sica.

1. Book. *Crazy Horse and Chief Red Cloud* by Ed McGaa, Eagle Man.

November 27, 1868

Our hearts so stout have got us fame,
for soon 'tis known from whence we came,
Where're we go they dread the name,
of Garry Owen in glory.[1]

When any soldier, anywhere, in the 7th Cavalry salutes an officer, they sound off with "Garry Owen, Sir!"

"Garryowen," a limerick drinking tune sung by Irish soldiers in the 7th Cavalry, is a marching song with a brisk cadence and a favorite of Lieutenant Colonel George Armstrong Custer, who has his regimental band play the marching tune quite deliberately right before attacks.

As twilight turns to daylight, the men of the 7th Cavalry pull a sneak on the unsuspecting Cheyenne winter camp of Chief Black Kettle on the Washita River. A Cheyenne baby cries, enabling Custer to pinpoint the tribe's exact location. Looking down from the heights over the Indian village, Custer has his band strike up the opening notes of "Garryowen" to signal the attack.

A Cheyenne child hears faint strange sounds: *Enemene*,[2] "sing noises." Suddenly the camp explodes in turmoil. Horse hooves pounding around the tipis are followed by shots, screaming, running, blood, and death, and for the child, now silence.

Chief Black Kettle and his wife try to escape across the Washita River and both are shot dead.

1. Lyrics of the Irish version "Garryowen"

2. Cheyenne word for sing

January 15, 1869

The Territorial county of Big Horn is split in half, with the northern half given the name Dawson, which includes the badlands named Mako Sica.

1871

George Armstrong Custer's 7th U.S. Cavalry is led by Brevet Brigadier General Lewis Merrill in South Carolina to quell the violence and break up the Ku Klux Klan.

1876

The 7th Cavalry under the command of Lieutenant Colonel George Armstrong Custer leaves Fort Abraham Lincoln on his way to the Little Bighorn. As they depart the sight of their fort, Custer's band plays "Garryowen."[1]

1. Niall O'Dowd, IrishCentral.com, 11/15/2017

On their way to the Rosebud, Custer and his men travel past the badlands named Mako Sica.

June 21, 1876

Newspaper reporter Mark Henry Kellogg wires his last dispatch: "We leave the Rosebud tomorrow and by the time this reaches you we will have met and fought the Red Devils with what result remains to be seen. I go with Custer and will be at the death."

June 22, 1876

As Custer's men leave the Terry column at the Rosebud River and ride on toward the Little Bighorn, the last song the band plays is "Garryowen."[1]

1. Custer Battlefield Museum, Garryowen, MT

June 25 and 26, 1876

The army's horses, exhausted from the long march, are no match for fresh Indian mounts and are unable to effectively flee the counterattack. The battle results in the defeat of the 7th Cavalry Regiment of the United States Army. The Plains Indians capture the United States flag and massacre Yellow Hair (Lieutenant Colonel George Armstrong Custer) and more than 200 men, including 34 Irish soldiers in his battalion. Custer, the most ardent and wasteful buffalo hunter in the 7th Cavalry, has met his match.

Payback in part for the "Dakota 38."[1]

1. Smooth Feather Productions (shown at North Dakota Heritage Center)

June 27, 1876

General John Gibbon, who arrives at the site of the massacre a day late, discovers the body of reporter Mark Kellogg.

On a U.S. Army supply that runs past the badlands named Mako Sica and up the Yellowstone River, Captain Sipes' boat arrives at the Big Horn Post. He is one of the first to learn the bloody results of the battle.

February 16, 1877

The territorial legislature changes the name of Big Horn County to Custer County following "Custer's Last Stand" in June of 1876.

October 1, 1878

Major General Franklin Bell is assigned to the "all-white" 7th Cavalry at Fort Abraham Lincoln, Dakota Territory.

June 25, 1880

The Sioux have their own name for the Battle of the Little Bighorn. Each year the Sioux commemorate their victory over the United States Army at the "Battle of the Greasy Grass."

July 13, 1880

By executive order, the Indian Territory area 620 is taken possession of by the United States. This area includes the badlands named Mako Sica.

October 6, 1880

Articles of incorporation for the new town of Glendive are filed by Lewis Merrill, Jas A. Burns, Henry J. Nowlan, William A. Mann, and Herbert J. Slocum.[1]

Lewis Merrill is the commander of troops guarding Northern Pacific Railroad construction crews as they lay tracks up to the Yellowstone River near Glendive. He was not highly regarded by his peers in the 7th Cavalry. Major Marcus Reno labeled Merrill as a "notorious coward and shirk." Captain Frederick Benteen, who disliked Reno, commented, "Poor a soldier as Reno was, he was a long way ahead of Merrill," whom he also labeled a "chump."

Merrill's efforts to quell Klan violence eventually leads to the dismantling of much of the Ku Klux Klan in the country.[2]

Henry J. Nowlan is a major in the 7th Cavalry.

William A. Mann had been appointed to the United States Military Academy, graduating in 1875, and received a commission as a second lieutenant of infantry. He serves on assignment with the 7th Cavalry.

Major Herbert J. Slocum of the 7th Cavalry is the nephew of Ulysses S. Grant.

1. *OTOL* pg. 11

2. Wikipedia

1881

Henry F. Douglas became a sutler for Major Merrill's troops, who were guarding the construction of the Northern Pacific Railroad between Bismarck and Glendive.[1]

"Legend indicates"[2] General Lewis Merrill of the U.S. Cavalry names the town Glendive in honor of Sir George Gore, the eccentric nobleman who slaughtered buffalo in great numbers, just for the fun of it.

The north side of Glendive, which is actually west of the railroad tracks, has avenues named similar to Union officers in the Civil War: George G. Meade, Lewis Merrill, and Charles S. Kendrick.

The area of town east of the railroad tracks is commonly referred to as the South Side and also has some avenues with similar Confederate officer names, such as Colonel Thomas Rosser, Lieutenant General Richard H. Anderson, and Lieutenant General Richard Taylor. As these south-side avenues make a charge for College Hill they are intersected by Grant Street.

Thomas L. Rosser was a West Point classmate and close personal friend of George Armstrong Custer. Rosser was a Confederate major general during the American Civil War and is now a railroad construction engineer.

James Franklin Bell of the 7th Cavalry married Sarah Buford.

1. *An Uncommon Journey* pg. 375

2. *OTOL* pg. 11

1882

James Franklin Bell serves with the military escorts for the Northern Pacific Railroad construction crews.

Henry Douglas of Glendive ships 250,000 buffalo hides back east. This concludes the last of the major buffalo hunts in the nation.[1]

1. *OTOL* pg. 11

1883

To the Sioux, the buffalo is the staff of life—much more than just an animal.[1]

Hide hunters wiped out the buffalo herds that the Blackfeet Indians depend on for their culture and subsistence.

1884

More than one-fourth of the twenty-three hundred Blackfeet in the United States starve to death.

1885

The great herds of buffalo on the northern plains have been mostly exterminated by hide hunters. Diseases such as anthrax, brucellosis, and tuberculosis carried by cattle provide another death sentence for the once prolific bison.[2]

Gone are the days when the buffalo graze the grasses and herbs, wallow out dust bowls, and stampede across the highland and lowland short-grass prairie in Mako Sica.

Hereafter the sound of thunder, is thunder.

1. *Land of Nakota*, James L. Long

2. *Buffalo Nation* pg. 26, Ken Zontek

1889

A spiritual movement known as the Ghost Dance gives the Plains Indians hope. The ceremony has four key elements. First, the earth will regenerate. Second, the buffalo will return. Third, the Euro-Americans will go away. Fourth, the Indian population will multiply.

November 8, 1889

Montana becomes the 41st state.

December 29, 1890

At Wounded Knee Creek in South Dakota, the 7th Cavalry soldiers massacre 350 men, women, and children of the Lakota tribe led by Chief Big Foot. The Bluecoats successfully muzzle the battle cry of the last free band of Sioux.

The sacred Ghost Shirt is confiscated from among the dead for a souvenir. This tragedy marks the rock-bottom depths of Native American existence.

———————— ∞C∕∽∞ ————————

March 31, 1905

It's Friday, and 21-year-old Roy Chapman Andrews, along with his 23- year-old friend Monty White, decide to go duck hunting on the Rock River in Wisconsin. Monty accidentally drops his paddle in the river, lunges to retrieve it, and the boat capsizes, dumping both hunters in the icy water. Monty tries to swim for shore, his legs cramp up, and that's it: he sinks like a stone. Roy is swept downstream, manages to grab a submerged tree limb, and is able to drag himself to shore. It takes more than an hour for Roy to slosh through flooded fields and finally find help. Eventually, Monty's body is recovered from the river, leaving the young Andrews full of grief and remorse.[1]

1. Book published by National Geographic: *Dragon Bones and Dinosaur Eggs*

June 8, 1906

President Theodore Roosevelt signed the Antiquities Act into law; any person who appropriates, excavates, injures, or destroys any historic object of antiquity situated on lands owned or controlled by the U.S. Government needs permission from the Department of the Government having jurisdiction over the lands on which the antiquities are situated or they will be subject to fines or imprisonment or both.

The act is signed largely to prevent the looting of archaeological Native American structures and objects on land not privately owned.

March 23, 1910

Major General J. Franklin Bell, Chief of Staff of the United States Army, is injured in an automobile accident in Washington D.C. Mrs. Herbert J. Slocum, the wife of Major Slocum of the 7th Cavalry, was killed instantly.

The passengers in the car were Major General Bell, Mrs. Herbert J. Slocum, and their chauffeur. The chauffeur was unhurt in the accident.[1]

1. *Sacramento Union*, March 24, 1910

1910

Four nurses from North Dakota join forces and homestead just north of what shall soon become the town of Richey. Elinor Marshall, one of the four homesteaders, pens their group as "The Four Old Maids of List Creek." [1] According to family legend, they built a four-bedroom house right on the corner of the four quarter sections homesteaded, each having their own bedroom on the corner of their prospective quarter section. In reality, they each built shacks on their land with supplies gathered up in Poplar, Montana. All the maidens have a nickname. Bergit is called Ole, which was her dad's name and common in Norway. You can imagine, with four pretty, young, single ladies living together out on the Montana prairie, it won't take long to attract suitors. One of the four List Creek homesteaders is Edith Keefe. She is engaged to Bud Mayes, who jilted her. Heartbroken and depressed, Edith disappears, never to be heard from again. John Knauff homesteads near Richey at the age of 22, and it is there he meets Bergit (Ole). They are married in 1914.[2] When the last of their four children is born she is given the name of Edith, most likely in memory of Bergit's vanished friend.

1. Elinor M. Porter obituary from 1978

2. Knauff family history book

—◦○⟨∽⟩○◦—

In the same year a Norwegian immigrant by the name of Peter Hans Hagenston files on a homestead two miles southwest of Banks, North Dakota. They are latecomers; most of the land in western North Dakota has already been taken. Peter has been working as a carpenter in Dazey, North Dakota—a good trade if you're hankering to build a prairie shack. He finally decides it's time to pack up the family and head out to greener pastures. It's fall 1910 by the time a team of horses, cows and chickens, wagon and rack, heavy tools and household goods have been acquired and loaded in a boxcar for the trip west. The railroad has not yet reached McKenzie County, so they make it as far as Ray, North Dakota. Peter's wife Anna and their son Ernest, age 8, take the passenger train, while Peter and the elder son Arthur S. Hagenston, age 10, ride the freight train. It's a tough go: by the time they arrive at Ray they are greeted by a howling northwest blizzard. They unload everything off the freight train, and load it all back on the wagon and rack, and then wait for the blizzard to let up. Unfortunately, they find out that the ferry to cross the Missouri River has already been pulled out for the winter. The ice is too thin to cross; it would be weeks before they could attempt an ice crossing. They decide to go to Williston for the winter with hopes of getting work. It takes 3 days to go 30 miles by wagon in the snow and drift. Arthur spends those 3 days prodding the cow to lessen the drag on the horses as they make their wagon trip to

Williston. The plans are to begin proving up their homestead after they get through the winter. Peter has to work in the summer to make ends meet, and when time allows, logs have to be hauled by wagon eleven miles to their home site. By the following winter, with their homestead shack only partially built, the family spends most of the winter living in two small adjoining tents while Peter keeps working on the log house. The boys bank snow up beside the tent walls to cut the wind, to create an igloo effect. Food gets a little scarce at times, and eating jackrabbit, living in tents most of the winter, with coyotes howling outside every night, leaves the family a lasting impression of pioneering.[1]

1. From Hagenston family history written by Arthur S. Hagenston.

<hr />

April 6, 1917

The United States declares war on Germany, finally entering into World War I.

Volunteering for military service is an opportunity for the American Indian to get away from boarding schools. A mass exodus from boarding schools causes some to close.

The United States federalizes National Guard divisions to quickly build up an army. Major General William A. Mann becomes the first commander of the 42nd Division, which is composed of National Guard units from 26 states and the District of Columbia. Colonel Douglas MacArthur, who is Major General Mann's chief of staff, said such an organization would "stretch over the whole country like a rainbow." The rainbow name sticks and the 42nd Division is granted the special designation nickname of "Rainbow Division."

Major General William A. Mann signs an autograph with a quotation from Hamlet: "To thine own self be true. Thou canst not then be false to any man.

"William A. Mann
Major Genl Natl Army
Comdg 42nd (Rainbow) Division"[1]
1. Greg Hagenston owns the original autograph.

September 26, 1918

After the greatest artillery bombardment in U.S. history, 350,000 American soldiers get to their feet and advance across no-man's-land toward the German trenches in the Meuse-Argonne offensive. In this largest American battle in history, over a million American soldiers participated. The Choctaw code talkers are instrumental in the U.S. victory by using their Indian language in place of regular military code. A captured German officer confirms they were "completely confused by the Indian language and gained no benefit whatsoever" from their wiretaps.[1] This key battle "cut the German throat"[2] and was the beginning of the end of World War I.

More Native Americans served per capita in the armed forces than any other group of Americans. General John Pershing wrote, "The North American Indian took his place beside every other American in offering his life in the great cause, whereas a splendid soldier, he fought with courage and valor of his ancestors."[3]

November 11, 1918

Fighting ends at the 11th hour of the 11th day of the 11th month. The Great War is over.

1. Wikipedia

2. Quote from historian Geoffrey Wawro

3. *TIME*, Olivia Waxman, 11/23/2018

June 2, 1924

President Calvin Coolidge signed into law the Indian Citizenship Act, which granted full U.S. citizenship to the indigenous peoples of the United States, called "Indians" in this act.

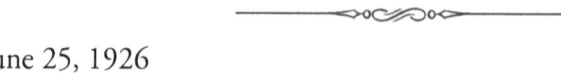

June 25, 1926

A solemn ceremony is held on the 50th anniversary of the Battle of the Little Bighorn in front of fifty thousand attendees. To dedicate a granite memorial at the Tomb of the Unknown Soldier in front of the Custer Battlefield Museum in Garryowen, Montana, White Bull, a Sioux Indian chief, and General Edward Godfrey "bury the hatchet" and remember those who died that tragic day five decades earlier.[1]

1. Custer Battlefield Museum

1934

Roy Chapman Andrews becomes the Director of the American Museum of Natural History in New York City. During his many years as an adventurer and explorer, he can remember ten times where he narrowly escaped death. "Two were from drowning in typhoons, one was when our boat was charged by a wounded whale, once while my wife and I were nearly eaten by wild dogs, once we were in great danger from fanatical lama priests, two were close calls when I fell over cliffs, once was nearly caught by a huge python and twice I might have been killed by bandits." On one occasion in the Gobi Desert, Andrews and his team of explorers unknowingly camped near a den of poisonous pit vipers which invaded their tents in the night, slithering into their shoes and caps, coiling around the posts of their cots, and stretching out among their guns. The cold temperature was their saving grace, making the snakes slow to strike. The men killed 47 snakes in their camp that night and left everyone skittish and wary. This experience caused Roy to develop a phobia about snakes, culminating one day when he stepped on something soft and round, causing him to immediately jerk back and scream. To his relief, the coiled rope his foot lands on poses no danger.

Andrews' close escapes and knack for surviving adventures had no logical explanation other than, as Roy says, "I must have been born under a lucky star."

1943

General Douglas MacArthur is the commander of the 1st Cavalry Division in the Pacific Theater. The 7th Cavalry is part of the 1st Cavalry Division.

Young Sioux men volunteer in droves to leave the reservation and enlist in the service during World War II. Aware that they will go into battle, these proud young warriors, many of whom joined up with the 7th Cavalry, have been taught from an early age by their elders to hold no grudge against any man. While training in Australia General MacArthur orders seven cavalry soldiers, all Sioux Indians, pulled aside for new orders. They are sworn to secrecy and their assignment is to become scouts and code talkers, communicating by radio in Lakota, their Sioux language. These Lakota Code Talkers work as a team and earn a nickname in the 1st Cavalry: "MacArthur's Boys."[1]

1. *Sioux Code Talkers of World War II*, Andrea M. Page

September 2, 1945

The official end of World War II takes place as Japanese officials sign papers in front of General MacArthur.

August 3, 1946

The Donner Party is guided through the Badlands Park by Glendive pioneer Andrew Larson, who is credited with naming Maco Sica Park—a slight variation in spelling from the Sioux dialect of Mako Sica, or sometimes Maco Sika. The travel group of university students is led by Professor Henry F. Donner, head of the Department of Geology and Geography at Western Reserve University, Cleveland, Ohio. The party is very thankful for the tour and "bewailed" of the fact their itinerary will not allow several additional days in the park, where they would like to explore by saddle horse.

As a token of appreciation, a warm letter and a "box of man-size linen handkerchiefs" is sent from Professor Donner to Andrew Larson for his "courtesy and generosity" in guiding the party of 17 through the badlands.[1]

One hundred years after the ill-fated Donner Party spends the winter of 1846–47 snowbound in the Sierra Nevada, "the virtual father of Maco Sica Park," Andrew Larson, successfully guides a different Donner Party through some badlands.

1. *Dawson County Review*, 10/3/1946, and book *As I Remember* by Gladys Kauffman

1953

Roy Chapman Andrews publishes his book *All About Dinosaurs*. This book for young readers will inspire a new generation of future paleontologists.

July 20, 1953

Mr. and Mrs. A. J. McCarty donate land to Dawson County, which in turn donates the said land to the state of Montana for a park. The Badlands Park had been named Maco Sica, and now the official name will be Maco Sica State Park.

March 24, 1955

The State Land Board votes to change the name of Maco Sica State Park to Makoshika State Park.

March 1955

Dr. Hiatt clips an article by the National Water Well Association from the *Wibaux Pioneer Gazette*. Pondering the lack of water situation in Makoshika, this is just the type of information needed to make plans going forward for a well in the park.

———⋙∘〰∘⋘———

March 31, 1955

Ed Lewis builds two latrines according to rigid Board of Health standards.

A letter from the Chairman of the Makoshika State Park Committee with an itemized list of materials charged to Ed Lewis along with a receipt from Guelff and Son is mailed to the State Park Division of the Montana Highway Commission for reimbursement. The lumber, shingles, nails, screws, and hinges total $93.52, and the four metal toilet seat covers which have been ordered and paid for by Ed Lewis from Wickland Mfg. Co. in Pasadena, California, for $20.10 are added to make the total expended for materials $113.62. Dr. Hiatt requests the check for this $100.00 authorized expenditure be made out to Ed Lewis and mailed to Dr. Hiatt.

"Thank you, R.W. Hiatt."

———⋙∘〰∘⋘———

April 7, 1955

Ashley Roberts replies to the request for reimbursement, encloses the proper forms, and instructs Dr. Hiatt on the procedure for Mr. Lewis to submit for payment: have him sign the three copies, sign the affidavit, both the white and pink copies, have both copies notarized and returned to the State Highway Commission, Park Division, for further processing.

A limited amount of roadwork for the park has been authorized and Ashley suggests to Dr. Hiatt that he get in contact with Mr. W. K. Brittain, the Division Maintenance Engineer in Glendive, about the job. "Mr. Brittain will be receiving information from the Maintenance Engineer Mr. W. E. Bawden and it would be a good idea to review the work and make suggestions. Once the recommendations have been reviewed we can procure final authorization and get started on the work. Sincerely, Ash."

Edwin Lewis receives a letter addressed to his home address at 409 South Sargent Avenue in Glendive from the Wickland Manufacturing Company in Pasadena 1, California, manufacturer and distributor of Sierra Sanitation Equipment. His money order for $19.80 is returned. The two M-40 toilet seats Ed ordered cannot be shipped—that model has been discontinued. The current model #1789-SS stool which is interchangeable with the M-40 is priced at $23.76 each net. F.O.B. Pasadena, California. Signed: Norman Wickland.

—————∞————

April 11, 1955

Dr. Hiatt sends a letter to the Wickland Manufacturing Company to plead for a better deal on the toilet stools. The letter reads as follows:

Dear Mr. Wickland,

Do you have ten minutes? Although we're two busy executives, and chances are remote we'll ever get within a thousand miles of each other, I'd like to bypass titles, position, and conventional business ethics and talk personally with you.

Enclosed is a copy of your letter to Ed Lewis and the reason for this letter. Also within is a report of our committee's activities during 1954. The "Come to Montana" refers to our new state park, now officially named "Makoshika."

We're trying to do as much to develop and promote Makoshika as possible with but token appropriations from the young State Park System and the local Chamber of Commerce. Ed donated his time and labor in constructing two latrines for the Park. The State went for most of the materials bill, the Chamber will pick up the balance.

The $23.76 per stool, however, is way out of proportion, and it is here where you come in. Can, <u>will</u>, you help us? I haven't the guts to ask for them at cost, but I thought you're in a position to know whether we can obtain metal toilet stools, new or used, for considerably less money. Thanks for what time, efforts and satisfaction you can give us. It seems no one in this country can help. Sincerely, Robert Hiatt.

April 22, 1955

Committeeman Haag consults for two hours with State Administration of Federal Land Board in Billings on the transfer of the public domain to Montana State Parks.

April 24, 1955

Ed Lewis and Dr. Hiatt borrow Jack Milne's truck along with the city of Glendive gas-powered pump and help Mr. McCarty pump out and cement his well, which the McCartys consent to for public use.

April 25, 1955

This time John Wickland replies to Dr. Hiatt's letter requesting help with the cost of the durable toilet stools. Writing to the Glendive Chamber of Commerce and to the attention of Dr. R. W. Hiatt, he refers to Hiatt as the Chairman of the Maco Sica State Park Committee. He would like to help, and after explaining the actual cost to manufacture the #1789-SS Stainless Steel Stool runs approximately $20.00 a unit, to sell them at cost would not be much less expensive than what was quoted to Mr. Edwin Lewis.

However, he found two "seconds" of the stool in a storage room that were manufactured in aluminum and painted in white baked enamel. John would be willing to put these units in serviceable and presentable condition and sell them for the cost of material only. "The material cost was $8.33 each, so if you would care to write us a check for an even $16.00 we would be glad to forward these to you on notice from your office. These units originally sold for $17.95 each net. We can ship these units within five days from receipt of your order. Wickland Manufacturing Company, John V. Wickland."

⊸◦◖◌◗◦⊶

April 28, 1955

Dr. Hiatt draws out some SIGNS FOR MAKOSHIKA ideas on a sheet of plain tablet paper.

The first series of signs he titles "Burma Shave Series":

For a Psychological/ For a Geological/ For Just a Plain Logical/ Thrill/ See Makoshika.

The next series of signs he sketches say, *Follow Signs to Cold, Safe Spring Water.*

Then six arrow signs to be painted with the words: *Spring Water.*

The sign posted next to the cemented-in, hand-powered pump jack to say the following: *PRIVATE PROPERTY/ If We, The Public/ Respect This Private/ Property We May/ Continue To Enjoy/ This Privilege Of/ Spring Water.*

Smaller letters across the bottom of the sign to read: *Glendive Chamber of Commerce/ Makoshika State Park Committee.*

On the bottom quarter of his tablet paper, Hiatt makes some notes and directions. He has two water witchers listed: Fuzzy (Leonard) Raisl from Bloomfield and Olaf Waag from Savage. Olaf is retired from farming and is now a renowned willow-stick water witcher.

On a smaller piece of paper Doc makes notes he can stick in his pocket. *To find Olaf's place go right into Savage, take the first left. His turn is just a little off the highway.*

Also noted on a small sheet of notepaper is: *Fritschie has a water tank with wheels he will donate. The problem is the wheels are no good and it's awfully heavy. I will have to use a truck. To find his place turn left at the first opportunity after crossing Burns Creek (Where store used to be). Go five miles from the highway and you will come to the stucco house of Charles Basta. Go a short distance beyond the Basta place (there is a woven wire gate), turn right on the gravel road for two and a half miles and then it's a left turn at the Fritschie mailbox.*

April 29, 1955

A pleased Dr. Hiatt sends a money order along with a letter to John Wickland:

Dear John,

Hope you don't resent the familiarity, but I like to address my friends by their first names, and you have certainly proved yourself a friend in need. I'd even say you went overboard with kindness in making your offer, which, of course, we accept and herein enclose the $16.00 M.O. It's just exactly that sort of spirit in action that's going to make Makoshika State Park what it should be.

I'll no doubt remember your letter for a long time because of its date, which just so happened to fall on precisely the tenth anniversary of (1) the birth of the UN in San Francisco, (2) the historic handshaking of Russian and American GI's at the Elbe River, and (3) my parting glimpse of the Golden Gate Bridge which, en route to the South Pacific, many of us wondered if we'd be privileged to see it again. Thank you very much, Robert Hiatt.

May 2, 1955

A mimeographed <u>Acknowledgment</u> is mailed to the Glendive Chamber of Commerce, P. O. Box 930 in Glendive and to the attention of R. W. Hiatt.

The purchase order letter dated 4/29/55 is for 2 only #1789-A Stools (Seconds) @ $8.00 each net.

The material will be shipped 5/16/55 F.O.B. Pasadena, California. Terms: Net 10th Proximo.

"Wickland Manufacturing Company, Jane Curran for Norman Wickland."

After what Dr. Hiatt refers to as a 6-week stalemate due to difficulty in securing metal stools, he makes himself a note that they are supposed to be shipped from Pasadena on the 16th of May.

May 8, 1955

Dr. Hiatt clips an interesting article from the *Billings Gazette* about some recently discovered copies of the *Frontier Scout* weekly paper which were printed at Fort Union, Dakota Territory, on July 14 and August 17, 1864. This was the era of miners trying their luck prospecting on the headwaters of the Yellowstone. Not encouraged by the dangerous Sioux Indian hostilities and the lack of good diggings, the miners are waiting anxiously for the government to send troops. Travel is precarious as passengers and freight ply the Missouri River between Fort Union and Fort Benton. The steamers *Yellowstone* and the *Effie Dean* both have serious problems getting laid up on sandbars in the river. Smaller flat-boats out of Fort Benton come to the rescue and pick up freight including passengers from the immobile steamers.

The editors of the *Frontier Scout* make a correction to the June 22nd issue where they said the Fort Union Army post was built in 1832 by Major Culbertson, when in fact the first old fort was built in 1828 by Kenneth McKenzie, president of the American Fur Company, who came up the Missouri River with his construction party of 50 men. Fort Floyd was what they called it at the time. It burned down and a new fort was built in 1831. McKenzie left in 1834, which was the year Congress barred sale of liquor to the Indians. He had constructed a still for making "merchandise" to sell to the Native Americans. Unfortunately, the act of Congress doesn't take hold and liquor trade with the Indians in the area continues.

The North-Western Indian Expedition led by General Alfred H. Sully left Sioux City on June 4, 1864. The army of 3,500 men set out to punish the Sioux, force them onto reservations, and build military forts to strengthen the peace. In the short term, they manage to stir up a hornet's nest of angry Sioux, who increase their attacks on the steamboats coursing the upper Missouri River.

Fort Rice in Dakota Territory was established by General Sully on July 7, 1864 as a field base for his expedition. The fort, named after Brigadier General James Clay Rice of Massachusetts who was killed at the Battle of the Wilderness during the Civil War, becomes one of the most important military posts on the upper Missouri River.

The expedition lasts four months and terrible destruction is done to Sioux lodges, setting fire to the camps and surrounding woods. Fifteen steamboats were hired to transport men and supplies part of the distance, and three steamboats were retained to support the expedition.

It was the Mauvaises Terres (Badlands) of the Little Missouri that stopped the soldiers in their pursuit of the Sioux. The Mauvaises Terres was described as "a succession of pinnacles, ravines, buttes, and mounds of every conceivable size and shape." The Sioux were able to find refuge and melt into the landscape that another writer described as a scene that "beggars description; it is only such a scene as can be realized in some wild, distorted nightmare dream; buttes of every possible shape, size, description, and color from grey to bright red and from 5 to 400 feet high, piled in inconceivable confusion by nature in one of her very wildest freaks."

The expedition reaches the Missouri-Yellowstone Confluence August 12th. Steam-boating up the Yellowstone about 50 miles and bypassing the small fur trading post of John Brasseau, they then progress all the way upriver to near Glendale Creek. This trip "demonstrated the practicability of steamboat navigation on the Yellowstone."

The short-lived *Frontier Scout* weekly newspaper gives a glimpse of early frontier life from the vantage point of soldiers from the Company I, 30th Wisconsin Volunteers. The paper offers dominant space to Patrick & Hull, fort bakers who provided pies for the printers. Barely a mention and with less print affords the news that a soldier from Company L of the 7th Iowa Cavalry drowned while swimming the river at Fort Union.

———⊙◦C〰つ◦⊙———

1964

One hundred years after that *Frontier Scout* weekly paper is published, Albert Jeremiah McCarty passes away. His wife Catherine McCarty lives to the ripe old age of 107. She worked for the Red Cross for over 50 years taking care of war veterans. She becomes friends with the Indians and they give her the name Winona, which in the Sioux language means "mother." Mr. and Mrs. A. J. McCarty donated land to Dawson County to form Maco Sica Park, which for spelling and pronunciation purposes was changed to the scientifically equivalent Sioux word "Makoshika." So in effect, you could say Catherine McCarty is the mother of Makoshika, for without her gift of the land, Maco Sica Park would not have been born.

To commemorate her 100th birthday Catherine McCarty is awarded the title to a square inch of land at the headwaters of the Missouri River. That's quite a small parcel even though only a symbolic gesture. More appropriately it should have been for a title to a small plot of land near where the Missouri and Yellowstone rivers meet, with enough space to place a small headstone for her namesake—the soldier that drowned in 1864 at the confluence. The soldier's name: Jerome McCarty.

———⊙◦C〰つ◦⊙———

November 27, 1968

On the 100th anniversary of the Washita Massacre, a reenactment takes place. Descendants of the 7th Cavalry known as "Grandsons of the Seventh Cavalry" are in attendance as reenactors. Relatives of the Cheyenne at Washita, wearing their traditional garments, are also present for the commemoration and have set up tipis on the original site of the battlefield. They have not been told that the Grandsons of the Seventh Cavalry will be there. The Cheyenne hear the battle tune "Garryowen" just as the Grandsons thunder in on horseback firing their blanks. The Cheyenne children present are terrified, screaming and running. The Grandsons of the Seventh Cavalry ride up and salute Chief Lawrence Hart, who is horrified they would tread on this hallowed ground.

A museum has returned the body of a child killed at the attack 100 years ago. The tribe members and the 7th Cavalry descendants gather together for a ceremony to bury the child victim's remains in sacred tribal ground with dignity and traditional Cheyenne songs. The mood is somber as the collection of small bones is passed hand to hand down the lineup of Cheyenne relatives. A Cheyenne woman, in a spontaneous act of kindness and goodwill, removes her shawl and wraps the coffin with the beautiful woolen garment as it is passed by. At the end of the line, Lawrence Hart, a Cheyenne Peace Chief, unwraps the blanket from the coffin, and as it is a Cheyenne tradition to offer the coffin wrap to a guest, with trembling hands, walks up to the 7th Cavalry Captain and places the blanket on his shoulders. With tears running down his cheeks the Captain approaches the chief, removes a pin from his uniform, and says as he extends his hand, "Lawrence, this is the Garryowen pin worn by the original members of the 7th Cavalry. It is the signal to attack. I have taken it off my uniform and I want you to have it on behalf of the Cheyenne people. We are sorry that 'Garryowen' was played that day 100 years ago and never again will it be played against your people."

Oh, give me a home where the buffalo roam,
Where the deer and the antelope play;
Where seldom is heard a discouraging word,
And the sky is not cloudy all day.

MAKOSHIKA

CHAPTER 3

Mr. Makoshika (1955)

May 22, 1955

First, they use Jack Milne's truck to load up the 18-foot wooden power pole and bring it to town. Then using George Urbanec's truck and Montana Dakota Utilities and Montana Highway Department equipment, four men and a boy go to work to haul the pole and tools to the top of what Dr. Hiatt describes as the "Matterhorn" in Makoshika. At the top of the badlands peak Dr. Hiatt and his son Bob, Lars Buvik, Fred Littell, and Roger Smith proceed to dig a hole 5 feet deep, and after attaching the 6 ½-foot cross arms to the pole they erect a cross. The bottom of the cross is set in the ground with the remaining 13 feet above the ground.

A little more than three months after Clifford Harsh's funeral the memorial cross atop the Amphitheater Peak is completed. It soon becomes affectionately referred to by the locals as "The Cross of the Bad Lands."[1]

Sketches of early Glendive history from 1881 to 1956 Diamond Jubilee Pictorial.

———◦◦C⌒Ɔ◦◦———

May 27, 1955

The *Glendive Daily Ranger* publishes three photos of Makoshika in their Friday issue. On the front page are two photos; the lunchtime caption shows a Hereford cow and calf in a pasture near the entrance to the park. The second is of one of the heavy-duty picnic tables that Dr. Hiatt and Kenneth Haag brought to the park from Bozeman. Inside the issue is the scene of the park road after a recent rain. The first two captions have Makoshika spelled wrong as "Makochika." On the photo description of the inside issue, Makoshika is also spelled wrong. The publicity for the park is much appreciated and the misspelling is a minor hiccup—no big problem.

May 30, 1955

Traffic counters in Makoshika State Park register 400 times during a 24- hour period on Memorial Day.

June 1, 1955

State Park Director Ashley Roberts writes to Dr. Hiatt and lets him know he will be in Glendive June 16th. He would like to get together for an inspection tour of the park and discuss plans for improvement.

"The roadwork has been approved and will be underway very soon. Sincerely, Ash."

June 2, 1955

The State Highway Department begins conditioning the main Makoshika road.

Friday, June 3, 1955

The *Daily Ranger* publishes a short news clip titled "Makoshika Park Roads Improved by State Agency." Hiatt reports drainage will be improved, roads widened, the trail to McCarty's well will be bladed, and a turnaround will be made at "eyeful" vista point which Hiatt describes as the most panoramic view of the park.

Dr. Hiatt makes himself some notes about the amount of gravel to be hauled, the culvert improvements, the switchbacks and perennial mudslides.

June 5, 1955

Billie Haag completes the painting of 16 new signs.

June 6, 1955

Ed Lewis and Hiatt post Makoshika signs and plant 7 new supports.

June 7, 1955

More signs posted.

June 8, 1955

Dr. R. W. Hiatt types up a midyear report on the activities of the Makoshika State Park Committee, Glendive Chamber of Commerce, for 1955 to date. This report is twofold, serving as a written report which also can be presented verbally by Dr. Hiatt as a formal speech:

Although Makoshika State Park has been developing here in our back yard for 20,000,000 years, I'll limit my report to its development during the past five months. I might remind you, too, that a year-and-a-half ago it wasn't a State Park, and three months ago it wasn't Makoshika.

We learned in January that the State Highway Commission was kicking around our request to improve, simplify, and authorize the name of the park Makoshika instead of the original Maco Sica which everybody murdered in pronunciation. So we proceeded to persuade

Commissioner Otis Waters that our request had merit, and he, in turn, convinced the Commission at their February meeting. The Commission then recommended the change to the State Land Board where the authority was granted in March by the Governor, Attorney-General and Superintendent of Public Instruction—a testimonial that those two political institutions can be bipartisan.

Committeeman Ed Lewis, who, incidentally, is more familiar with the geology and paleontology of Makoshika than anyone I know, constructed two latrines for the Park during February. Installation of them has been delayed three months due to difficulty in finding metal stools which the strict Board of Health specifications recommend. They were reportedly shipped from Pasadena May 16th (by way of Suez Canal?). Ed donated his time and skill, the State Park Division chipped in $100 and the Chamber will pick up the balance of $30 or so on the materials. Guelff Lumber allowed Ed the use of their building in which to work, and Hagenston's are donating storage space until the stools arrive.

In April Committeeman Kenneth Haag spent two hours with the Federal Bureau of Land Management in Billings getting familiar with the red tape necessary to acquire title to the public domain in the park area. Law limits such transfers to 640 acres per party per year. My request for 7,000 acres last year must have raised an eyebrow. So we're starting over again, and Kenny already has our 1955 application prepared for 640 acres, some contiguous to present State Park land, some which include the main road.

Also in April two committeemen helped A. J. McCarty drain and clean out their 20'-deep spring water well. The job was much facilitated by a motor pump which the City was kind enough to lend. McCarty's have generously welcomed the public to use this well so long as it is respected as private property.

A conservative estimate based on a traffic counter of the number of visitors to Makoshika on Memorial Day was 400.

The big news and the good news is now manifest in Makoshika. In May the local division of the State Highway Department received authority to improve the road, as of now they have spent seven days at it. To date they have:

1. Widened and smoothed the eight miles of main road from the St. Bernard dog to the declivitous drop to the flats.

2. Bladed the road leading to the McCarty cabin, making a new extension off to the left to the well where they cut into the hillside to facilitate cars turning around, and branching a new road off to the right where the most panoramic view in the area may be beheld.

3. Dozed a considerable segment off the summit of switchback hill which perennially landslides onto the road. This they have shoved across the road to build up the eroding lower bank.

4. A turnaround has been leveled off at the last Vista Point.

5. Today and tomorrow are gravel days. The State supplies the gravel and trucks, and the County Commissioners volunteered their drivers for two days.

Fourteen new signs have gone up since Billie Haag finished a fine job of painting them last Sunday. A dozen more will go up later this month.

Time's up, but the committee wishes to thank the three publicity media— the radio, the newspaper and you individual people for all the good work you have, and will have, disseminated in behalf of Makoshika State Park.

And let's not forget it was Cliff Harsh who forged the first and second links of the chain of progress for Makoshika.

Dr. R. W. Hiatt, Chairman
Kenneth L. Haag
Ed Lewis Doug Holm
Cliff Harsh (in memoriam)

No mention of the cross erected on the butte in the badlands. It's too personal.

Dr. Hiatt writes himself a note: *Clay Peters, State Highway geologist.*

"State Badlands Are Top Subjects for Photographers Seeking Color" is the heading on a news clip Dr. Hiatt finds worth saving. Besides the description of vivid coloring, freakish shapes, giant toadstools, the weird construction and patterns of light and shadows, the article goes on to talk of one of the "few places left in the West where one might come across a band of wild horses, roaming the rugged country."

Early explorers found an abundance of bighorn sheep in the badlands. The *Ovis canadensis auduboni*, commonly known as the Badlands bighorn or Audubon bighorn, is thought to be an extinct subspecies of the Rocky Mountain bighorn. The Montana Fish and Game Department is working on transplanting some of the Rocky Mountain bighorns to their former range.

The article states the "amateur or professional rock and fossil collectors will find a wealth of material in the badlands." In areas near Fort Peck and Ekalaka important fossil finds have been discovered, and Ekalaka has a nice display of dinosaur fossils.

The town of Ekalaka was named in honor of Ijkalaka, the Indian wife of pioneer David H. Russell. She was the daughter of Eagle Man, an Oglala Sioux and a niece of War Chief Red Cloud. She was also related to Chief Sitting Bull. Her name has the Sioux meaning of [The Swift One] "for her skill in getting packed and moved when the Sioux were in a hurry to move camp. She lived in the town named in her honor until her death in 1901."

The paper also states: "The Sioux Language is also represented in another badlands area just east of Glendive—Maco Sica State Park."

There is no date on the article that Dr. Hiatt cut out, but evidently, the news of Maco Sica changing to Makoshika has yet to catch the eye of the Miles City (U.P.).

The *Glendive Daily Ranger* writes in their "AS WE SEE IT" section under the heading Makoshika a "well done" for Dr. Hiatt and a "thank you" to the Montana Highway Department. The article goes on to say now that better roads and improvements have been made in the park, we need to work together to publicize this "outstanding attraction."

⌁⌁⌁

June 15, 1955

Ed and Lars plant six more signposts that were discarded city signs and now have been refurbished and repainted.

⌁⌁⌁

June 16, 1955

State Park Director Ashley Roberts along with Glendive Chamber Manager Bill Vondrashek and Dr. Hiatt tour Makoshika.

⌁⌁⌁

June 19, 1955

Lars and Ed plant more signs.

⌁⌁⌁

June 1955

The Glendive Chamber of Commerce sends the June bulletin to its members. The paper is folded in such a way that the two-cent postage stamp seals the fold, saving time, tape, and staples.

Below the list of dates and programs for the summer is typed in capital letters:

JUNE -- JULY -- AUGUST -- SEPTEMBER --- MAKOSHIKA STATE PARK IS OPEN!!!

On the back of the bulletin Dr. Hiatt staples a couple of news clippings. The first clipping from the *Billings Gazette* June 29th Wednesday morning edition is titled "Funds for Park." An announcement is made that $109,000 has been allocated to improve Roosevelt Memorial Park. A new park highway, new headquarters building, and a Theodore Roosevelt museum are in the plans.

Dr. Hiatt would be thinking to himself, must be nice—we had trouble enough scraping up a hundred bucks for materials to voluntarily build two outhouses.

The next news clip is from the *Glendive Daily Ranger* Friday, July 1st. Friday night at about 7:30, Mr. and Mrs. A. J. McCarty were returning from their cabin to Glendive and stopped to put out a fire that was getting out of control. Before it got to some trees, they were able to use a shovel from their car and spread dirt over the blaze until the fire was extinguished. It was a close call, could have been a lot worse. They report the area is covered with picnic litter and paper debris. The park is becoming more unsightly every day due to the litter. The subheading underlined above the "Couple Extinguishes Fire in Makoshika Park Last Night" says: "Paper being strewn everywhere."

July 3, 1955

Art Hagenston and his son Dennis along with Dr. Hiatt and his son Bob spend two and a half hours tidying up around picnic table numbers 4 and 5 in Makoshika Park. They dig two disposal pits, then fill the pits with about 700 beer and oil cans and burn all the paper trash scattered around.

July 5, 1955

The Railway Express Agency delivers the 21-pound box containing the toilet stools that were ordered by letter on 4/29/1955.

July 8, 1955

A couple from the town of Belt tour Makoshika and stop to see Dr. Hiatt to locate an area that was pictured in a *Great Falls Tribune* photograph they spotted in the paper. They state this is the cleanest park they've seen in the northwest. The roads they describe as excellent and claim that trash barrels don't minimize litter.

July 9, 1955

Dick Hampton from Montana Dakota Utilities uses company equipment to dig two holes for the outhouses. Holm Construction donates four sacks of cement, sand, and gravel and pours the slabs.

July 11, 1955

Lars, Ed, and Dr. Hiatt work on digging crib pits for the toilets and get rained out.

July 12, 1955

Lars and Ed finish the digging and crib installation with N.P. spade and spoon.

Dr. Hiatt serves as Toastmaster at the regular meeting of the club, this time at the Ming Farm in the Bloomfield area. The novice city folks had some fun attempting to judge 4-H beef on the hoof, finally admitting they would be much better judges with the beef on a platter, knife, and fork in hand.

J. J. Ming is the topic-master and speakers include George C. Johnson, Dr.

A. C. MacDonald, Henry Schwartz, and Joe Hathaway. John Cook is the chief evaluator.

July 13, 1955

With the help of Art Hagenston, his son Dennis, two Milne Implement Company employees, Milne's farmhand tractor and flatbed truck, the two concrete slabs are loaded on the truck and transported to Makoshika for placement on cribs. Also helping are Ed Lewis, Lars Burdick, and Dr. Hiatt. Unloading the slabs are Ed, Lars, Jack Lamb from Billings, Dr. Hiatt, and his son Bob.

In the Wednesday *Glendive Daily Ranger*, an article is headed: "Makoshika is Praised by Florida Man." Bill Engleman and his wife from Orlando, Florida, on their way to a vacation in Yellowstone Park, stop by Makoshika and take some movie pictures of the scenery. It is the Kiwanis Club plaque at the edge of town that draws them into Glendive. Bill, a Florida Kiwanis member, attends the regular weekly meeting at the N.P. Lunchroom and "told Members that he thought Makoshika was one of the finest Parks he has ever seen."

July 14, 1955

Art, Dennis, Ed, Lars, R. W. Hiatt, and Bob load the "houses" on Milne's truck to be transported to Makoshika. The toilets are affixed to the slabs and Ed will install a screen and pipe to finish the installation.

Dr. Hiatt gets a plug for Makoshika in the *South Dakota Mail* (*Plankinton Herald*) newspaper. Of course, it helps that his dad is the editor. The short article summarizes the midyear report of the Makoshika State Park Committee which Dr. Hiatt had sent to his father in Plankinton. The article explains the change in spelling and pronunciation of the name of the park. "The Indian name, Maco Seca[sic], had a number of pronunciations, with no absolute agreement on any one, so Dr. Hiatt figured it would be better to Americanize the name to Makoshika, which is easy to pronounce."

July 22, 1955

Dr. Hiatt applies a prime coat of linseed oil to one toilet.

———◦○◯◯○◦———

On Glendive Chamber of Commerce letterhead, Dr. Hiatt types up a two- page letter to the Chamber Board of Directors.

The custom letterhead is worthy of mention. "glendive" is spelled out in red cursive letters with an un-capitalized *g* for aesthetics, followed by the smaller block letters "CHAMBER OF COMMERCE." The address and phone number in red print behind red bullet points read "P.O. Box 939 PHONE EMpire 5-4235 Glendive Montana." In the lighter green background the four bullet points represent the artistry of an airplane in flight, an oil derrick, a locomotive, and a farming scene. Badlands form the background scene at the top and bottom. The bottom of the letterhead has block-letter red script that says: "Eastern Montana's Agriculture—Railroad and Power Center."

Gentlemen,

Thanks to the brains, help, generosity and cooperation of several Glendive citizens several dollars will be saved of the thirty contributed by the Chamber toward material costs of the two new toilets in Makoshika State Park.

Ed Lewis, who has donated so cheerfully and so many hours' skilled labor, paid out $112.72 for materials. The State Park Division reimbursed him with $100.00, leaving a balance due him of $12.72, which you may mail to him at 409 S. Sargent.

Two bills from Hagenston Hardware (for two gallons of boiled linseed oil and for two toilet paper holders) should complete payment for materials.

Those whose contributions were much appreciated in the construction and installation of these "25-year-guaranteed" institutions include: Dick

Hampton, who dug the disposal pits with a 22" bit on MDU's post-hole digger; Joe Morasco[sic] and Holm Construction Company for help, advice and materials in making the concrete slabs; Bob Feisthamel and Ready-mix for working overtime and donating sand and gravel; Jack Milne for use of his truck and four of his employees who helped in loading operations; Guelff Lumber and Hagenston Hardware for storage space; Wickland Mfg. Co., Pasadena, California, for making special metal stools at less than cost for us; Lars Buvik and Bob Hiatt (Jr.) for helping in installation and Ken Haag for helping to apply two coats of linseed oil.

It is estimated that somewhere in the neighborhood of $275 has been saved through the goodness of the hearts of above-named businesses and individuals. Committeeman Lewis deserves special commendation, and it is my hope that if and when the opportunity arises each one of you give Ed a pat on the back.

You may remember in his last report as Secretary-Manager that Cliff Harsh made the statement that there were five men who were good for the Chamber. Bold as that sounded, I think he must have been thinking about men like Ed Lewis.

Sincerely,
R. W. Hiatt, Chairman
Makoshika State Park Committee

Dr. Hiatt saves an article in the *Glendive Daily Ranger* titled: "Millions of Americans Flock to the 28 National Parks." The national parks budget is up over 36% from the 1953 budget.

Unfortunately the increase for state parks is just not there; nonetheless, the beauty and serenity of the unspoiled badlands wilderness is unaffected.

July 26, 1955

Ashley Roberts writes to Dr. Hiatt to thank him for sharing a copy of the letter he wrote to the Chamber of Commerce giving thanks to the many individuals that helped install the two new toilets in Makoshika State Park.

Ashley is planning on being in Glendive July 31 and August 1 to do some photography with Bill Browning. They like the idea of a park-in-action photo shoot and ask if Dr. Hiatt and Ken Haag could meet them at the Jordan around 10 A.M. Sunday morning the 31st. "Very truly yours, Ash."

July 31, 1955

Due to a "schedule conflict" Dr. Hiatt was unable to meet up with Ashley and Bill on Sunday morning to prowl through the park for their photo shoot.

August 12, 1955

A letter from the Glendive Chamber of Commerce accompanies the check for $12.72 to Mr. Ed Lewis. The officers of the Chamber are Vic VanHee, President; E. P. Holm, Vice President; Pete Abler, Treasurer; W. J. Vondrashek, Sec'y Mgr.

The Board of Directors sends a vote of thanks for his generous efforts building the restrooms for the park, and along with the check they send their expression of gratitude for "A good job—well done. Sincerely yours, Dr. R. W. Hiatt."

August 18, 1955

Dr. Hiatt receives a copy of the Montana Chamber of Commerce publication titled *Montana Affairs*, and on the cover page is a nice picture of Makoshika. Inside the 8-page magazine, Bill Browning writes a half- page column: "Makoshika State Park High on Scenic Parade."

In a quick letter to Bill Browning, Dr. Hiatt says, "Excellent job with Makoshika in the August Montana Affairs!" The publication makes a big hit in Hiatt's reception room, and he asks Bill to send him a dozen or even a half-dozen copies of the August issue.

"Sincerely, R. W. H."

August 30, 1955

Right above a brief notice in the *Glendive Daily Ranger* where City Engineer Claude Eyer announces the end of water rationing in Glendive, there is a notice that the Toastmasters Club will meet in Makoshika Park tonight. Dr. Hiatt will give a slide show presentation featuring 36 Kodacolor slides to illustrate the "beauty and utility of Makoshika."

The toastmaster will be Ken Haag; Roger Smith will act as Topicmaster, and Dr. A. C. MacDonald will be the master commentator. Other speakers besides Dr. Hiatt will be Al Pontrelli, Hank Schwartz, J. J. Ming, and John Cross.

Sept 7, 1955

The next project: Fireplaces in the Park. Dr. Hiatt writes to Doug Holm the following:

Dear Doug,

Our post office boxes must be neighbors. Usually I "sort" half my mail into the wastebasket before leaving that institution, but not today. Your "letter" almost went into file 13 too. I would have opened and read it, except that I received one just like it.

Did Doris ruin your dinner the other day by bringing up the subject of Makoshika fireplaces? We have some State Park money to spend now, and there are 115 days of 1955 left. All we need now is Committeeman Holm's know-how released to tackle "Operation Fireplace."

Although I have complete faith in your own individual judgment, if you prefer committee counsel, I think we could all spin out there with you and pool ideas.

Thanks for what you can do,

Bob.

November 1955

The one-page legal-sized Glendive Chamber of Commerce newsletter is mailed out to the members again using the 2-cent stamp to seal the four- way fold. No staples, no tape, no envelope; very frugal. Again, as usual, there is an appeal to the members who have yet to take the time to send their Chamber investment to do so soon. The Chamber always wisely asks for an investment in the Chamber and not dues.

A brief paragraph reports on the Montana State Chamber of Commerce Convention and mentions those who attended from Glendive were: Noel Carrico, Dr. R. W. Hiatt, Bert Hilger, Art Hagenston Sr., and Glendive Chamber Manager Bill Vondrashek.

"The speaker at <u>YOUR</u> annual Chamber of Commerce Dinner to be held January 11th at 7 PM at the Elks Hall will be Bill Browning. He will be showing his pictures of beautiful Montana scenes."

President VanHee asks all Committee Chairs to submit their final committee reports for 1955 by December 1st.

November 15, 1955

Ashley Roberts, Secretary of the State Parks Advisory Committee, sends an invite to the Committee members to attend a meeting called by Mr. Rockwood, Chairman of the Committee. The meeting is to be held at 1:15 P.M. in Helena at the Historical Library meeting room on November 29th. The goal of the meeting is to review the last season and discuss plans for next year.

Attendance this past season at Montana's state parks was at an all-time high. Roadwork and many other improvements were accomplished as funds permitted.

"We realize that this is rather short notice, but we hope that all members of the committee will plan to be in attendance or send someone to represent you.

"Will be looking for you on the 29th. "Sincerely, Ashley C. Roberts."

The secretary (ap) who typed the above letter for Ashley C. Roberts spelled Hiatt wrong. The letter is addressed as "Dr. R. W. Hyatt, Glendive, Montana. Dear Dr. Hyatt."

The error is understandable, and Ashley may have been in a rush to sign a stack of letters to Committee members and overlooked the typo.

Dr. Hiatt is very particular and would have noticed the error, yet also very forgiving and will brush it off and move on. He might even have cracked a smile over the spelling, joking to himself that it should be an easier task to get the state to change Hyatt to Hiatt than it was to change Maco Sica to Makoshika.

Short notice or not, the end of November can be a terrible time of the year to travel back and forth across the state on old Highway 10. Maybe train travel is the way to go.

November 19, 1955

William H. Browning, the Manager of the Montana Chamber of Commerce, sends a scathing letter to Mr. Frank Connelly, Chairman of the Montana Highway Commission in Helena. He cc's the letter to Jack Hallowell, Noel Carrico, Bill Vondrashek, and Margaret Renshaw. In the end he states we are not complaining but asking to bring our state attractions up to better standards. He is confident the commission, despite the lack of money, can solve the problems. In part his letter reads:

Dear Frank,

I have several suggestions to bring before your commission for their consideration.

The first is in regards to <u>Makoshika State Park</u>. The Chamber at Glendive and Glendive citizens have shown their good faith in trying to improve the Park with signs, picnic tables, interest points, planning and even roadwork to an extent. This Park is gaining more attention annually but people still don't like dangerous roads. Some there have washouts, very steep pulls and lack of safety guards. At one spot this summer water from a run-off completely washed over part of the road. A culvert and higher grade would have prevented this. I'm hoping your State Parks Division can devote more to improvements including a few points of interest signs, road and drain off work, picnic tables and water. There is also a lack of a large historical sign or attractive entrance into this Park. I'm sure the Park deserves more attention.

Bill also comments on <u>Medicine Rocks tourist attraction</u>. "There is not even a small sign naming the place. Cattle guards are needed, road blading, at least one or two picnic tables, and since gates closed off the area the tourists assume it's not open to the public.

"We need more roadside tables across the State and east of Missoula there is a filthy roadside area with toilet facilities unsafe for human use.

"Regards, W. H. B. (William H. Browning)."

November 21, 1955

A multipage review of 1955 Parks Division Activities is prepared for the Highway Commission meeting on November 28th.

November 22, 1955

Ashley Roberts sends a copy of the report to the Advisory Committee for discussion at their meeting on November 29th.

A postcard from Carolyn Antonides written in ink pen on November 15th and postmarked November 22nd at 7 P.M. in Louisville, Kentucky, is addressed to the Montana State Chamber of Commerce, Noel Carrico, Glendive, Montana. Noel makes a pencil notation on the card and turns it over to Dr. Hiatt.

The card says the following:

Dear Sirs,

I'm a member of Girl Scout Troop 56 in Louisville, Kentucky. We are a Senior Troop and interested in camping. We are considering a trip west. I would appreciate it very much if you would send me some information concerning camping sites available on State Parks and otherwise. We are experienced campers and are more interested in primitive or near primitive sites. Would you please send some information on pack trips also. Thank you, Carolyn Antonides. (ADDRESS over)

After writing all of the above in cursive on the 3 ½-inch-by-5 ½-inch postcard, Carolyn runs out of room for her address, directing the reply to her return address on the front of the card: 2703 Field Ave., Louisville, KY.

November 27, 1955

Dr. Hiatt pays a personal visit to see Doug Holm. Doug has too many irons in the fire and lets Doc know he will be stepping down from the committee. Doug says, "cattle take all my spare time." He suggests his dad, ex- contractor-mayor John Holm, for active committee work in 1956.

November 29, 1955

Traveling by Northern Pacific Railway to Helena, Dr. Hiatt attends the Advisory Committee meeting.

Nine committee members are in attendance along with State Park Director Ashley Roberts serving as Committee Secretary.

Considerable roadwork and other improvements were made at most of the parks this year. Attendance was the largest in the history of the parks with the exception of the two parks on the Fort Peck Reservoir. The attendance was down at Fort Peck due to the low level of the water in the reservoir. Fourteen individual reports on the various parks were included in the summary of activities, and consideration for future operations at Fort Peck, The Pines, Tiber Reservoir, Medicine Rocks, and an area in the Crazy Mountains was discussed.

The Makoshika State Park summary is fairly brief. Major improvement of roads was accomplished and the Chamber of Commerce reports attendance at the park was considerably higher than ever before. "The Glendive Chamber also cooperated in the erection of several directional signs and the erection of two new toilets."

A caretaker is not maintained in Makoshika.

Dr. Hiatt suggests the idea of allowing camps for different groups in Makoshika.

A resolution was passed calling for a study of different methods of financing state parks.

On the meeting summary which Advisory Committee Secretary Ashley Roberts put together, the spelling of Dr. Hiatt is still printed as "Dr. Robert Hyatt."

November 30, 1955

A small news clip in the *Daily Ranger* with a heading "Park to Study Raising Money" mentions Dr. Hiatt's attendance at the State Park Advisory Committee meeting in Helena.

Bob Tomalino talks to Dr. Hiatt about a ten-acre archery range in Makoshika.

Hiatt makes a note about the possibility of Youth Campgrounds to be located on a Dawson County section.

December 3, 1955

Dr. Hiatt addresses a letter to the Board of Directors of the Glendive Chamber of Commerce and encloses a check.

Gentlemen,

My investment in your program for 1956 is enclosed.

As is the following statement for your investment (for transportation only) in Makoshika State Park's representation at the 1955 meeting of the State Park Advisory Committee in Helena, 29 Nov 55:

R - T, N.P. Ry Gl - Hel $42.57

Sincerely, R. W. Hiatt, Chairman, Mak. St. Pk. C.

Round-trip Glendive to Helena on Northern Pacific Railway is an economical, safer, and much more relaxing mode of transportation as opposed to white-knuckle car travel on icy Highway 10. It beats a road trip confronting Deadman's Curve between Glendive and Miles City, which is all the deadlier on icy roads with zoned-out drivers.

December 1955

The newsletter begins with a "Seasons Greetings" from Glendive Chamber of Commerce President Victor VanHee, Vice President E. P. Holm, Treasurer Pete Abler, Sec'y-Manager W. J. Vondrashek, and "The Chambermaid" D. C. Coleman.

The Vital Information section of the one-page legal-sized newsletter cites a traffic count by the Montana Highway Department on the Marsh Road November 4th and 5th. Friday morning to Saturday morning the count is 731 vehicles. Saturday morning to Monday morning shows 3,687 vehicles. "Surprising isn't it?"

Christmas shopping hours: the stores will be open until 8:30 P.M. Friday evenings December 9-16-23.

In your ads and cards remember to "keep the Christ in Christmas."

"Santa Claus will be on the streets of Glendive at 1:00 PM Saturday, December 17th, giving free colored popcorn balls to all the farm and city kiddies that day."

The following members have already sent in their Chamber investment for 1956:

Joe Kelly, Claude Eyer, Dairy Queen, Noel Carrico, Don Wright, A. A. Stark, E. W. Popham, Roy Bruce, Cook Sign Co., (Miles City), Riverview Trailer Court, Western Oil Well Service, Glendive Steam Laundry, Triangle Trailer Court, Glendive Transfer and Storage, Valley Motor Supply, Tony's (Carter) Service, Joe Crisafulli and Sons, Dr. R. W. Hiatt, Pontrelli's Cafe, Dr. James Hurning, Judge F.S.P. Foss, Tom Bakker Construction Co., Dr. A.

C. MacDonald, Kalloch Service, and Schwartz Construction Co.

The Annual Banquet is set for Wednesday the 11th at 7:00 P.M. at the Elks Hall. "Plans are to keep the speeches short and show films on Glendive and the whole HUGE TREASURE STATE."

December 13, 1955

The letter on Glendive Chamber of Commerce letterhead from Dr. Hiatt to Ashley Roberts (State Park Division Director) and cc'd to Forrest Rockwood (Chairman of the State Park Advisory Committee) says the following:

Dear Ash,

It was another interesting and enjoyable experience meeting with you, Chairman Rockwood, other members of the Committee and the Highway Commissioners a fortnight ago.

Thanks for the report of the meeting, too. Probably one reason I like Makoshika is its variety. Is that why your stenographer likes me because my name can be spelled a variety of ways? Or is this reciprocity for changing Maco Sica to Makoshika?

Speaking loudly as the lone eastern committeeman there I should like to commend "Full steam ahead" in early actuation of the thought contained in the sentence atop Page 3 of the Report beginning "One major need is…" Can this have <u>top</u> 1956 priority?

MERRY CHRISTMAS and HAPPY NEW YEAR!

The one major need Dr. Hiatt is referring to is a program for more adequate signage to call tourists' attention to the various parks and their locations.

December 15, 1955

In the Thursday edition of the *Wibaux Pioneer Gazette*, most of a column is devoted to a summary of the State Park Advisory Committee meeting. The HELENA (AP) article emerges after the heading that says: "PARK INVESTMENT IS SUGGESTED TO BRING TOURISTS. Top Advisor

Urges More Lures." The Chairman of the Advisory Committee, Forrest Rockwood, comments and shared the bullet points of the meeting, including the need for "more signs directing tourists to parks, tables, shelters, and fireplaces." A list of the committeemen attending the meeting finishes off the column. The last four words give credit to Dr. Hiatt for attending. Of course, the spelling of his name is incorrect again: "Dr. Robert Hyatt, Glendive."

On the column to the right of the State Parks article is The Professional Directory advertising a listing of eight professionals. The most populous are eye doctors, of which four are in the listing: Dr. John Dix, Chiropractic Physician, Glendive; Dr. R. S. Zuroff, Optometrist, Glendive; Dr. Melvin Rogstad, Optometrist, Baker; E. F. Noonan, M.D., Physician and Surgeon, Wibaux; Dr. Robert W. Hiatt, Optometrist, Glendive; Dale Cox, County Attorney, Glendive; Raymond Hildebrand, Lawyer, Glendive; Dr. C. W. Hadley, Optometrist, Miles City.

———⋙oⳡ◦Ɔⳡ◦⋘———

In other news the Wibaux paper reports that early pioneer Mrs. Cora Appenzeller, age 84, has died. Her father was Captain Sipes, the captain of a boat supplying the U.S. Army along the Yellowstone River and one of the first to learn of the demise of Lieutenant Colonel George Armstrong Custer.

———⋙oⳡ◦Ɔⳡ◦⋘———

Ashley Roberts types up a pleasant "Dear Bob" letter to Dr. R. W. Hjatt on State of Montana Highway Commission letterhead:

Thanks for your very nice letter and sorry about the spelling of your name. I do think, though, that y instead of I adds certain flair and is distinguished even if it isn't correct. Excuse, please. On the other hand, if Chairman Connelly were writing I hesitate to say just how your name would be spelled. He still has a most difficult time with MAKOSHIKA and sometimes the results have been almost a disaster. Give him time and I think he'll make it.

A good signing program appears to be a __must__ so far as our parks are concerned.

The Commission has also emphasized this point so it would appear that some priority will have to be given this phase of our program. Beginning now we are doing some planning and any ideas you have will be most welcome.

The Yuletide season approaches with its usual rapidity and, as usual, am in a complete quandary as to what to get the wife for Christmas. Why this problem always perplexes me I don't know but the fact remains that it does so will have to give it my undivided attention for the next few days. Before I go into my trance, however, I want you to know how much I appreciate your efforts on behalf of MAKOSHIKA and to wish you and yours a very happy Holiday Season.

Regards,

STATE PARKS DIVISION

"Ash"

Ashley C. Roberts Director

December 1955

The Glendive Chamber of Commerce tabulates a list of eighteen projects in order of importance for Glendive in 1956.

1. Improve Marsh Road
2. New Hospital
3. Oil Richey Road
4. New Yellowstone Bridge
5. Water and Sewer Improvements
6. New Industry
7. More Street traffic and parking improvement
8. New Schools and gym
9. Truck By-pass
10. New Courthouse
11. Better Agricultural program
12. Annex West Glendive
13. New Swimming Pool
14. Increase Chamber Budget
15. Oil Wibaux-Baker Road
16. West Glendive dike
17. Music Festival on streets
18. Daylight Savings time

Glaringly absent from the list of importance—Makoshika.

CHAPTER 4

Mr. Makoshika (1956)

The Glendive Chamber of Commerce Budget for 1956:

COMMITTEES

Planning	$1,000
Merchants	1,500
Agriculture	500
Highway	1,000
Education	500
Makoshika	250
Public Relations	500
Finance & Membership	250
Youth Advisory	150
Industrial Development	1,000
Hospital	<u>100</u>
Subtotal	$6,750
Salaries	$7,000
Maintenance and Repair	300
Stationery, Postage & Supplies	600
Travel	950
Taxes and Insurance	<u>150</u>
Subtotal	$9,000

Total Budget $15,750

December 27, 1955

Ashley Roberts sends a notice to the Advisory Committee presenting plans for reorganization of the State Park Advisory Committee as per discussion of the State Highway Commission at their last meeting. The Commission is of the opinion a larger group will help when it comes time to work with the legislature. They intend to select a plan at their January meeting and put it into action by early April. Ashley asks for comments no later than January 20th.

Two plans are suggested with the first plan being the preferred model.

Plan 1. One representative from each of these groups:
Montana Chamber of Commerce
Montana Automobile Association
Montana Wildlife Association
Highway Association –
> Highway 10
> Central Montana
> Highway 2
> Highway 93
> Highway 6

Dude Ranchers Association
Montana Historical Society
Sons and Daughters of Montana Pioneers
(Other organizations would be added as agreed upon)

One statewide representative for the approximately fifty local chambers.

The entire committee would be called in for discussion of the overall program and an Executive Committee composed of three members at large and one representative from each financial district would do the actual work and make recommendations to the State Highway Commission.

Plan 2. The same groups as in plan 1 plus a representative named by a civic group from a community nearest each of the existing parks.

Commercial organizations would be asked to name a representative from the 12 financial districts.

1. Kalispell
2. Havre
3. Glasgow
4. Sidney
5. Lewiston
6. Great Falls
7. Helena
8. Missoula
9. Butte
10. Livingston
11. Billings
12. Miles City

To represent the State:
Fish and Game Department
State Forester
State Water Board
State Land Department
Board of Health
(Possibly others)

The entire committee would be called in for a discussion of the overall program and an Executive Committee would be selected to do the actual work and make recommendations to the State Highway Commission.

Respectfully submitted, Ashley C. Roberts.

March 5, 1956

Ashley Roberts writes to the State Parks Division Advisory Committee to inform them of the meeting set for Friday April 6, 1956 at 1:15 P.M. in the Commission Room of the Highway Building. This important meeting is called to discuss budget, operations, and plans for development. "Will be seeing you. Sincerely, Ashley C. Roberts."

Enclosed for review is the Suggested Budget for Fiscal <u>1957</u>.

Of the $41,568.00 Parks Division Budget, Makoshika State Park is allocated $750.00 for Maintenance and Operations.

March 24, 1956

Dr. Hiatt writes a letter to Gary Cook, Cook Outdoor Advertising Company, in Miles City. Mr. Cook has been hired to repaint "MACO SICA" with "MAKOSHIKA" on two signs—one at the Chamber office and the other east of town on Highway 10.

"The purpose of this note is merely to encourage you to expedite this assignment as much as possible so that it will be ready for the tourist season. The Committee will be grateful. Sincerely, Dr. R. W. Hiatt, Chairman."

March 25, 1956

The Saturday Evening Post on page 124 has a Rand McNally & Co. quiz titled "Where Do You Think You Are?" Dr. Hiatt loves newspaper crossword puzzles and always works on the puzzles and quizzes in the reading material he is involved with. This quiz has 12 numbered boxes with a map circle in each box showing a small area from 12 different states. The puzzle asks, "Can you identify the states?" To Dr. Hiatt's delight box number 6 shows an intersection of highways with the highway sign 10 on the road to the east. Going north from the center of the circle, the highway on the west side of a river shows the town of Stipek, and along the north margin of the one-inch- diameter circle it says "Intake." To the west edge of the circle the first letter of the town is off the map so the location is identified as "lendive." Toward the south-southwest edge of the circle is a location identified as "Hoyt." To Dr. Hiatt's dismay, the middle of the circle south of Highway 10 has an elevation marker of 2069 and an area of the map identified as "MACO-SICA."

To straighten out this mapping error Dr. Hiatt has a letter telegram sent to:

Editor,
Letters,
Saturday Evening Post
Independence Square
Philadelphia 5, Penna.

MACO SICA, MAP 6, PAGE 124, SATEVEPOST 17 MARCH WAS OFFICIALLY CHANGED TO MAKOSHIKA ONE YEAR AGO.

Dr. R. W. Hiatt, Chairman
Makoshika State Park Committee
Glendive (Montana) Chamber of Commerce

(Bill Glendive Chamber of Commerce, EM5-4235)
R. W. Hiatt

———————— ∽०cᏣᎧ०∽ ————————

April 4, 1956

On the top of the 7-by-6-inch notepaper is printed "Editorial Rooms," and centered directly below on a ¼-inch square embossment it says "The Saturday Evening POST," and in smaller letters "Founded by Ben Franklin." Harley P. Cook, associate editor, types a note:

My Dear Dr. Hiatt,

Thank you for your wire about the official name of Makoshika Park. I am forwarding the information to Rand McNally, whose Maps we use for our quizzes.

Yours sincerely, (signed with a fountain pen) H. P. Cook.

———————— ∽०cᏣᎧ०∽ ————————

April 6, 1956

At 1:15 P.M. Director Ashley Roberts calls the State Parks Advisory Committee meeting to order and reviews the State Parks 1957 budget, discusses the proposed changes in the Advisory Committee, explains a problem at Yellow Bay, discloses the six proposed sites that are considered for addition to the park system, and clarifies plans for next fall.

Mr. Roberts reads a portion of a letter from the "Keep America Beautiful Organization." They want to support the state's parks with a nationwide antilitter campaign along the highways.

As far as the proposed "Advisory Committee Change" goes, Mr. Roberts is pleased at how active the current committee is, how everyone shows great interest and everybody is doing an excellent job. He is going to recommend to the Commission we keep the committee structure as it is now and add new members as we add new parks.

Each committee member gives a report and makes suggestions for the park in their area. Dr. Hiatt reports that Makoshika expenditures have been low. Roads have been constructed and maintained by the Highway Department. The biggest problem is lack of signs to guide tourists. He reports that different community groups have participated in bettering picnic areas and camping sites.

The meeting concludes with a brief slide presentation.

Dr. Hiatt makes notes beside each of the six proposed park additions.

A. Indian Caves - 6 miles south of Billings
B. Tiber Reservoir - South of Shelby
C. Medicine Rocks - Ekalaka
D. Old Fort Owen - Stevensville
E. Missouri River Crossing - Upper end of Fort Peck Reservoir alongside new Missouri River Bridge - highway connecting Malta with Roundup.
F. The Pines - Montana State College summer camp north shore Fort Peck Reservoir.

A paper from the meeting lists expenditures to February 29, 1956 on each of fifteen park sites. Makoshika State Park has a budget of $750.00 and has had no expenditures.

On a separate sheet Dr. Hiatt makes a few additional notes about the meeting.

$2,500 roadwork left until July 1st.
Of $750.00 budget for fiscal '56 unspent, can be applied to '57
Ashley will be down next week.
Commission will grant another $20,000 in highway funds for parks.
(40 - Hour week - Highway Department.)
Meeting next in late October.

⟫⟳⟪

April 9, 1956

In the colorful Northern Pacific Railway itinerary envelope with a picture of a Northern Pacific train sporting the vista-dome on one side and a route map from Minneapolis to Vancouver on the other, Dr. Hiatt tucks his two Pullman passenger check receipts. Round-trip rail fare between Glendive and Helena is

$29.81 plus the two Pullman receipts of $6.38 and $6.11 for a total of $42.30. A letter to the Glendive Chamber of Commerce from Dr. Hiatt says: Gentlemen:

Request your approval of reimbursement of $42.30 for round-trip rail-Pullman fare to Helena, 5-7 Apr 56, where I represented Makoshika State Park at the Spring meeting of the State Park Advisory Committee meeting 6 Apr 56.

Through this committee (1) Makoshika is constantly gaining recognition statewide, (2) we gained permission to apply all of our budget allotment not used in fiscal 1956 to 1957, (3) one ambitious State Park representative was cooled off in their attempt to gouge out a $4,000 contribution from State funds for their project, (4) more Highway Department funds will be available 1 Jul 56 for further roadwork similar to that accomplished in 1955, which was a blessing to Makoshika.

Park Roads in Makoshika are far better now than they've ever been in April. Although picnicking hasn't started, smooching season is well underway......

Sincerely, Dr. R. W. Hiatt, Chairman, Makoshika State Park Committee.

April 10, 1956

The First National Bank of Glendive publishes their Statement of Condition with a photo of Glendive's Makoshika Park on the front cover of their folded 10-by-7-inch leaflet. The back cover describes Makoshika Park as "56,000 acres of rugged badlands grandeur." The three-paragraph description mentions fossils, mule deer, a band of "plumb wild" horses, and Fish and Game Commission plans to consider restocking the area with bighorn sheep.

April 18, 1956

Lew Keim, the Public Relations Director of the Montana Chamber of Commerce, sends letters to local Chamber managers across the state to recruit articles for their May issue of the *Montana Affairs* magazine in the Travel and Vacation edition.

We hope you will write a story for Montana Affairs of about 100 words in length on your city's <u>newest</u> tourist attraction. A story about what your city is doing now to keep the tourists one day longer. Please keep the story on the basis of <u>new attractions</u>, <u>new efforts</u>.

The deadline is May 1st, absolutely. Sincerely, Lew.

The Glendive Chamber manager, after reading the letter, writes in pencil across the paper in bold block letters: *DR R W HIATT.*

The letter is hand-delivered to Dr. Hiatt, probably at his office.

April 30, 1956

Between the 18th and the 30th of April Dr. Hiatt ponders, makes notes, handwrites, and finally at the last minute types up his story for the *Montana Affairs* magazine.

His notes are made on the blank side of a Toastmasters International Speech Contest Worksheet and Ballot for Judges. This Judges Official Ballot is a spare from the District 17 contest in Miles City last year on the 23rd of April.

There are seven categories scored by judges in a Toastmasters speech contest. Each category has a weighted score, and when all seven categories are judged excellent the total perfect score will equal 100 points.

Dr. Hiatt challenges himself to write a 100-word story that if given as a short speech would be judged excellent. The top score for an OPENING to a speech is 15 points. VOICE (pitch, tempo, volume, and enthusiasm) has a maximum score of 10 points. PLATFORM DEPARTMENT (gestures, poise, eye contact, and mannerisms) also has an excellent score of 10 points.

The first three speech items have to do with appearance and delivery, and for those fortunate enough to have heard Dr. Hiatt give a talk, they witnessed these categories delivered to slam-dunk perfection. Next is ORGANIZATION at 20 points (logic, clarity, suitability) followed by MECHANICS with 10 points (diction, grammar, pronunciation, word pictures), the Close has 15 points, and finally EFFECTIVENESS has the top point value at 20 points (was purpose achieved? to impress, to inform, to persuade, to entertain).

Using the flip side of the worksheet, Dr. Hiatt begins by printing a column of hot buttons.

Fantasty[sic]
Grandeur
Peace
Awe
Unique
Raw
Virgin
Makoshika
Change of Pace
Solitude

Challenge
Opportunity
Change
Time, space & Motion

Next to the column of words, Hiatt writes his rough draft:

*If you're looking for something <u>NEW</u> in scenery, if you'd welcome a change of pace from the traffic-cluttered city and the ~~monotonous long stretches of monotonous highway~~ monotony of highway travel. ~~(3)~~ if you **crave** an hour, or two, or eight, to get away from it all, MAKOSHIKA STATE PARK in GLENDIVE'S backyard is the place.*

Its topography is unique and awesome. It is a cameraman's, geologist's, artist's, and tourist's paradise. Mother Nature, unmolested by Man, has carved grotesque formations throughout. Park roads were improved and extended in 1956.

These Montana badlands are generally conceded to be more exciting, more colorful, and more accessible to the tourists than their counterparts in ~~North Dakota and South Dakota~~ other states.

~~*108 words*~~

Now satisfied that this story of about 100 words is ready to go, Dr. Hiatt types up his letter on Glendive Chamber of Commerce letterhead below his comment to Lew.

Dear Lew,

If you pick up mail in the afternoon, this should meet your absolute deadline of May 1st.

After the body of the script Dr. Hiatt signs off as, "Sincerely, R.W. Hiatt."

May 1956

The eight-page glossy black-and-white publication of the Montana Chamber of Commerce, Volume VI, NO. 5, titled "Montana Affairs" focuses on the tourist industry. The goal is to put up "Road-Blocks" in the way of attractions for tourists to stumble over and stay longer to enjoy. In the center of the brochure, the Makoshika tripping point is highlighted as **Improvements at Makoshika** by R.W. Hiatt.

The first paragraph touts Makoshika's improved accessibility, and the next two paragraphs quote Hiatt's first and third paragraph submissions.

Mission Accomplished!

———⊸o⟡o⊷———

On page 3 of the May issue of the *Montana Motorist* magazine, a 2-column article called "Travel Montana with John Willard" touts the eastern Montana badlands. He writes, "There are hundreds of gulches as yet unexplored in this wild country, of which Makoshika State Park, south of Glendive, is only an example." He talks about prospecting for fossils and describes it as an "incurable disease, like fishing or duck hunting."

Doc doesn't know it yet, didn't even feel it, but the fossil bug just bit. It won't take much now: when the time arises and he is decoyed by something that looks like a fossil and discovers it is a fossil, he will be hooked.

It was a hundred years ago that the Irish Nobleman Sir George Gore and his entourage scoured this area for game, and now a hundred years later another noble man will soon begin hunting this locality, although the prey Doc Hiatt will stalk has been dead for 65 million years.

It appears on newsprint, this 5-paragraph continuation of a section on camping. Dr. Hiatt's eyes are glued to the 4-by-6-inch article titled "Minnesota State Parks Offer Choice Camping." Not taking time to find the scissors or even his pocketknife, he uses his fingers to tear around the edges and remove this important clipping from the paper.

After reading and rereading he stews over the article for a while, does some research, and writes in ink pen on bottom margin of the article, *John H Martin, asst. Director, Division of State Parks.* Barely finding

118

room on the irregular torn bottom edge, he writes, *Department of Conservation, St. Paul Minn.*

The article states, "CAMPING FACILITIES at 18 Minnesota state parks include tent sites, tables, fireplaces, water and garbage disposal pits." Also, "trailer sites with electricity and water have been constructed at six state parks. Cabins that you can rent by the day or week are available in five state parks."

In 1956 the Minnesota camping fees are 25 cents a car, 25 cents for a tent, and (depending on the size) either 25 or 50 cents for a trailer. In 1954 the Minnesota camp fees raised $10,000 and increased to $14,000 in 1955.

Camping is on the upswing, especially with all the modern equipment available nowadays like nylon tents, air mattresses, compact bedrolls, and efficient cooking utensils. "Campers still have the spirit of outdoor adventure but they no longer have to rough it very much."

Dr. Hiatt is well aware that Minnesotans love to camp and how exciting it is for them to head out to the wilds of Montana for a vacation. They are flatlanders—they've never seen any place like Makoshika before!

A nice fourfold glossy brochure compiled and distributed by the Montana Chamber of Commerce and Montana Highway Advertising in cooperation with local Chambers of Commerce is called "A Round-up of 1956 VACATION EVENTS." The back fold has basic hunting and fishing information, tentative season dates, and nonresident license fees. The four sections inside the publication list the March through November "goings on" across the state. The only item listed in March is the Northern Plains Spring Exhibition on the 28–31 in Glendive. Likewise, the one event in April is the Annual Music Festival in Glendive on the 20–21. May kicks off with a Miles City event, although the dates haven't been set yet for the Annual Bucking Horse Auction Sale. Twenty other events across the state are listed in May, including the opening of Makoshika State Park in Glendive on the 1st. June takes up a whole quarter section with events all over the state. Sidney has the Shrine Circus, Miles City Roundup, and Range Riders

Museum, and Glendive had the Annual Rod and Gun Fish Derby. July is another eventful month across Montana with the Shrine Circus making its way from one town to the next. There is the Flathead Indian Pow Wow out West in Arlee, the 40th Anniversary Celebration, Parade, and Rodeo in Richey, the Annual Boat Regatta in Poplar, on the 13–15 it's the Wild Horse Stampede in Wolf Point, and Glendive has several events on July 4-5-6. It's the 75th Diamond Jubilee Celebration of the Railroad arriving in Glendive. July 4th is Pioneer Day, July 5th is Railroad Day, and July 6 is Western Day. There will be parades, a carnival, dances, and a pageant. August has a lot of fairs, stock shows, and the annual Crow Indian Tribal Fair and Pow Wow. Glendive has September 2–4 set for the Dawson County Fair. After September things are winding down, Miles City has their Montana Ram Sale, and by October only a few events are listed across the state, including a Big Buck Contest in Columbus. November ends the listing with ski runs opening at Belmont and Big Mountain.

The final section of interesting places to see has a brief listing for Makoshika State Park. It says, "Badlands. Off U.S. 10 east of Glendive city limits."

—◦○◦—

May 11, 1956

Bill Browning writes to Noel Carrico and says in part the following;

"… I've sure been plugging hell out of Makoshika. I've shown the slides to a number of Montana audiences, one group at Lethbridge, and had Makoshika on T.V. at Des Moines. Lots of people told me they didn't know a place like that existed in Montana. You should get some more visitors this summer. Hope you can drop this word to Bill V......"

On Montana Chamber of Commerce letterhead, Noel writes to the Glendive Chamber Manager:

First he quotes Bill Browning and then adds: "Hope the roads can be improved some out there, while not impassable, they could be helped. Sincerely, Noel."

May 15, 1956

The Public Relations Director of the Montana Chamber of Commerce writes to Mr. R. W. Hiatt, Chairman of the Glendive Chamber of Commerce Tourist Committee.

He appreciates the cooperation through Hiatt's article in the "Travel and Vacation Edition" of *Montana Affairs*. He sends a copy of the publication and implores Dr. Hiatt to request additional copies if he desires. Any comments or suggestions on the subject of travel promotion are welcome.

"Sincerely, Lewis P. Keim."

The *Glendive Daily Ranger* gives Makoshika State Park and Dr. Hiatt a mention for the latest feature in the *Montana Affairs* publication.

May 18, 1956

An informal letter from Dr. Hiatt to Ashley Roberts: Dear Ash,

What do you think about Minnesota's favorite fireplace? (Study attached correspondence and plans.)

Architect Hauck agrees they can be prettied up simply enough to blend into the landscape.

Shall I put Ed to work building a model or a batch of them? Or did you mention something about your supplying the grate or steel component?

I think the railroad could make some excellent grates at very reasonable cost here.

Hauck suspected the dimensions of the grate might be too small. My first reaction concurred but not my second thought. What do you think?

Sincerely, Bob

P.S. "Not safe for trailers" sign going up shortly. I watched another one stall on the second switchback Sunday from atop the Cross Butte.

P.P.S. Did Browning tell you he had Makoshika on Des Moines TV?

P.P.P.S. Local Makoshika appreciation and enthusiasm increasing … rwh

May 24, 1956

Three dozen copies of the May issue of *Montana Affairs* are mailed along with a letter to Dr. Hiatt from Lew Keim. Lew says it is a pleasure to send you these additional copies, and he is looking forward to meeting. "Sincerely, Montana Chamber of Commerce, Lew."

Ashley Roberts responds to Dr. Hiatt's letter about the Makoshika fireplaces. He likes the Minnesota State Parks fireplace plans and wants to use the diagrams for comparative purposes before he returns them. He thinks the ten- by-twenty-four-inch size is large enough but is not sure about the revolving feature of the grate.

He hadn't heard about Makoshika on Des Moines TV. *The "Not safe for trailers" sign is a good idea—should eliminate a lot of bad words and distraught tempers.*

What about Ed? Is he going to be on our payroll? We discussed employing him as a part-time caretaker at $100.00 per month. Let me know what his situation is so that we can get the necessary papers signed. Our May payroll is already in and the checks made out—would have to employ him effective June 1st.

Will let you know about the fireplace soon. Sincerely, Ash.

———— ≪⁂≫ ————

June 6, 1956

Dr. Hiatt personally delivers copies of the *Montana Affairs* publication to Hilltop Motel, Rock Log Lodge, Best Motel, Uptown Motel, El Centro Motel, Main Motel, Derrick Motel, and Stan's Agate Shop.

June 10, 1956

Doc's "13th Wedding Anniversary"

A busy Dr. Hiatt types up letters to Ashley Roberts and Ed Lewis and then sends a carbon copy to Ken Haag.

Dear Ash,

Thanx[sic] for your good letter dtd[sic] 24 May 56. Wish I were as prompt as you in replying. On both sides of June 1st I was calling on eleven O.D.'s between Libby and Hamilton and attending the Western regional conference of the President's Committee on Highway Safety in San Francisco …And Tuesday family and I head for Chicago and Miami for ten days……Suggest until 21 Jun you direct correspondence to either Ed Lewis or Ken Haag, with a carbon mailed to me Box 1086.

Ed started 1 Jun 56. (I was waiting for your confirmation.) He's now setting six brick-red oil-drum refuse barrels (courtesy Shell Oil) into gravel-bedded holes in the picnic area. He'll gather firewood supplies for same, and tidy up area. He'll get and paint a few more signposts and prepare more sign boards for Billie Haag to letter.

Architect Phil Hauck went for his virgin trip through Makoshika the other evening. He's real enthusiastic, is already thinking ten years ahead, and has ideas for blending fireplaces and surrounds. He plans to submit Makoshika to Bozeman's school of architecture where some 35 students may compete in developing the park next fall.

Ash, if you get this Monday and want to call before our departure, O.K. Otherwise, I'll advise Ed he'll hear from you or Ken……Sincerely, Bob.

Not skipping a beat, Dr. Hiatt types up a letter to Ed Lewis with a carbon copy to go to Ken Haag:

Ed Lewis, c/o Lawrence Vashus, 418 Hemlock
Forest Park
W. Glendive, Montana

10 Jun 56

Dear Ed,

I thought it a good idea to get some of our Makoshika ideas down in black and white so we know what's going on and what needs to be done. From June 12th thru June 21st our family will be out of the country. During that time feel free to use the facilities in our garage and get the gravel. State Park Director Ashley Roberts, Helena, will correspond either direct with you or Ken Haag until our return.

I have told Roberts you started work June 1st. He'll no doubt send some papers to sign. For June at least the job is defined as "Part-time" caretaker @ $100 per month. If we get going more on a full-time scale, I'm sure we can hoist the pay-scale.

Five projects which would be worthwhile during June are:

Install six refuse barrels as started already. (Not too close to tables.)

Collect and dispose of scattered refuse along roadsides and within 50' radii of tables.

Supply each table with a couple good logs for kindling.

Pick up about six old city street signs between water plant and river (tell Joe Wester it's for Park; we have City's and Claude's authority), clean and paint with black screen enamel in our garage. Plane off the wood signs and apply two coats of white enamel which we'll need for new and replacement signs.

Scrub down toilet seats and equip each toilet with two rolls tissue.

Good luck and we'll see you when we get back. Use your good judgment, and if you need help, friend Haag down the hall is the man to ask. R. W. Hiatt.

Dr. Hiatt types a note on the carbon copy to Haag: "Dear Vice-Chairman Haag,

"Or didn't you know? …. I believe you are 'young enough to appreciate the job and experienced enough to do the job.' (My favorite of all political slogans, just for the record.)… Possibly nothing will come up while I'm gone, but should it, you had no competition in the election… Thank you, Sir!"

June 16, 1956

It takes five paragraphs and two postscripts for Anoka, Minnesota, tourist Ted Frederick to scathingly vent his vacation experience in Montana. He addresses his letter in this order to: "State of Montana, Conservation Dept., Highway Dept., and Chamber of Commerce, Glendive Montana."

The body of his typewritten letter says the following:

The wife and I and three children have just finished a 2700-mile trip thru Minnesota, Iowa, Nebraska, South Dakota, Wyoming, Montana, and North Dakota. We pulled a two-wheeled van-type trailer behind a gear-driven 53 Plymouth. For the most part we had a wonderful time.

When we came to the Montana State line there was a sign saying "Welcome." I want you to know that in your state we were the least welcome of anywhere on our trip. At the first store we came to we bought groceries and asked where

we could find a roadside park to cook a meal. "Oh you won't find any of those in Montana." I guess we didn't. We drove all day in 100-degree heat without a chance to stop anywhere.

We kept looking at the map though. Boy there is one good park ahead—if we can just get to Glendive—there is Makoshiko[sic]. We will surely have a chance to get cleaned up and have a hot meal.

If you have ever driven through the other states I mentioned you will find that a state park means to turn a little way off the main road and you have a place to camp, cook, and clean up. And you don't climb any mountains to get to them!! How were we to know that your Mako was any different? Once we got in that oversized cow-trail, what chance was there to turn around with a trailer? Then we came to that mountain-climbing hair-pin it was so steep that our motor stalled out before reaching the top. If you want a thrill sometime, just hook a two-wheel trailer behind your car and go up and stop about a hundred feet from the top of the grade and kill your motor. Try looking over your shoulder wondering if you can clear the car door in time to keep from going over cliff with it. Now I suppose you people are used to such mountain- climbing. Well there are a lot of us that are not. Will you PLEASE put up a sign or something at the entrance to sort out the "are nots" so they won't get in the same trouble we did?

I would like to invite you to come to Minnesota on a trip sometime. You will find a table along the road every few miles. There are way-side parks about every twenty-five miles. State Parks are not over one hundred miles apart. For the state parks you buy a dollar sticker that admits the car to all state parks. Camping is fifty cents a night extra. Then go home and see what you have to offer on the road from Sturgess[sic] to Miles City to Glendive to the North Dakota line.

Regretfully, Ted Frederick.

The joker of your hospitality was one of those information signs as big as a dinner-table on the end of a bridge where the speed was zoned Min 30/Max 50.

Again—PLEASE—put some sign of information on that Mako trail that will give a dumb plains-country guy a chance to turn around in time.

June 19, 1956

Ashley Roberts confirms in a brief letter to Dr. Hiatt that Ed Lewis is on the payroll as of June 1st and he will be getting his first paycheck soon. He is glad to hear about the students' project at the state college. He is not sure when he will make it back to Glendive again; hopefully soon. "Best Regards, signed Ashley C Roberts, p by his secretary:ap."

June 23, 1956

A letter to the Chamber of Commerce in Glendive from the field trip leader of the Geological Society of Minnesota in Minneapolis, Minnesota, says the following:

Dear Sirs,

Some years ago Ed Bump took me into the Bad Lands near Glendive.

In July I am taking a group of 25 members of our society on a geology field trip, and we will stop overnight at El Centro Motel on July 26. I would like to take the group for a look on the morning of the 27th.

We are using a 41-passenger bus for transportation.

Can you give me some information on the possibility of this side trip and the roads to take.

Yours very truly, Bert Carlson

June 25, 1956

Dr. Hiatt is back home and fires off a letter to Ashley:

Dear Ash

Thanx for yours of 19 June 56, signed by "p."

Boy, did Makoshika get a play yesterday! Never seen so many people and cars out there. We were forced to find our own new private picnic spot, and then we were beat to our first choice.

Ed and the Highway Department are going to town on their projects. He wants to get going on a fireplace or two (or six). Can you spare the plans, or were you planning to have one batch made up centrally?

Mrs. Sundling's family is putting the heat on her to sell her spread. A property buyer is also nibbling at her. She'd like to see the Park have it (Lodge as is with 160 acres), she doesn't want much down, and her first and rather shyly-quoted figure is $20,000, which "Cliff thought was right."....You, Ken, Phil, ~~and~~ Ed, she and I should go out there together your next trip here, methinks. ~~I'll supply you with a copy of my~~ In the meantime we can cogitate.---- I'll supply you with a copy of my answer to the Minnesotan's letter when I write him, probably within 30 days.

See you, Bob

———— ⤞◦⟋⟍◦⤝ ————

June 28, 1956

Ashley responds:

Dear Bob,

The fireplace plans are still tied up. After several conferences with the plans department, plus a conference in the field with one of our caretakers, it has resulted in much confusion in just what we want in the way of a fireplace. My mind was all made up once—then the man in plans came up with a suggestion that utterly confused me again. Now, however, I believe we are on our way. The plan will be similar to the Minnesota plan with a few variations. We hope to have the job done by the middle of next week. Will return your plans, plus a copy of our conception. Sorry for the delay, but a fireplace can be a cantankerous thing.

After our plans are completed, we will be making up these fireplaces here in Helena. There will be additional delays, however, and if you can put something together down there for two or three fireplaces, it might be wise to do so.

Will cogitate on the idea of purchasing the Sundling property—and cogitation maybe[sic] as far as I'll get. Do you have any ideas where the money will come from? Am planning a frontal assault on the Legislature next year, but don't know whether it will produce $20,000 or not.

Will be seeing you soon. If not before—will be there to greet the travel editors on July 16th and start them through the state.

By the way, have you been able to get a "No Trailers" sign on the Makoshika road?

Regards, A3sh,

Again, signed by his secretary.

Dr. Hiatt responds to the Minnesota Field Trip Leader Bert R. Carlson. Dear Bert,

Willard VonDrachek, Secretary-Manager of the Glendive Chamber of Commerce, handed me your letter, dtd 23 Jun 56, yesterday.

I know your group will appreciate your routing them through Makoshika State Park the morning of 27 July 56.

Since the park roads are not designed for bus traffic, we'll be happy to provide five or six cars with drivers to take you and your party through. Perhaps you know Dr. A.C. Selke, long-time head of geology at Dickinson State Teachers College and brother of Dr. George, head of Minnesota conservation. You might write him, asking if he'd like to join your party from Dickinson to Glendive and serve informally as a guide.....And you'll want to spend an hour or so in our museum in the library with Ed Lewis, who owns most of the geological finds. Let me know your schedule so we can organize.

Sincerely, Bob Hiatt.

June 30, 1956

The First National Bank of Glendive, "A Bank of Cordial Service" as stated on the front cover of their 5-by-7-inch "Statement of Condition at the Close of Business June 30, 1956" brochure, has a "Welcome to Glendive" sign across the top third of the publication. Across the bottom of the sign's outline is a row of brands. Above that, silhouetted on the prairie, is the action of a cowboy roping a steer on the right side of the words "Gateway to Historic Montana." The top of the artwork has a border with "ASK ABOUT OUR MACO SICA (Badlands) PARK."

The cover also promotes "Glendive's DIAMOND JUBILEE CELEBRATION, July 4th, 1881 – July 4th, 1956."

The inside pages have the financial statement and a listing of officers and directors.

On the back page are five paragraphs of "SOME FACTS ABOUT THE GATE CITY."

The first two paragraphs deal with theories of how Glendive received its name. The first said the name derives from Glendive Creek which was named by the "Irish playboy" Sir George Gore, who passed through this territory on an extravagant hunting expedition a hundred years ago, guided by the renowned frontiersman Jim Bridger.

Another piquant theory for the source of the name "Glendive" is derived from an informal reference to scruffy old Bob Glenn's filthy-dirty saloon down the road a short way. The whiskey establishment was referred to by the locals as "Glenn's Dive."

The leaflet's next paragraph says the first industries in this area were trapping beavers and trading in furs and hides. It says the last big buffalo hunt in the nation happened in 1882 out on the Fallon Flats about 30 miles southwest of Glendive.

The second to the last paragraph gives the Northern Pacific Railroad, which has its Yellowstone Division Headquarters in the "railroad town" of Glendive, credit for the area's growth and development. Besides our livestock and agriculture industries, the oil industry is a new player and has tremendous economic potential.

The final paragraph above a Glendive Montana Diamond Jubilee emblem at the bottom of the page says: "Makoshika (formerly Maco Sica) State Park, is within two miles of Glendive, and a popular scenic and geologic attraction for thousands of tourists each year."

July 2, 1956

Dr. Hiatt hears back from Bert Carlson:

Dear Bob,

Thanks for your welcome letter of June 28.

My only trip into the Bad Lands of your area was in 1950 with Ed Bump, formerly of the Northern Pacific. We went into the area late in the afternoon for a picnic lunch and could see clouds and lightning to the north. We decided that we had better get out because we had crossed two washes. We went over the second one just as the rain started and I have never seen it rain so much. Getting back to the El Centro Motel (where we are stopping this trip) the manager told us we should know better. Anyway I would not have missed the experience and needless to say I did not get any pictures, which I hope to do this time. You see I have a personal reason for wanting to go back.

We are coming from the west and have reservations in Jamestown on the night of July 27. If I can get the group into at least part of the area, I know the time will be well spent.

Thanks for your interest. Yours,

Bert Carlson

July 16, 1956

During a quick visit to the Hiatts' residence, the travel editor Frank Freeman is ushered into the garage and shown a "sizeable petrified turtle plus petrified seaweed and fossilized leaf prints" that Dr. Hiatt found in the badlands.

July 23, 1956

Dr. Hiatt clips news articles reporting on the Travel Editors two-week tour which began in Glendive. Participating were editors from the Fort Worth Press, Detroit Free Press, Salt Lake Deseret News Telegram, and the San Jose Mercury News.

Forrest Rockwood, the Chairman of the State Parks Advisory Committee, thanks Hiatt for sending a set of clippings and acknowledges the good job and good publicity for the State Park system.

July 25, 1956

Ashley returns to Dr. Hiatt the loaned fireplace plan file along with a copy of the fireplace drawing designed in Helena. According to Ashley, both should work nicely and some will be pre-fabricated in Helena; however, it will take some weeks to accomplish. In his letter to Hiatt, Ashley says: "In the meantime you may wish to see what you can do in Glendive." Ashley also says he will see if he can scrounge up more picnic tables for Makoshika.

Ashley finishes off his letter with the following paragraph:

Many thanks for sending the news releases covering the Travel Editors trip to Glendive. I am so sorry you were omitted from two of the major published pictures! I am quite sure your countenance or at least your figure would have enhanced the scene considerably. Nevertheless the checkered shirt was not entirely lost and perhaps the general public will get the idea that there are many beautiful sights that may be seen at Makoshika State Park.

Sincerely yours, Ashley C. Roberts p

ACR:ap

July 27, 1956

Friday morning at precisely 11:30 ante meridiem (A.M.), Dr. Hiatt delivers a news release to KXGN and then strolls over to the ranger and hand-delivers another copy at 12:05 post meridiem (P.M.).

The press release on Glendive Chamber of Commerce letterhead reads as follows:

Thirty-four members of the Geological Society of Minnesota toured Makoshika State Park Friday morning. The group, under the leadership of Dr. Bert R. Carlson, Field Trip Leader, have visited points of geological interest between Minneapolis and Yakima, Washington, during July.

Following the ~~Makoshika~~ tour the geologists went to the Glendive Museum where Ed Lewis, local geologist and member of the Makoshika State Park Committee, explained and identified many fossils. Local hosts for the group were Ed Bump, a personal friend of Carlson, Dr. R.W. Hiatt, park committee chairman and Lewis.

....

.

.

.

.

....Submitted noon Fri., 27 Jul 56, By R. W. Hiatt

The *Glendive Daily Ranger* prints Dr. Hiatt's news release this same day under the heading: "Minnesota Geologists Visit Makoshika State Park Today."

The paper says pictures of the tour will appear in a future issue.

———————<>o<^~>o<>———————

August 6, 1956

Ashley writes to Dr. Robert W. Hiatt, Optometrist:

Dear Bob:

Thanks for the clipping on the tour of the Geological Society of Minnesota. You and Ed are having a busy time. Am anxious to see the pictures and (more important) did you get in any of them and, if so, are you properly identified?

Am hoping to get down your way again soon. I'm not certain exactly when it will be, but probably the latter part of this month. Will want to talk fireplaces, picnic tables and signs and get down to facts and see just what we can do.

Thanks again for the clippings and send the pictures when they appear.

Very truly yours,
STATE PARKS DIVISION
Ash
Ashley C. Roberts
Director

August 10, 1956

In a booklet put out by the Montana State Highway Commission, the front cover says, "What the TRAVEL EDITORS WROTE about MONTANA, 1956." The first article written by Miller Hollingsworth is titled "Montana Badlands Look Pretty Good," and the caption below the photo of a cap rock against the summer sky reads, "Montana's Maco Sica badlands—real sweet." He covers several areas of the state in his article, and in one paragraph about Glendive he writes, "The Badlands have been converted into a state park and named Macoshika[sic]. A local optometrist, Dr. Robert Hiatt, is leading the movement to attract tourists to the badlands."

Dave Hall from the *Fort Worth Press* was impressed with the fantastic shapes in the eroded badlands. "The land was bad, but the roads were good. And there were picnic tables too."

Kay Aldous of the *Deseret News - Salt Lake Telegram* makes a brief mention of the badlands area of Glendive and then raves about the overabundance of antelope in the Miles City area, quoting a game official who says "they're running out our ears." The nonresident antelope fee has been reduced to $20, and she writes, "The prongs simply aren't being harvested in great enough numbers."

Frank Freeman from the *San Jose Mercury News* must have had a good conversation with Dr. Hiatt about Makoshika on the tour through the park. In his write-up about the Glendive badlands, he refers to the area as "56,000 acres of geological nightmare or, as one once said, 'Hell cooled over' …" Frank pretty much hits all of Dr. Hiatt's talking points and ends his lengthy paragraph with the comment: "The pity of it all is that so few travelers know of the two- year-old park & sail by one of the country's most unusual examples of erosion by water & wind."

Under the subheading "The Wide Open Spaces—GLENDIVE—" Frank gives his rundown of Montana, where the buffalo used to roam, and some still do on a federal bison range. It was 150 years ago this month that Lewis and Clark traveled this territory.

Montana is known for its big game: "moose, elk, deer, antelopes, bighorn sheep, Rock Mountain goat, bear and caribou." He mentions "five reservations for Injuns—Assiniboine, Sioux, Blackfeet, Chippewa, Salish, Kootenai, Crow & the Northern Cheyenne." The multiple-page write-up of Frank Freeman covers the tour from one end of the state to the other, beginning in Glendive. He says Glendive is named after an Irish nobleman's "estate over on the auld sod." He was Sir George Gore, the buffalo hunter here in 1855.

A quarter-page photo in Frank's section of the Travel Editors booklet shows Mr. Freeman peering at a formation in Makoshika State Park. In the background is the prominent peak Dr. Hiatt referred to as the Matterhorn in Makoshika. Doubtful that anyone will notice, however to the discerning eye a very faint outline of the cross on the hilltop is visible.

August 12, 1956

It's Sunday, and from 3:30 P.M. to 6:30 P.M. Dr. Hiatt and Ward Barthelmess go on a photo safari in Makoshika with plans to pick out eight pictures for a lithograph tourist brochure.

The first shot is on Taylor Avenue with the Makoshika sign and Hungry Joe Cross in the background. Another photo has more sky and a person pointing to the cross.

The next is of a high butte on the right as they drive on the park road into the badland valley.

They wanted to get a photo with Haag standing on a razor back. They were going to call that one "Old Razor Back." This brings on a hearty laugh following the standard gestures of Doc Hiatt's hands reaching first toward his red bow tie and suddenly outstretching downward, the laugh reaching its crescendo as he arches forward at the waist and hands dangle near ankles sporting his ever-present red socks. Recovering, and since Mr. Haag is not with them to pose, they take a photo and drive on up the road.

Before they get to the switchbacks, they stop and take a photo of the Cross Butte up to the left. Doc stands still for a moment and looks up at the cross as his mind registers a silent memory of Cliff Harsh.

They first plan to take a photo from atop the Cross Butte and then change their minds as they get a shot from the last right turn on the switchbacks. It's a good shot of a yellow car coming up the switchbacks and a blue car going down.

Picnic tables and privies catch their attention, and even though extremely proud of the finished outhouses, they skip those photos for the tourist brochure and get some of picnickers enjoying the picnic tables.

Up on top they stop and ponder a photo of the radio antenna.

From the first left past the vista point and looking down to the right, they spot a columnar spire. Hiatt hops down over a couple humps of gumbo to get positioned for a shot.

Next stop will be the classic. Dr. Hiatt poses on the left side of the Baked Potato formation.

They get over to the scoria butte and get another shot of the yellow car approaching.

They take several more photos on the way back, starting with a panorama off to the right of the scoria butte. They take one more photo and name this one "Ducks in Rock."

After the film is developed they will pick out the choice eight pictures for their brochure.

August 19, 1956

Most of a full page of print and several pictures of Makoshika State Park are featured in the *Sunday Daily Ranger* under the headline "Travel Editor Tells about Visiting Glendive and His Tour of Makoshika State Park." Frank Freeman of the *San Jose Mercury News* is impressed with the three murals done by J. K. Ralston on display in the Jordan Hotel. From the age of 10 until he joined the United States Army in 1918, the young Ralston cowboyed from the Capital P Ranch, headquartered in Dawson County.

Of the three photos about Makoshika angling across the page in the paper, the first one shows an artist's drawing of Makoshika in prehistoric times next to four of the original wooden signs for the park. The first sign says "Maco Sica Park," and the next two signs say "Maco Sica State Park," and the final sign in the progression says "Makoshika State Park." Another photo from atop the switchbacks shows part of the road and the scenic view of badlands down the valley. The center-page photo features two cap rocks with the cross on top of the hill in the background.

———⊸∘〇✧〇∘⊶———

August 21, 1956

Dr. Hiatt decides it's about time to touch base with Ashley Roberts again and types up a letter:

Dear Ash,

Good to hear from you recently.

Also glad to learn you'll be here in a week or two. Since I've been unreasonably busy day and night optometrically, and there seems to be no sign of a letup, could you schedule your arrival so that we could take a little 6:00 a.m. tour of Makoshika? The Park is pretty, the deer are numerous, and we could do some business minus the big rush.

It had a good play again yesterday. A good many tourists, and one picnic table had 30 (!!!) eastern Montana cars around it (Army Reserve party w/wives and kids). We picnicked the Baker C. of C. President and his family. He caught a "jet-propelled" sand lizard coming down the Cross butte which is now son Bob's pet in the garage and attraction of the neighborhood.

After getting a $20.00 estimate on the Minnesota grate from a local welding concern, Ed took my advice and headed for the N.P. The Asst. Supt. who said "I like to go up there," volunteered to make us one gratis! If it's successful, he rather apologetically explained that they'd probably have to charge a little for the others. Ed's bill for materials to make the form plus a sack of cement is enclosed. (If forms need to be made out for this reimbursement, return this invoice with them.) Ed may have it up by your arrival for your inspection.

Are you going to have ten tables we can move down here before the snow falls?

Ex-photographer Ward Barthelmess and I hope to have eight good shots which we plan to include in a four-page, non-verbose, offset lithographed brochure for Chamber distribution to tourists. This would be substantially, if not totally, financed by the Chamber.

Wife Lois and I missed you by hours August 8th when we enjoyed the final Caverns tour of the day.

Let me know when we can look for you...........
Sincerely
Bob

On the back side of the letter copy to Ashley Roberts, a quick brainstorm is scrawled out. Dr. Hiatt places the paper horizontally on a writing surface, and in the center of the page draws an arrow sign to the left and to the right. In between the two arrows he writes "7 miles." Above the arrow signs with two strokes across the page, he makes lines that represent Highway 10 going from the east on the right, to the west on the left, and ending at gl (Glendive).

Running slightly out of room on top of the page to register his thoughts, he slides the page at a right angle in front of him and in a catawampus fashion writes his idea for a highway sign seven miles east of Glendive. "Only 4 ½ hours to Billings / But only 15 minutes to Makoshika State Park and Glendive."

August 28, 1956

The Montana Chamber of Commerce submits a 21-point statement of recommendations to a legislative-created Montana committee. Advertising, better highways, and State Parks development are the key points in their report. Tourist traffic is way up with people visiting Montana from all over, including Canada. The State Parks plan looks a lot like a copy of the "Minnesota State Parks Offer Choice Camping" article that Dr. Hiatt tore out of a paper back in May. Umpteen millions of dollars are being spent by tourists in Montana, and presently the State Park Commission does not even have authority to maintain sanitary conditions in the state's campgrounds, parks, and roadside turnouts. Presently the maintenance division is responsible; however, the State Park Commission should be delegated authority and funds to "insure the safekeeping of its public areas."

One thought Dr. Hiatt has for Montana state parks is a decal that could be purchased and affixed to a car window that would allow all the occupants of the vehicle to visit any state park in Montana without having to pay a fee. The sample Hiatt has in mind is a decal 3 by 4 inches with an outline of Montana in green on a clear background with **MONTANA** spelled out below the straight part of Montana's southern border. The counties have a black border and a brown buffalo highlighted standing sideways, its head facing the west with the top part of its hump crossing the northern border of Montana into Canada.

⊸•◦⫸⟡⫷◦•⊷

September 1956

Dr. Hiatt studies the State Park Division Expense Account Detail Report for July 1, 1955 to June 30, 1956. Of the $51,991.44 expended on the state parks

in Montana, the Makoshika portion was $100.00, which is for the park caretaker salary of Edwin Lewis in June. At first glance it looks like Lewis & Clark Caverns had the bulk of the expenditures at $31,203.27; however, the park also had receipts of $30,782.80, therefore the net expense to operate Lewis & Clark Caverns was only $420.47—a bargain for the state. Operations for Headquarters in Helena totaled $12,179.27.

By 1956 Makoshika Park is on the *Montana Highway Map* and one of the 14 state parks highlighted on the inside cover. The Shell Oil Company publication that goes out to all Shell employees features Makoshika State Park on the front page of the September 1956 issue. The picture shows Dick Guenzi and Johnny Ray sighting across a canyon, using a new type of surveying equipment.

The eight photos selected for the tourist brochure are:

1. Taylor Avenue Makoshika Sign with Hungry Joe Cross in the background.
2. Dr. Hiatt pointing to the first high butte on the right as they drive in to Makoshika.
3. Partway up the switchbacks with the yellow and blue cars.

4. Picnickers using one of the picnic tables.
5. Hiatt down below posing on a columnar spire.
6. One more photo with Hiatt on a formation a couple humps down from spire.
7. Hiatt beside "Baked Potato" rock.
8. Scoria butte with yellow car approaching.

Other photos were taken and not used, as they only need eight. The photos debated and left out were the "Old Razor Back," "Radio Antenna," "Panorama," "Ducks in Rock," and "Cross Butte."

October 1956

Doc Hiatt is immersed in correspondence, maps, and drawings as he facilitates the early development of Makoshika. By October 1956 the park signage is finally completed to Hiatt's satisfaction.

Exploring the badlands and Doc Hiatt has become synonymous. Acquainted with a new Lutheran pastor in town who started an early morning church service in the park, Doc Hiatt and Pastor Jim Hanson are two of a kind.[1] Earlier this summer; Doc had a great idea to share with Pastor Hanson. It's a natural amphitheater—a perfect place to hold services. A trail is made and benches are set with a great view of the wooden cross on top of the butte directly above and in front of the seating. On the drive out to Makoshika the first good view of the Cross Butte is looking up to the left, before starting up the switchbacks.

1. Recollections of Avis Anderson

CHAPTER 5

Fast-forward to 1962.

Mr. Makoshika

Bill Browning, Executive Vice President of the Montana Chamber of Commerce, introduces freelance outdoor writer Edwin A. Bauer in a foreword on the Montana Travel Promotion publication put out for the Chamber's annual convention. The thrust of this speech put down in written form is that tourism is fast developing "into the greatest industry in the world."

Dr. Hiatt reads Ed Bauer's speech with intensity. In order to fully capitalize on this lucrative tourism industry it takes intelligent marketing, says Mr. Bauer, and "Montana has clean, fresh air and bull elk and badlands which you can't match any place else."

The amount Montana spends on travel promotion is "an incredible pittance. You ought to hang your heads in deep shame." Montana has "wonderful travel potential" in a "wonderful state." He repeats that "only through intelligent promotion will you ever reach anywhere that potential."

<hr>

Like a kid in a candy store, a gardener with a spring seed catalog, or a chicken farmer ordering spring chicks from a hatchery catalog, Dr. Hiatt is happily armed with a 1962 booklet listing publications available from the Montana School of Mines in Butte. This 14-page 5 ½-inch-by-8 ½-inch pamphlet is a gold mine of available Bureau of Mines and Geology Memoirs, Bulletins, Informational Circulars, Reprints, Miscellaneous Contributions, and Geological Investigations. All of these publications are available to the general public for a nominal fee and shipped postage paid.

December 14, 1962

The Highway Commission State Parks Director Ashley C. Roberts sends a cover letter to Dr. Hiatt thanking him for his help and cooperation as a member of the Advisory Committee, and he looks forward to working together during the next biennium. Ashley says they are forwarding a copy of the Biennial Report sent to the Governor and Legislature. Also included will be a "copy of the Expenditure Detail of the Parks Division for the past fiscal year."

With wishes for a Merry Christmas and a Happy New Year, Ashley signs off.

The Montana State Parks trifold color brochure has listings of the five state monuments and the eighteen state parks with amenities highlighted if available.

The cover has a photo of a lighted Lewis & Clark Cavern, and on the inside bottom right corner is a snapshot of Makoshika highlighted by caprocks framed against a cloudy sky. Each park and monument has a short write-up, and the last sentence and note of the Makoshika promo says: "The word 'Makoshika' (ma-KO-she-ka) is Sioux for 'hell cooled over.' (Note: Road beyond entrance is inadequate for trailers.)"

The five amenities available in state parks listed in columns of boxes are Drinking Water, Stove or Fireplace, Toilets, Camping, and Unusual Scenery. Activities available are F - fishing, B - boating, S - swimming. Makoshika has marks in all the boxes except Drinking Water and Activities. Hiking is not included in the list of activities available.

Expenditures for Makoshika State Park for July 1, 1961 to June 30, 1962 total $2,214.51. Broken down, the amounts are: Salary - Resident

Manager - $20.00, Salary - Caretaker - $1,500.00, Telephone and Telegraph - $4.05, Uniforms - $33.80, Subsistence - $84.00, Janitor Supplies - $35.00, Equipment Insurance - $10.89, Surveying - $40.00, Land Improvements - Recr. Fac. - $223.42, Mntce. of Recreation Areas - $109.90, and Mtnce. of Auto Equipment - $153.45.

Total expenditures for the State Parks Division are $141,705.11.

It's been nine and one-half years now since the State Park Commission was dissolved and the powers, duties, and activities were moved to the State Highway Commission. The State Parks Division now has twenty-four Advisory Committee members who serve without pay and attend meetings at their own expense. Without the Advisory Board there are many improvements that might not have been accomplished. With the support of the Governor and the Legislature, the State Park system can continue to grow, expand, and become a first-class operation that all Montanans can be proud of.

The back side of the *Glendive Tourist and Rockhound Guide* is sponsored by the following twelve Glendive businesses: Birdsall Tire Co., Degel Oil Co., Runway Cafe, Lulhaven Cafe, West Glendive Standard Service, Courthouse Texaco Service, Robbins' Mobil Service, Southside Tavern, and four businesses that paid extra for their advertising space to include photos of their businesses. Those four establishments are: The Hilltop Motel, The Cedar Grill and Lazy H & M Bar, the Jordan Hotel, and the Uptown Motel.

The front-page advertisers are Kampschror Implement Co. and The Beer Jug. Between their ads on the front page is a photo of Makoshika, and the message across the bottom of the page is: ------STOP... REST AND RELAX IN GLENDIVE, MONTANA------ The Gateway to the Historic Northwest and the Friendliest City in the West.

The front side of this guide for rock hounds has a map showing the best search areas around Glendive where agates, petrified wood, fossils, geological oddities, jasper, and stone artifacts can be found.

On the flip side below the advertisers are the words; SCENES IN MAKOSHIKA STATE PARK... THE LAND OF A MILLION YEARS

AGO! A Fossil Hunter's Paradise.

———⊸◦⌒◦⊷———

January 24, 1963

A letter from Jon David Hornyak in Caruthersville, Missouri, is sent to: Park Commissioner, Maco Sica State Park, Glendive, Montana. The mail carrier first delivers the letter to the city of Glendive, and the city marks "Not City" on the envelope and sends it back to the post office. The post- office clerk next slips the mail piece into Dr. Hiatt's post office box.

The letter says: "Dear Sir: I have heard a lot about your park with its remains of prehistoric animal remains. Could you please send me some information on your park? Yours truly, Jon David Hornyak."

———⊸◦⌒◦⊷———

January 30, 1963

A copy of a six-page plea from the Canyon Ferry Recreation Association for the support of House Bills 313 and 314 finds its way to Dr. Hiatt's desk. The first page summarizes the benefits of the two bills which are printed out on the following five pages. If passed, the boat gas tax refund would be abolished and 1% of the annual gas tax collections would be transferred to the State Park Fund. This money would be earmarked for "use in State Parks adjacent to water, on which there is motor boating, for on-shore facilities."

———⊸◦⌒◦⊷———

February 5, 1963

Ashley Roberts sends to the Advisory Committee a two-page report of what is going on with the Legislature. He explains the appropriations process for the state parks and some of the bills that are in the works. One bill the State Parks Division is opposed to is HB 383, which would appropriate $50,000 of park funds for repair and reconstruction of roadside parks. The bill appropriates one-third of the total park appropriations, and he says the state parks can't afford to give up that much for roadside parks, which is agreed are in need of attention.

—◦◦◦◦◦—

February 7, 1963

With piles of correspondence pertaining to the legislature to deal with, Dr. Hiatt stops and decides to do what he really wants to do. He reaches down and opens the stationery drawer on his desk, which is the drawer above the one with a soft cotton cloth and rubber squeeze bulb attached to a spray bottle he uses to clean spectacles. From the short stack of papers he retrieves a custom page of stationery six inches wide by seven inches and slips it into a typewriter, rolls the page up two and a half inches to get past his letterhead, and begins to type. The letterhead is a black-and-white photo of Makoshika on the left and Doc's name, address, and phone on the right.

He types: *Dear Jon, Your letter to "Park Commissioner, Maco Sica State Park" found its way into my post office box. Since our last park caretaker has moved away, and since the State Parks Director in Helena is very busy at this season with the Montana Legislature, I'm taking the liberty and a few moments to tell you at least a little about Makoshika State Park (formerly Maco Sica, both meaning badlands).*

The reason Makoshika scenery is more exciting and that fossils of prehistoric animals and vegetation are found here rather than in the North Dakota badlands to the east is that the earth's crust buckled many millions of years ago and upheaved so much land in depth that this is one of the few places in the world where six geologic formations can be identified right on the surface. Petrified parts of dinosaurs, triceratops, small horses, fig, ginkgo, and sequoia trees have been found in the area.

Enclosed are two brochures in which the pictures will acquaint you a little with the park which comes right up to our city limits. Sincerely, R. W. Hiatt.

P.S. Come visit us someday.

February 25, 1963

Dr. Hiatt sends a personal note to three Senators on the Highway Committee using the "tree" Makoshika cards regarding Bills 313 and 314, which have passed the House and now go on to the Senate. The three eastern Montana Senators on the committee are from Carter, Custer, and Prairie counties.

He reports the completed task to Mrs. John F. Casey, President of the Canyon Ferry Recreation Association.

March 3, 1963

The *Helena* (AP) reports Senate approval of the two bills providing about $175,000 annually in gas tax funds to be used to develop about a dozen waterside state parks.

Other appropriation bills expected to pass include the highway agency parks division of $326,000 for state parks and $252,000 for advertising.

Mid-March 1963

Dr. Hiatt decides it's time for a spring road survey, so he drives his car to the end of the Makoshika State Park road to make notes as he logs his mileage and motors back to his home on West Dodge Street.

At the very end of the Makoshika road is the "back road to Makoshika," and this is where Hiatt begins his course. As one reaches the end of the Makoshika road, the "back road" abruptly turns off to the right and the bulldozed trail makes its way down the steep badlands to the valley floor. From there it's a way across the prairie to meet up with the Sand Creek road, which follows Sand Creek until it meets up with the Marsh Road, and then its four miles back to Glendive. If you take a right on Pedersen Drive before the first railroad crossing, the cutoff road will take you to College Hill, and below the hill another right and you are back on the Makoshika road. It's a perfect loop road through and around the park with magnificent scenery.

The biggest problem with the "back road" is the state of erosion from where it turns off the Makoshika road all the way to the valley floor. The nearly indiscernible trail is full of washouts, ruts, sandstone boulders, and seemingly bottomless sinkholes. The formerly bulldozed path cannot be described as a road and is totally unsafe for car travel. To the adventurous like the Hagenston family this "back road" makes a perfect Jeep trail, and the heart-pounding, leaning, and bouncy navigation to the valley floor and back up the badland trail to the Makoshika road becomes the highlight of a Jeep outing in Makoshika.

Dr. Hiatt makes his first notation: *Should replace log to block "exit" road. Deep ruts just prior to turn around.*

Driving down the road .8 mile, he stops and makes another note: *Cliff Harsh's two "ducks on a rock" have eroded to duck carcasses by now.*

Motoring on to 1.5 miles he stops and scribbles: *Scoria peak....rutty.*

Two more tenths of a mile at 1.7, he makes a notation: *End of old scoria graveling. Dirt road starts.*

Moving on to 1.8: *1958 fire area (both sides of road).*

At 2.1: *Bur. of Recl. Ant. & Mak. Bowhunters Rng. Sundling & Murphy cabins to right.*

2.2: *Electricity to Sundling's.*

3.1: *V.P. - Potato & Radar. Slight scoria gravel prior to here. Dirt road good shape.*

3.3: *1961 fire area (on right).*

3.7: *Radio Hill.*

3.9: *McCarty-Water-Amphitheater Road (to rt.) Deep ruts impassable.*

4.2: *Right turn to new ('62) pic-camp area.*

4.6: *Left to water.*

4.9: Amphitheater. Two 9'x1' 2x12's needed for "pews." Silver paint handrails.

Returning to main road.

5.6: Do Not Enter new area Exit Road.

6.2: Return to main road. Road thru switchbacks needs graveling. 7.1: Start down switchbacks.

7.6: Bottom switchbacks. Gravel base good on switchbacks.

8.2 Registration booth. 10: John Dowson home.

10.3: Glendive pavement (Snyder & Rosser). 10.8: Corner Barry & Taylor.

11.2: Underpass.

12.1: Home, 314 W. Dodge.

Monday, April 1, 1963

On a 3-by-6-inch page from his April 1st daily planner, Dr. Hiatt writes in notes and to-dos. He removes this page from his 2-ring binder and stows it in his shirt pocket for quick retrieval.

H. L. Hunt Jr. Trust Estate, No. Prc. RR. Co#1.

NW ¼. NE ¼. Sec.25. 15N. 55E. Dawson County, Mont. Permit #.

Sign - [Gas City]? W/Holm Lewis, 7 Apr 63.

~~Call Irene Kalloch when at office. Expect cracked bridge. Order or fit frame.~~

~~Call Luke - Hamilton - Buechler for Holiday for Trumpets for SA/TM band.~~

Preprinted in small type on the bottom of this page from his planner is a quote attributed to Disraeli that says, "There can be no economy where there is no efficiency."

Benjamin Disraeli, born in 1804, was of Italian-Jewish descent. His father had a disagreement with the synagogue of Bevis Marks in 1813 which was unresolved and resulted in Benjamin and his siblings being baptized as Christians in 1817.

By the age of 20 the young Benjamin, feeling invincible and wise despite his years, convinced a friend of his father to launch a daily newspaper, *The Representative*. The paper was a complete failure and Benjamin was unable to pay his share of the capital. Despite that disaster he speculated heavily in South American mining shares and lost it all the next year.[1]

Though his aptitude was not in the direction of business savvy, he was a gifted orator and writer and decided to try his hand in the political arena. Even though Jews by religion were not allowed to participate in Parliament, this did not affect Benjamin since his father early on had him baptized as a Christian.

In 1868 Disraeli became Prime Minister and is quoted to have said, "I have climbed to the top of a greasy pole." He became a close friend of a lonely lady, widow Queen Victoria. The novelist hit it off big time with the Queen, who describes him as a Prime Minister "full of poetry, romance and chivalry."[2]

Dr. Hiatt's daily planner serves him both as a task organizer, and the simple quotes on the bottom margin of each page provide a tickle to his thought stimulator.

"The greatest good you can do for another is not just to share your riches but to reveal to him his own." — Disraeli

1. Web – *Encyclopedia Britannica*

2. Web – GOV.UK – Tom Crewe

———— ⋖∘c⟅⟆∘⋗ ————

April 14, 1963 Easter Sunday

Prior to the Easter breakfast at the Jordan Petroleum Room (Adults $1.00 and 50 cents for children 10 and younger), an Easter Sunrise service is held at "The Amphitheater" in Makoshika State Park at 5:30 A.M.

Hastily prepared programs are handed out as the parishioners take their seats on the wooden nine-foot-long pews made from boards two inches thick and twelve inches wide. A play by Don A. Mueller called *In the End of the Sabbath* is performed by the following cast members in the order of their appearance:

Reader – Diana Schuett
Man (Mocker) – Don Brownfield
Woman (Mocker) – Mary Nellans
The Other Mary – Paulett Biel
The Other Reader – Rick Blevins
Soldier – Bill ~~B~~Preimesberger (Dr. Hiatt takes a pen from his shirt pocket and corrects the spelling of Bill's last name.)
Ang~~l~~eel – Dian=e Leubke (Hiatt corrects two more typos on this line of his program.)

At the conclusion of the play the program says: "The congregation is asked to jion[sic] with the cast in the singing of the following hymns." (Believe it or not, Hiatt lets slip by the misspelled "join" without marking a correction with his pen.)

(Eyes zoned in on the first hymn title, he corrects the word WO$^\text{u}$NDED.) "O SACRED HEAD, NOW WONDED[sic]"

The first line of the hymn likewise needs correcting: "O sacred Head, now wo$^\text{u}$nded,"

The next hymn, "CHRIST THE LORD IS RISEN TODAY," on the second line needs to have the word "Ang~~l~~eels" corrected, and on the last line of the hymn, as Doc gazes up to the top of the mount in front of the pews, he adds an "s" to the word "cros": "Ours the cros[sic], the grave, the skies, Alleluia."

Feeling content and in his element at the conclusion of the service, Dr. Hiatt vertically folds the program to fit in his shirt pocket and proceeds to the Jordan for breakfast. Dr. Hiatt is a saver; though he doesn't save everything, this program is a keeper—it's not going anywhere except in his stack of important papers.

To him the Sunrise Service is a perfect start to this Easter Sunday morning, and "The Secret" printed on the front of the program soaks in like the morning rays of sunshine.

The Secret

I met God in the morning,
When my day was at its best.
And His presence came like sunrise
Like a glory in my breast.

All day long the Presence lingered,
All day long He stayed with me
And we sailed in perfect calmness,
O'er a very troubled sea.

And I think I know the secret
Learned from many a troubled way,
You must seek Him in the morning
If you want Him through the day.

CHAPTER 6

Red Socks Doc

⸺∘⧜∘⸺

One time when I was in grade school and my dad was out of town, I had something important to go to where I needed to wear a tie. I didn't know how to tie a tie and neither did my mother, so she made an emergency call to Doc's office to let him know we were on our way for assistance. She loaded me up in the car and drove me downtown. We hurried up the steps to the hallway leading to Doc's office, where he welcomed us in and listened to Mom explain the dilemma. Doc fumbled confidently as he attempted several times to tie an acceptable knot. He was adept at tying a bow tie; the problem was he hadn't tied a necktie for years. It was a struggle before a knot was cinched up successfully.

⸺∘⧜∘⸺

April 7, 1963

Christine Harbor from San Jose, California, folds a page of tablet paper in such a way as to make an envelope. She affixes two airmail stickers plus eight cents postage and tapes shut the letter written in perfect penmanship. The letter, which finds its way to Dr. Hiatt's post office box, is addressed to:

Makoshika
State Park
Montana

Dear Sirs,

In social studies class at school we are studying the Western States. I would be very grateful to you if you could send me some information on Makoshika State Park. Thank you.

> Yours Truly,
> Christine Harbor

April 11, 1963

A postcard mailed from Germany is addressed to: "Park Superintendent, Makoshika State Park, Glendive, Montana, U.S.A."

The Glendive post office knows that any piece of mail with a Makoshika address needs to go to Mr. Makoshika. The postal clerk sorting through a handful of mail deals this card into Dr. Hiatt's post office box.

Braunschweig, Germany, 4 - 11 - 1963

Dear Sir!

Planning to visit Montana and being a friend of nature beauty I should like to see Makoshika State Park. Would you kindly help me prepare my trip by sending me some information about features and facilities of your park maybe with a map of it if obtainable? Thanking warmly in advance I remain

Sincerely yours, John Doe[1]

April 23, 1963

A young Jim Freeman gives a speech in school about Makoshika and afterward sends a thank-you letter, written in lead pencil, to Dr. Hiatt:

Dear Dr. Hiatt,

Enclosed is the material on Makoshika you gave me. Thank-you very much for the use of this material for my speech.

I am pretty sure I got and held their attention when I showed them the pictures and told them of the many outstanding features of the Park.

I must have done well because I got a good grade on the speech. Thanks to you and the material.

Besides telling the audience the information, I learned many new facts about the Park myself.

Thank you again, Jim Freeman

April 25, 1963

On page four of the *Glendive Ranger Review*, Dr. Hiatt is pictured in Makoshika posing on his back as he is pointing up at the "Potato Rock" cradled above him. The huge rock—one of the many interesting features in the park—has the appearance of a mega-sized Idaho potato.

April 27, 1963

A curious Mrs. Nina Laurence from Philadelphia sends a letter via airmail to Dr. Robert Hiatt.

Dear Dr. Hiatt:

A few weeks ago I wrote the State Parks Division of the Montana Highway Commission requesting some information on Makoshika State Park. I received a letter in answer from a Mr. Ashley C. Roberts telling me Makoshika became a State Park in 1953, and that in '57 or '58 another 600 acres were leased bringing the total acreage to 760, etc. He was unable to give me additional information and referred me to you, saying you had a "keen interest in the area" and could give me "first-hand information about the name."

We were doing a draft of an idea for a story when we came across the word Makoshika and hoped, primarily because of the beauty of the word, that we might be able to use it. However, before determining how or even if it is possible to work it in we need additional information.

I am particularly curious and anxious to know how, why, and by whom the park received its name. Was there a Sioux by that name and if so what tribe? Is there a translation other than "hell-cooled-over" (meaning given in the Montana Highway Commission pamphlet) or, is that the most accurate? In general what is the terrain of the Montana badlands?

I should be most grateful and appreciative for any information you may be able to give me about Makoshika. Thank you so much for your courtesy.

Sincerely yours, Nina Laurence

———— ◇○⌒○◇ ————

May 3, 1963

Using his personalized letterhead and a fountain pen, Dr. Hiatt writes a one- page note to the "Editor, Ford Times, Dearborn Michigan."

Dear Sir,

I've been on a Ford-and-Comet diet the past 11 years, during which time your magazine has come to me via Urbanec Motors here. It's a popular item on my reception room table. I was the source of some of the information contained in the "Land of a million years ago" article by the Jansens in your July 1961 edition.

What is the maximum number of copies of said back issue that you can send, and cost there of? I will share them with the local Chamber of Commerce. (Coincidentally, George Urbanec, owner of Urbanec Motors, was Chamber President in 1954 and appointed the Makoshika State Park Chairman in that year.) Thanx[sic].

R.W. Hiatt, OD.

———— ◇○⌒○◇ ————

May 4, 1963

Using a method to, as Doc might say, "kill three birds with one stone," he carbon-copies three letters on legal-sized paper. The body of the letter is typed using black ribbon while the address and salutation are done with red ribbon. Each letter copy is individually signed with a fountain pen.

to: (1) Miss Christine Harbor San Jose 32, California

(2) Mrs. Nina Laurence

Philadelphia

(3) Mr. John Doe[2]

Braunschweig, Germany

Dear Christine, Nina, and John,

Please forgive the carbon copy, but to introduce myself I am a busy, practicing optometrist and father of two active teenage children. Among a variety of interests the promotion and development of Makoshika State Park has been one enjoyable, if unpaid, hobby the past nine years. Since the State Parks Director for Montana has his hands full with 24 other state parks to administer from Helena some 400 miles west of here, and inasmuch as Makoshika's third caretaker started work just this week and like the others doesn't write, your inquiries were channeled to me this week. We'll try to answer your specific questions, and some general comments, enclose a brochure or two, and possibly include a black-and-white print and color slide from my personal collection of Makoshika photos.

Mrs. Laurence, your curiosity about the name is best answered by quoting from Linguist Dr. J. P. Harrington, Bureau of American Ethnology, Smithsonian Institution, Washington, D.C., who wrote to me 2 Jul 1954 that "The word makoshika means badlands. The first two syllables, mako-, are the standard combining form of makoche, country. The syllable -shi- means bad, and appears independently as shicha, bad. The -ka means place. Therefore the whole word means Badlands Place. The name is in the Dakota Sioux language and refers to any badlands, not merely to the famous Badlands. The tendency is to write the name as one word both in English and in Sioux. The pronunciation is: "mah-koh'-shih-kah."…The State Advertising

Department's definition of Makoshika as "hell cooled over" is cute, but not authentic.

Mr. Doe[3], "Guten tag!" By all means you shouldn't bypass Makoshika. To again quote a letter, this time from Dr. Arthur Selke, head of the geology department of a nearby college, "In the 20 European and five Latin American countries I've been in I saw nothing like it, except in Mexico." In further referring to Makoshika he states that "Your badlands are not only extensive, but have variety as well, unlike the South Dakota and North Dakota national 'park' badlands."…. Regarding your request for a map I can say with both truth and humor that this country is so wild, so topographically grotesque, so "uneconomic," and so virtually uninhabited that federal, state, and county governments do a considerable amount of guessing when they do find it necessary to localize an area map-wise for legal purposes. However we have three large road maps posted at our tourist information booth, in the local Chamber of Commerce office, and at the registration booth in the park itself. We have 25 miles of park roads so marked, though, that you won't get lost, so don't let one of the brochure's "56,000 acres" frighten you.

Miss Harbor, back in 1956 we escorted four travel editors through Makoshika at the beginning of their statewide tour. They wrote about Montana for their home newspapers in Fort Worth, Texas, San Jose, California, Salt Lake City, Utah, and Detroit, Michigan. The writer from your city was Frank Freeman. Why don't you ask your teacher to invite him to talk to your class, if he's still in San Jose?

You might also write to the magazine Ford Times, Dearborn, Mich., asking for a copy of the July, 1961, edition which carried an interesting pictorial article on Makoshika. If you have further questions, write again. And if your travels ever route you within 500 miles of Glendive, come see Makoshika. It's an experience all by itself.

Sincerely,

Robert W. Hiatt

May 6, 1963

Dr. Hiatt reads a short 2-column editorial in the *Billings Gazette*. The heading "Making a Reputation" is a discussion about the upcoming tourist season and says "That cordiality and willingness to help travelers when they ask questions will not only add to their pleasure but also enhance the reputation of the West."

With a smile on his face, Doc takes the scissors from his desk drawer and clips the article. Reaching into another drawer he retrieves a page of his custom stationery, loads it in the typewriter, and as is customary he types the date, the salutation, and the valediction in red type.

6 May 63

Editor
The Billings Gazette
Billings, Montana

Dear Sir,

I couldn't help but smile as I read today's top editorial. It served as a reward for a couple hours of unsung efforts yesterday.

This "portfolio" isn't intended for publication. I just thought the coincidence of thought and timing of your editorial and my Makoshika letters might interest you.

Along with a copy of attached onion letter to each of the three inquirers enumerated atop I enclosed three brochures. In each of the Makoshika envelopes I inserted two or three black-and-white prints and two or three colored slides.

Please return onion letter (and the three inquirers' letters too). It's my only copy.

Sincerely,

R. W. Hiatt

May 8, 1963

The editor replies:

Dear Dr. Hiatt:
Congratulations, sorry we don't have a merit badge to bestow on you, as you deserve one. May your tribe increase.

Harold Seipp, editor
HS

And so the truth and sincerity Dr. Hiatt demonstrates in his letters, at their best, are capped at the beginning and end in Red. As in real life, the bold friendly greeting that first catches one's eye is the ribbon in Red, tied in such a way around Dr. Hiatt's collar as to form a perfect bow. And after the storytelling unfolds and the laughter subsides (whether you joined him in verbalizing his jest or not), eventually he leaves your presence and moves on to his next task. But one can't help but steal a glance—a quick one is all it takes—to observe his departing stride, and as a cuff at the bottom of his pant leg rises ever so slightly to reveal what none of us understands but are somehow relieved to see is still there, a Red Sock peeks out from the ankle, as if to say in unwritten words: Sincerely, Robert W. Hiatt.

1 John Doe is not the true name

2 Mr. John Doe is not the true name

3 Mr. Doe is not the true name

CHAPTER 7

Thread to the Badlands

May 6, 1963

Upon learning the State Advertising Director is arriving in Glendive and staying overnight at the Jordan Hotel, Dr. Hiatt hastily takes his pen and stationery, scrawls out a message, and hand-delivers a note to the hotel desk clerk.

Dear Mr. Tjare,

I'll stand by today (at home: dial 5-2148) in the event you can maneuver an hour to take a quick peek at Makoshika. If not today, any time between four and nine in the morning. (If later, call John D. Lewis, Chamber Secretary.)

Welcome to Glendive! Bob Hiatt

May 7, 1963

Dr. Hiatt types a short letter to Vern Soderberg and mails it to the Deaconess Home in Helena:

Greetings to you all from Glendive! (To Mr. and Mrs. John, too)

When I took the airplane glass over to the highway department yesterday, Tony said you left nothing there last fall.....for example, the registration book.

Can you help us?

I haven't seen Harvey Graber since he started as the new caretaker, but I'm guessing he'll like it and be good at it.

Did you ever tour the Hunt-N.P. oil-well road off Sand Creek? It provides scenery still different from the regular park roads.

You were a good park caretaker. Sincerely,
R. W. Hiatt

May 9, 1963

The Ford Motor Company letterhead has an address of "The American Road, Dearborn, Michigan." The circulation manager of the *FORD TIMES*,

E. C. Stephens, types up a reply letter to Dr. Hiatt.

Dear Dr. Hiatt:

Thank you very much for your letter of May 3rd, in which you express an interest in receiving a supply of Ford Times July 1961 issue, which contains the article "Land of a Million Years Ago."

While our library stock of this issue was low a month after publication date, we want you to have as many as we can spare, and we are therefore sending you 50 copies, with our compliments. We hope that this supply will be of some help to you and the Chamber of Commerce. The shipment should reach you in about a week.

We appreciate your interest in writing to us about this issue.

Sincerely,

E. C. Stephens

The *Ranger-Review* publishes a couple of caprock photos featuring Dr. Hiatt's pose as a method to demonstrate the size of the formations.

With April rainfall well above average, Makoshika will be an awe-inspiring colorful treat for the thousands of tourists who will soon be visiting.

May 11, 1963

FORTS and TRAILS of Old Montana and Wyoming is a multi-page travel feature inserted in the *Billings Gazette*. Dr. Hiatt is impressed with the Glendive advertisement featuring the photos of Makoshika, the maps, and articles that are the shiny lure for the tourist, and then the foot-stomping frustration when he reads about the 1850 scientific expedition where Thaddeus Culbertson was sent by the Smithsonian Institution to study the badlands, but not our badlands.

Inside the first page is a map of forts spanning the two states along with dotted and dashed lines representing the Bozeman and Bridger trails. The southernmost forts on the map are Fort Laramie and Fort Fetterman in Wyoming. In Montana, the northernmost forts stretch from Fort Assiniboine in the West to Fort Union and Fort Buford in the East.

Researchers for the related article titled "White Man's Toe Holds in the Red Man's Domain" on the bottom section of the page include J. K. Ralston.

The next full page features a "Welcome to Montana from Friendly, Colorful GLENDIVE." Along with the "welcome" message and a reminder not to miss the Dawson County Fair and Rodeo on August 1, 2, and 3 are several photos of Makoshika. The bottom third of the page features the ad sponsors, including a lodging ad for the Hilltop Motel highlighting the amenities of "Air Conditioning, Kitchenettes, and Phones."

Flipping the page brings one to an interesting feature about Fort Union. A sketch of Fort Union in 1833 is shown at the top of the page. The original drawing was done by Swiss artist Karl Bodmer, who accompanied Prince Alexander Philipp Maximilian to the fort.

Bodmer painted landscapes and portraits to illustrate the writing of Prince Maximilian.

The feature article by H. M. Shoebatham dominates the page below the picture of the fort with the exception of a Smirnoff Vodka ad, a Miles City Saddlery ad, and a thumbnail advertisement by the Press of the Territorian in Santa Fe, New Mexico. For a buck mailed to The Territorian, you will receive a pamphlet number 3 of a series: "Little Known Facts About **BILLY THE KID**."

Around 1833 Kenneth McKenzie, who is called the "King of the Upper Missouri," heads the American Fur Company at Fort Union. Trade with the Indians for furs and pelts is crucial to the success of the fur company. Each year an estimated 25,000 beaver skins, thousands of muskrat pelts, 50,000 buffalo hides, and 30,000 deer hides are floated down the river. Beaver is shipped in packs of around 50 skins. The packs weigh 100 pounds and the beaver sells for $2.00 a pound.

Kenneth is aggravated with his situation and makes a trip to Washington D.C. to argue for relaxing the law banning liquor trade with the Indians. He cannot compete with the British traders who traffic in liquor. His request is turned down, so to remedy the situation he has a still shipped from St. Louis to Fort Union. McKenzie sets up his own whiskey manufacturing operation using corn raised by Mandan Indians.

Eventually, word of the still operation makes its way to William Clark, Superintendent of Indian Affairs. This is it for McKenzie. Fur Company officials, who had known about the whiskey-making operation, tell him he is done, start packing. The American Fur Company is able to retain a license to trade, as long as they boot McKenzie.

In 1837 the steamboat *St. Peter* visits the fort, bringing with it the smallpox scourge. Diseased Indians die by the thousands. The stench from rotting corpses carries 300 yards from a nearby Indian camp to the fort. "Some of the victims go crazy and others are half-eaten by maggots before they die."

In 1838 Pierre Chouteau, Jr., gains control of The American Fur Company. The company's official name is Pierre Chouteau, Jr., and

Company; however, the firm continues to be known as the American Fur Company. Some of his company's more well-known partners and employees include Alexander Culbertson, Andrew Dawson, Malcolm Clarke, and Kenneth McKenzie.

In the fall of 1840 Father DeSmitt was a guest at Fort Union. Before departing for St. Louis he said Mass and baptized the half-breed children.

On June 12, 1843, on board the steamboat *Omega*, John J. Audubon arrives at Fort Union to spend two months at the fort collecting specimens, artifacts, hunting, and making observations. He makes passing mention of the Mauvaises Terres while describing in detail the bighorn sheep that frequent the badlands. Keep in mind the term "Mauvaises Terres" is descriptive for badlands and does not refer to any particular region. The son of a sea captain and his mistress, John spent his growing-up years engrossed in hunting, fishing, drawing, and music. As a young businessman with a family, his fortunes take a turn, and bankruptcy resulted in a jail sentence for debt. To make ends meet he turned to drawing portraits, mainly deathbed sketches, which before photography gave the families a lasting remembrance of their loved ones. He finally decided to do what his passion was in life and develop his talents for taxidermy and painting. Audubon's greatest work, *The Birds of America*, required more than 14 years of field observations and drawings, not to mention the promotion and management of the project, to make it a success.[1] During his trip to Fort Union, John J. Audubon is working on his next large-scale project: "The Viviparous Quadrupeds of North America." When his summer work is completed in the West, the expedition drifted downriver to St. Louis, arriving before winter on October 19, 1843. It is but a few years until Audubon's mental state deteriorates to a point that he is unable to complete his quadruped project. His sons help him, and the later mammalian drawings can be credited to his son, John Woodhouse Audubon.

The prints are dated from 1845 to 1848.

1. Wikipedia

In 1846 Alexander Culbertson, who is an agent for the American Fur Company, begins construction of Fort Benton on the north side of the

Missouri River. This is the last fur-trading post on the upper Missouri. In 1848 Major Culbertson, deciding to change to a more durable fort, begins the reconstruction of the fort using adobe bricks made from Missouri River clay.[2]

2. www.fortbenton.com/fbrestore/history.html

Hunters and adventurers from England arrived at Fort Union, where they headquartered for their trophy-hunting expeditions. After hunting all fall, winter, and spring, the English hunter John Pallister, in July 1848, boarded the steamboat *Martha* with his trophies and steamed down to St. Louis.

In 1850 Thaddeus Culbertson stopped by Fort Union on behalf of the Smithsonian Institution. His mission was a scientific expedition to explore the badlands of what is now South Dakota. Thaddeus and his party of three voyagers along with a servant were accompanied by his brother, the renowned fur trader Alexander Culbertson.

Thaddeus had received a Bachelor of Arts degree in 1847 from the College of New Jersey (Princeton) and for a time taught school. He was interested in botany and fossils, and prior to the scientific expedition he studied at the Princeton Theological Seminary.[3]

From *Journal of an Expedition to the Mauvaises Terres and the Upper Missouri in 1850* (Forgotten Books)

With an appropriation of $200 from the Smithsonian (founded in 1846 for the increase and diffusion of knowledge) and the rest of the trip's expense to be covered by his fur-trader brother Alexander, the party set off from St. Louis on board the steamer *Mary Blane* on Thursday, March 21, 1850. They also brought with them 10 horses to assist with the overland travel and a trusted little companion: a dog by the name of Carlo.

Thaddeus has been suffering from a distressing cough, congestion, and weakness. On a personal note, it is his hope that this journey will help bring relief from his ills, revive his health, and renew his strength.

After a tedious forty-five-day trip from St. Louis, on Saturday morning, May 4, 1850, the party of travelers called a halt on the opposite side of the Missouri River from the trading post of Fort Pierre. They had been traveling overland since they landed the steamer at St. Joseph, Missouri, about midnight on March 26th. It was there at St. Joseph where the party rested for a couple of days and prepared for their trip cross-country. Thaddeus kept a daily journal of this journey, and on occasion when he was at a stop and the chores were finished up, and if he had enough energy and daylight, he would comfort himself by reading the Bible. He was always a slight bit distressed when they kept plodding on without recognizing the Sabbath. On Thursday, March 28th, he writes in his journal: "Read a chapter to-day in 1st John and found much pleasure and profit in thinking of the train of thought which was probably in the Apostle's mind—hope that I understood his sentiments and was brought nearer to the cross by sympathizing with him."[4]

4. Ibid

It is 9 o'clock in the morning when they set off from St. Joe with a buggy, horses, and mules on the 29th of March. At first, it was settlers that would take the travelers in for the night, giving them shelter and sharing their food. Further to the west, it was the occasional trapper's cabin that hosted the party, and eventually it was the Indians who fed them, hunted with them, and helped them ford the streams and rivers. The buggy would have to be dismantled and floated across the waterways, the horses and mules had to swim, and the men and gear were taken across by Indian canoe.

The explorers finally arrive at Fort Pierre after waiting patiently for a portage across the river, and now having rested for a couple of days, Thaddeus is feeling well and strong and is ready to start out on Tuesday, May 7th, for the Mauvaises Terres. With a buggy, provisions for about three weeks, and a pair of stubborn mules, Thaddeus and two others set off for the Bad Lands. The two men going along to assist include a man named Joe, who is an experienced hunter from the fort, and Owen McKenzie, who is the son of Kenneth McKenzie of Saint Louis and an Indian woman. Owen is a very fine and talented young man, a first-rate shot and a splendid rider. With only mules and no available horses for this side expedition to the Mauvaises Terres of White River, Owen will have to demonstrate his riding skills at a later date.

Monday, May 13th, the party arrives at their destination and spends the whole day in the Bad Lands. Satisfied with their discoveries of several well- preserved specimens, including turtle shells, some petrified bones, jawbones, and teeth, and due to the blistering heat, lack of water, and indifferent mules, the group decides to head back to the fort. Thaddeus describes the Bad Lands: "Fancy yourself on the hottest day in summer in the hottest spot of such a place without water—without an animal and scarce an insect astir—without a single flower to speak pleasant things to you and you will have some idea of the utter loneliness of the Bad Lands."[5]

5. Ibid

Incidental to his thorough description of the Mauvaises Terres, Thaddeus mentions the bighorn sheep that frequent nearly every prairie on top of the badland buttes. "They love to roam around the very brink and along the steep sides and seem to think themselves secure in these heights."[6]

6. Ibid

Back at Fort Pierre, Thaddeus works on packing his specimens. He writes in his journal detailed observations of the Indians and their mannerisms and customs. One custom he is thankful for deals with feast etiquette (table manners), in that it is impolite to not consume all the food on your plate while a guest during Indian festivities. However, it is common practice and acceptable to leave the gathering with leftovers and take them back to your own tipi to eat with your family.

One of the customary foods served by a host at an Indian feast is boiled dog meat. The Indians considered dogs as livestock, and after a dog has faithfully served out its usefulness as a pack animal it will be killed and boiled for a feast. A young pup boiled, and with the water changed out several times, is considered a delicacy and doesn't have the strong dog taste of boiled adult dog.

Thaddeus and his brother Alex, being polite and appreciative guests at a dog-fest featuring a couple of boiled work dogs, take the ribs handed to them and upon getting a whiff of the strong dog aroma, gracefully exit the festivities with their leftovers.

Another entry in his journal describes the Indian recipe for dried plums. During the season when the wild plums have ripened the ladies delight in gathering them, and then they sociably get together for an afternoon of "sucking out the plum stones, saving the skins, which are carefully put away and dried, and when cooked with the scrapings of a buffalo skin, are esteemed a most rare dish."

On Wednesday, June 5th, Thaddeus was happy to receive a prairie dog an Indian had killed with a stick. The skin of the animal had not been injured and the coat of hair was in excellent condition, making this a fine specimen to skin and stuff. The prairie dog is very difficult to catch, and the ones shot are ruined for taxidermy purposes. After hearing that Audubon had failed to secure a specimen, Thaddeus felt very fortunate to have successfully secured one of the little viviparous quadrupeds.

The next day, on board the American Fur Company steamboat *El Paso*, the Culbertson brothers set off from Fort Pierre for Fort Union at the mouth of the Yellowstone.

Sunday, June 16, at four o'clock in the afternoon, the steamship "landed at Fort Union having made the trip of 2,500 miles in thirty-six days, 4 hours, the quickest one ever made."

The next morning the ship's bell is ringing to notify of preparations to start still higher up the river.

On Tuesday, June 18th, in the early afternoon, about 80 miles from the fort, Thaddeus goes on a short excursion to investigate "Elk Horn Prairie." A half mile from where the boat stopped, the object of attraction appears as a white monument off in the distance. Upon arrival at the strange feature on the landscape, it's discovered the white pyramid consists of bleached elk horns rising 15 feet high and 25 feet in circumference. The traditional custom of Indians that pass by contributing to the heap began prior to the knowledge of Indians living in these parts.[7]

7. Ibid

It's noontime some 15 to 18 miles above the mouth of the Milk River when the captain nails a board to a large cottonwood tree by the shore, stating the *El Paso* landed here June 20, 1850. The freight for Fort Benton is unloaded on the bank, soon to be retrieved by smaller boats from the fort.

By half-past three o'clock the steamer is headed back towards Fort Union. Thaddeus has reached his journey's high-water mark, and his thoughts turn toward home as he ponders his future. He writes in his journal: "Should it please Divine Providence to restore me to my home and my studies, it is my sincere prayer that it may be to employ my powers and my knowledge as a minister of the Gospel."[8]

8. Ibid

The aged Mr. Picotte on board the ship had earlier tried to stab a buffalo swimming beside the boat, but his sword would not penetrate the hide. To the amusement of the crew, upon inspection, they found the tip of his sword as "dull as a beetle."

Only one grizzly bear was seen and Kelly, an old hunter, explains why. This is the time of the year the bears are out "on the prairies after the "pomolanche" or prairie turnip, of which they are very fond."

The river has started to fall and the boat has no time to lose getting back to Fort Union. Getting hung up on a sandbar now would be the end of the line for the boat. Upon a serious grounding the *El Paso* would be stuck through the freeze up and the spring breakup, likely rendering the steamer useless by the time next spring when the water would be high enough to float it off the bar. As they pass by Elk Horn Prairie, "Mr. Picotte has a notion in his head" to stop and load up the whole pile of sun-bleached elk horns and take them to St. Louis. All others on board prefer to leave the revered landmark untouched. For now the strange savage structure is safe, but eventually, by the time the prairie grizzly, the badlands bighorn sheep, and the buffalo vanished from the prairies, vandals will surely have captured the stack of horns to be sold in St. Louis for handles of knives, forks, and daggers.

As the *El Paso* nears Fort Union on its return from the freight delivery for Fort Benton, they pass by large veins of coal cropping out of steep banks cut by the river channel. Mr. Picotte remarks the sight of burning coal veins and smoking hills from this area in years past. A large cave-in snuffed out the smoldering coal a few years ago and the hills finally broke the smoking habit.

A skiff from Fort Union meets up with the *El Paso* a few hours upstream from the fort. On it are a Crow interpreter, Malcolm Clark, and two other men. Malcolm is a military man now working as a trader for the American Fur Company.

On Friday, June 21st, the *El Paso* arrives back at Fort Union. On this, the June solstice, the longest day of the year, Thaddeus says his good-byes to his friends at the fort and his two relatives: Cousin Ferdinand Culbertson and his brother Alexander. The stay-over is brief and the next morning the steamboat moves across the river from the fort to gather wood. Some men from the fort have come across the river in a boat to help bring in the fuel. At seven thirty in the morning, the *El Paso* moves off, firing a salute to the men pushing off to row back to the fort. Thaddeus gets one last glimpse of his brother standing up in the boat.

Wednesday, June 26th, the going has been slow zigzagging back and forth across the river looking for the channel. They disembark to go wooding again; the cottonwood is plentiful but burns fast. Ash is preferred, however not near as easy to procure. The boat keeps grounding on sandbars and has to back up, find the deeper channel, and slowly try to gain a few miles. They lay up for the night at a place they say should be named "Mosquito Hollow." All night men are in misery, incessantly attacked by the ravenous insects.

On Thursday evening when they landed for the night, the men watch in awe as old Mr. Picotte scrambles up a "very steep, high bluff" rising from the bank of the river. On top, he is waving his arm and hollering for the men to join him. The crew, thinking he has spotted game, in a mad rush and with a few weapons hastily assembled, clamber up the hillside to see what there is to see. Once all are on top the men roared in laughter as Mr. Picotte hollers "follow me," plops down on his rump, and slides down the hill all the way to the water's edge.

On his way down the hill, Thaddeus, for the first time in his life, is pleasantly surprised to see a cactus in bloom. He secures a specimen for the Smithsonian.

It is nine o'clock in the morning on Friday, June 28th, when the boat reaches Fort Pierre. Mr. Picotte disembarks here, and Thaddeus enjoys one last chat with Owen McKenzie and his other friends at the fort. At two in the afternoon they depart.

On Saturday a boat from another fur company is met on its way upriver. As the boats pass all hands are on deck, but neither side raises a hand or utters the slightest greeting. After all, they are the competition. Thaddeus notes in his journal the pleasant sight of several ladies on board the other steamer.

July 6th, 1850: The *El Paso* has landed and the expedition to Indian country and the badlands has ended. Thaddeus prepares reports on the badlands, fossils, flora, and fauna for the Smithsonian. He also writes details of the principal tribes of the Sioux Nation on the upper Missouri River.

The renewed strength gained by the journey did not last long for Thaddeus. Shortly after his return home, he is stricken by a fatal form of dysentery and dies in a matter of weeks.

John James Audubon dies of Alzheimer's disease on January 27, 1851.

At Fort Union, Alexander Culbertson becomes acquainted with Andrew Dawson and is impressed with his negotiating skills and abilities to perform business tasks. Dawson is transferred to Fort Benton in 1854 and put in charge of completing the fort, which was being made more formidable with new construction techniques using sun-dried bricks. Major Andrew Dawson is put in charge of the Fort Benton Trading Post in 1856. After the new fort was completed, it is at a special Christmas dinner with many in attendance when Dawson suggests the fort be named Fort Benton in honor of Senator Thomas Benton of Missouri, who is a close friend of his.[9]

9. Historical Society of Montana

It was 1856 by the time the Irish Nobleman Sir George Gore concludes his extravagant hunting expedition and arrives at Fort Union. There he was treated like the foreign snob that he was, which enraged him greatly. He was accustomed to being waited on hand and foot. So much so that he didn't even load his own guns: he would shoot, hand off the rifle, and be handed another firearm by one of his servants, loaded and ready to fire, then repeat the process until his wild game was down.

In 1858, after having amassed a fortune in the fur trade, Alexander Culbertson left the plains to take up farming near Peoria, Illinois.[10]

10. Wikipedia

It is the severe winter of 1858 when disaster strikes Andrew Dawson. The bitter cold caused mercury to freeze in all the barometers and no one was able to verify the actual temperature. Andrew had a trapdoor over a cellar where he kept his important documents, and he had forgotten to close it. Outside in the dark, as he was hastily walking to retrieve some papers, he fell into the opening and lay there all night. He barely survived the fall[11]

11. Ibid

In 1863 Owen McKenzie gets into an argument over money matters with Malcolm Clark and is shot and killed. Malcolm hightails it in order to escape revenge by McKenzie's friends.

Having never fully recovered from his injuries, Andrew Dawson is forced to retire, and in 1864 he settles his affairs with the American Fur Trading Company.[12]

12. Ibid

Fort Union, the upper Missouri's most important and longest-lasting trading post, ended its reign by 1867. The hide and fur market has collapsed; the prairie grizzly, the beaver, the badlands bighorns, and the buffalo have become more scarce. In less than twenty years they will have mostly or completely vanished from the West, joining the former monument on Elk Horn Prairie as a memory of an era gone past.

Bad investments and too much money spent on the farm forced the Culbertson family to return to Fort Benton in 1868, where Alexander returns to trading.[13]

13. Ibid

Finally, the doomed Malcolm Clark meets his fate in 1869 and is killed by the Indians.

It was on January 15, 1869 when Dawson County, Montana, was created and named for the former manager of the Fort Benton Trading Post, Major Andrew Dawson. Dawson County is home to the Mauvaises Terres of eastern Montana, better known in 1869 as Mako Sica.

Over the next century, the Western landscape is completely transformed by railroads, highways, cities and towns, barbed wire, ranches, and farms. Yet, still to this day, the Mauvaises Terres offer our souls a step into the past in real time, for the badlands landscape has been left undisturbed, and to tread through with an alert eye will reveal itself eons ago while remaining true and unchanged from the Old West.

The *Gazette* travel feature concludes with a full-page Northern Pacific Railway advertisement on the back page. The North Coast Limited Vista- Dome route takes it from the Twin Cities, Billings, Spokane, Portland, Tacoma, and Seattle.

May 13, 1963

While using both sides of a 5-by-8-inch recipe card, Dr. Hiatt pencils notes of his three-hour-and-five-minute excursion to Makoshika Park using military time. Converting to civilian time, he starts his trek at 2:00 in the afternoon. Four minutes after leaving the intersection of Snyder and Rosser, his car arrives at the registration booth. Traveling 1.2 miles on down the road, he makes a panorama stop and there he takes a photo using regular Kodak film. At 2:19 P.M., arriving at the "Mushroom" formation, he switches cameras and takes a shot using Kodak Verichrome Panoramic film.

It's 2:23 P.M. when he arrives at Radio Hill and then five minutes later he is at the Amphitheater. Using both cameras he photo-shoots using regular Kodak film and the Verichrome film. Back to Radio Hill and then another three-tenths of a mile he stops and exits the vehicle.

Oh my God, he loves this.

As he takes it all in, he reaches into his shirt pocket and pulls out his pack of filterless Lucky Strike cigarettes. In an automatic motion, he knocks the pack on the back of his hand to partially release one "Lucky." In a swirl of motion akin to a magician's sleight of hand, the pack lands back in his shirt pocket while the single cig cylinder is deftly tapped on his wrist, gently packing the tobacco in the paper tube. Out of nowhere, a flame appears and he puffs the bent yellow fire into the weed, beginning the burn and setting off the flavor and aroma of tobacco smoke. After a deep satisfying drag on the cigarette, he begins his journey to go below "trailblazing" to the formation known to a few as "Camel."

Upon reaching a sandy tower he had named "Lanky Mr. Sandstone," Doc is surprised to find its sandstone cap blown off. He shoots numerous Kodak and Verichrome photos at this location, and then hikes "downstream." Later on, he finds a gentle return up climb to meet his down climb and begins the ascent. On the hike up and about 150 feet from the top, he reconnects with his down trail and finishes the trek on the old trail back to his point of origin on Radio Hill Vista Point. The return climb takes 26 minutes including a generous rest for a "40-year-old."

It's now 4:45 P.M. and he writes, "Home we go, utterly satisfied with photographic conditions." The day was very windy on top, perfect for climbing "down below." Despite the breeze, he sweated "like hell" at the end of his "jacketless" sojourn.

Recording the exact return time, he is back to the registration booth at 4:56 P.M., to Glendive pavement at 5:00 P.M., intersection of Taylor and Barry at 5:01 P.M., the Chamber of Commerce at 5:03 P.M., and finally home at 5:05 P.M.

Back home Dr. Hiatt takes an ink pen and records further observations on the blank space remaining on the back of the index card.

He saw one of the trio of deer that Reverend Jim Hanson and he had seen the previous day between 7:00 A.M. and 8:30 A.M. in the same location.

He witnessed the sight and sound of erosion as an avalanche of rocks and dirt rumbled down a hillside.

He watched a crazy bird climb a vertical clay eroded cliff with no strain. He noticed Graber had silver-painted several signposts.

He noted the Highway Department has scoria-graveled the top third of the switchbacks.

He waved at a wide-eyed Minnesota tourist as their cars met on the switchbacks.

With his thinking cap on, Dr. Hiatt studies a postcard featuring an open-air, covered shelter made with petrified wood and natural rock formations of the badlands, and the view looking over Painted Canyon in North Dakota. He attaches a portion of the Chamber of Commerce May newsletter which discusses plans to reopen the Tourist Information Booth again this year. There were some operational problems with the information center last year that need to be corrected. Already there are applications filed by eight high school girls that would like to work at the booth this summer.

Today is the day "Social Studies Student" Christine Harbor types up a thank-you note to Dr. Hiatt.

Dear Dr. Hiatt,

I don't know how to thank you for the information on Makoshika State Park. I am sure it will improve my Social Studies grade (though it needs no improving). But most of all I am thanking you for the snapshots of the park. Also, for the slides, because no one else in my class has any slides on any other state park. Thank you again.

Yours   Truly,

Christine Harbor

May 14, 1963

Ashley Roberts writes a short memo to Dr. Hiatt:

Dear Bob:

As of now, we will not plan a spring meeting of the State Parks Advisory Committee because of conflicting activities on the part of so many of our members.

We will follow with a letter to report to all members within the next three weeks or so.

At the time we would try to bring you up to date on our accomplishments and plans for the coming year.

Sincerely,
STATE PARKS DIVISION
Ashley C. Roberts, Director

May 16, 1963

Dr. Hiatt takes his scissors and snips the envelope Christine Harbor mailed him. The usable cut-out portion includes Christine's return address, the San Jose postmark, the canceled stamp, the typewritten address to Dr. Hiatt, and an inch and a quarter of blank space below the address. Using the blank space, Hiatt types up a note to *Billings Gazette* editor Harold Seipp.

Glendive
16 May 63

Dear Hal,
I don't mean to annoy you with trivialities, but young "smarty-pants" letter of appreciation qualifies your May 6th editorial as prophecy. Return, thanx, RLH

May 17, 1963

Harold returns the envelope cut-out and the thank-you note to Dr. Hiatt along with a two-inch strip of paper with a single typewritten sentence that says, "what wonders little attentions to others will do for the soul. hs."

⎯⎯⎯⎯⎯◦◦◦◦◦⎯⎯⎯⎯⎯

May 20, 1963

Itching to go on another excursion in Makoshika, Dr. Hiatt looks for a hiking companion to share the experience with. John D. Lewis declined, saying he is tied up, and John S. Lewis left town until Thursday. James H. Hansen is tempted to join but the invitation is too impromptu. It's midday with a cold (raw) wind; fortunately, the badlands cut the wind and occasional warming sunshine breakthroughs make the five-hour exhausting expedition a pleasant one. The hike-looping takes Doc from "Eyeful" slightly off-right, toward the east and circuiting to the left on the return. His photography is principally shots of formations and flowers. He sees a sand lizard, a bluebird, a magpie, a rabbit, deer tracks, and a human shoe print way down below. Tucked away in the valley is a wild horse grazing area. The two most outstanding discoveries are the formation that looks like a battleship gun (howitzer?) and the outstanding solo white-and-pink flowers.

Finally back where he began the hike, Dr. Hiatt is suffering from what he describes as a "40-year-old exhaustion headache." Basically, after the vigorous hike he is ready for the cure to solve the problem, which he describes as a "bath, aspirin, and 2030 (8:30) bedtime."

Plopping into his car seat, before he fires up the car engine, Doc pauses to read a nine-inch-by-four-inch cardboard note that was propped in his steering wheel while he was out on his hike. The new Makoshika State Park caretaker, Harvey Graber, says the following on the note:

Hi, Doc,

Are you having a good time down below the hill? Looked for you but could not see you. I am making the rounds. Now I want to check the water well and see just what I will need to clean it out. Also, am gathering some firewood.

Be seeing you Harvey"

May 21, 1963

Shortly after last week's memo to Dr. Hiatt, Ashley Roberts receives some photos and newspaper clippings of Makoshika in the mail. He writes:

Dear Bob,

So …. Dr. Bob strikes again …. And this time with some excellent pictures of Makoshika. Very good.

How prophetic can you get? I would have suspected that the cap on the formation would have eventually been dislodged …. But never did I suspect that I (or you) would live to see the day that it happened.

How is Harvey getting along? I expect to be in the Glendive area during the second week of June. Please arrange for some nice dry weather so I can get around. (And maybe we can get the steak cooking job done.)

Thanks again for sending the clippings.

Sincerely,
STATE PARKS DIVISION
Ashley C. Roberts
Director

May 23, 1963

A few of Dr. Hiatt's photos from his excursion on May 13th show up on the front page of the *Ranger-Review*. He likes to give imaginary names to the eroded formations, such as "Lanky Mr. Sandstone" to the pillar that flipped its lid and lost the caprock. "Sea Horse" and "Castles in Makoshika" are fitting names for some others. On page six in the paper, a caption under "A Beached Whale" says, "Shutterbugs have been having a field day in the park recently."

Another item is an announcement of the sixth annual archery tournament sponsored by the Makoshika Bowmen, which is slated for Sunday, May 26th, at the archery range in Makoshika State Park. About 60 archers are expected to attend from Montana and North Dakota.

Featured on the front page is a photo of Mrs. Harold Sterhan, immediate past president of the Glendive Women's Club, handing over a $300 check to Mrs. John Cross, secretary of the Frontier Gateway Museum, for the purchase of sheetrock to be used on the museum's basement ceiling. Observing the check presentation in the photo is Jim Carter and Mrs. W. D. Murphy.

In reply to Ashley Roberts' note from May 21st, Dr. Hiatt types the following:

Dear Ash,

Today would be the day to cook the meat. But the second week in June should be the best in the year, too.

On the subject of prophecy remind me to show you my little portfolio of correspondence with Makoshika-inquirers from Germany, San Jose, and Philadelphia followed by a couple of chit-chats with the Editor of the Billings Gazette.

Makoshika graduated to page one today. It's still in my cameras, but I found the prize formation last Monday afternoon! You have to "turn a corner and stumble onto it" to find it, and it's possible only the mustangs and I have seen it, but it's a classic.

Harvey's eating it up. When he says he's going to do something, it's done a day or two later.

Sincerely,
Bob

The copy of Hiatt's reply to Ashley is typed on the blank side of a Glendive Swimming Pools, Inc., bond application. On the 3rd of June, the city of Glendive is offering $18,500 in bonds to be sold for the purchase, installation, and construction of a bathhouse for the swimming pool located at Lloyd Square Park.

It's finally time for me to step in.....

As I wade through these letters and articles Dr. Hiatt saved, I wonder why he attaches the "Beached Whale" clipping to the Glendive Swimming Pools, Inc., bond application. The photo is only one column by three inches; however, Doc has snipped the whole fourteen-inch strip with, of course, a skinny side-strip at the top showing page (6) and the date. Inspecting the long column above the "Beached Whale," I see there is an unrelated article listing the award winners announced at a school assembly. These kids all graduated in the '60s, and I find myself interested in reading through the list of accomplished students—many with familiar names. Doc didn't cut out the complete school assembly article, so it's doubtful he preserved this portion other than to connect his "Whale" with the May 23, 1963 date on the top left strip. This still doesn't completely explain why this clipping is attached to the "Glendive Swimming Pools, Inc.," bond application. Regardless, some students will be getting a mention here, except, missing from the rest of the article that was not cut out is the name of the outstanding band student of the year who received a special reward. Since the name of this special student was not saved on this clipping, I will leave it up to the inquisitive vintage-newspaper sleuths to find out who it is.

Other band students receiving awards were: Duane Neiffer, Bonnie Feisthamel, Merrikay Slagsvold, Kathy Stetson, Barbara Odenbaugh, Virginia Landers, Jill Hendrickson, Mary Joan Hasche, Shirley Franklin, Betty Birdsall, Myrna Meidinger, Dara Ann Kaul, Carol Meyer, Ann Bjerkreim, Karen Hadzor, Kathy Temple, and Suzanne Norton.

Mr. Prescott presented chorus certificates to: Linda Swift, Carol Meyer, Merrikay Slagsvold, Vicki Killworth, Dara Ann Kaul, Cathy Stetson, Brenda Hanson, Joy Foss, Diane Kolberg, Toni Mertens, Carol Hansen, Glenda Kruger, Vicki Selman, Sandy Mortinson, and Bonnie Feisthamel.

Mrs. Harstad gave 2-year sweater patches to 22 students for their work in the library. She also gave out 1-year certificates to 16 students.

Emblems were given to the winners of each weight class in wrestling by Mr. Hodgson. The awards went to: Floyd Wing, Tim Zody, Joel Leite, Danea Wing, Steve Opp, Dick Kolstad, Ed Miller, and Curtis Powell.

On the bottom of the clipping below this list of student award winners is the "Beached Whale." It all makes sense when I flip the paper strip over, for here is the legal notice for sale of city bonds to construct the bathhouse at Lloyd Square Park. Loren E. Stott is the Mayor and Liala Green is the City Clerk. I'm sure Doc Hiatt considered it an inside joke to himself that the "Beached Whale" photo is connected to the same piece of newsprint as the Glendive Swimming Pool bond notice, which is related to the swimming pool bond application on the reverse side of his letter copy to Ashley Roberts, which brings him back to Makoshika formations and the "Beached Whale."

As long as Doc put me on the subject of the Glendive Swimming Pool, I'll close this chapter with a personal anecdote about the old round cement swimming pool at Lloyd Square Park.

I was born in 1952, and at the time we lived up in the "Heights" on Ames Avenue, which is a few blocks up from the swimming pool at Lloyd Square Park. When I was four years old we moved out to the country on Dry Creek. My rural wading pool was a little irrigation ditch and the creek bottom, which only flowed after rain and usually left a few puddles in the aftermath of a thunderstorm. When I was six years old we moved back to town and lived on Slocum Street, which is only a couple blocks down from the "Swimming Pool Park" [Lloyd Square Park].

The cement swimming pool in the park was shaped like a huge funnel with the deepest area at the bottom being ten feet below the surface. The wading area was marked off by a rope that floated all the way around the pool. There was a high dive that had a platform built a few feet above the water surface on each side of the structure. The platform extended out into the deeper part of the pool past the rope. I seldom waded all the way out to the rope because the water was up to my neck when I ventured out that far.

I didn't know how to swim; nevertheless, I liked to wade around looking for my little black water-bug friends. I could never catch one, but I observed how their miniature arms worked like fins as they darted around underwater. I decided to try to copy them, and before you knew it, I was swimming around underwater with my eyes open, inspecting the big cracks in the concrete and dodging other kids' feet and legs. I'm in my element as long as I have the footing to stand upon when I need a breath.

My mother signed me up for swimming lessons, which I wasn't too thrilled about. This is like boot camp, having to hold on to a paddleboard and kick my feet on command—how boring. And we weren't practicing underwater swimming, where I would shine. All the other kids in the class are older than me, so I feel out of place. I don't pay too much attention in class.

The teacher calls to me several times and points toward the other kids getting up on the high-dive side platform. I stand in the back of the line and get "butterflies" as I watch the kids, one by one, jump off the end and swim back to the rope. Hey, I think to myself, I'm not ready to discover a whole new world. Finally, all the kids have jumped in except me. I stand there at the end of the platform staring into the deep blue. The class is about over and the other kids have all waded out of the pool to get their towels. I jump and sink like a rock all the way to the bottom. Instinctively I push up with my feet, and as my head breaks through the surface, I yell "help" at the same time I'm trying to take a breath. Back to the bottom, I sink, and again I push up with my legs and get half a help out before I sink again. I repeat this several times, all the while I'm trying to figure out how to turn sideways so I can swim underwater to the rope. I don't have time, I'm too busy pushing up for air. As I burst to the surface again I see the teacher slowly wading out to me. By the time she retrieves me I'm exhausted. I'm carried and laid out on a park bench where I stay until my mother arrives to pick me up. Someone must have called her since I usually walk home after the swim class.

She let me quit swimming lessons, and the first thing I taught myself on my own was how to tread water.

I knew Doc Hiatt at this time due to the fact he had been over to my house to inspect the oddities I collected while we lived out on Dry Creek. I remember him telling me I didn't need to call him to my house; I should just stop by his house when I discover something I need to have identified.

In a few short months from the time of the "Beached Whale" in May of 1963, Doc and I will be stepping out together into the dried gumbo of Makoshika to investigate a dinosaur bone I discovered.

That's when we became "fossil hunters."

Stay tuned.

CHAPTER 8

Summertime in Glendive

CASEY AT THE BAT

BY ERNEST LAWRENCE THAYER

(Taken from the *San Francisco Examiner* – June 3, 1888)

The outlook wasn't brilliant for the Mudville nine that day;

The score stood four to two, with but one inning more to play, And then when Cooney died at first, and Barrows did the same,

A pall-like silence fell upon the patrons of the game.

A straggling few got up to go in deep despair. The rest Clung to that hope which springs eternal in the human breast; They thought, "If only Casey could but get a whack at that —

We'd put up even money now, with Casey at the bat."

But Flynn preceded Casey, as did also Jimmy Blake, And the former was a hoodoo, while the latter was a cake;

So upon that stricken multitude grim melancholy sat;

For there seemed but little chance of Casey getting to the bat.

But Flynn let drive a single, to the wonderment of all, And Blake, the much despised, tore the cover off the ball;

And when the dust had lifted, and men saw what had occurred, There was Jimmy safe at second and Flynn a-hugging third.

Then from five thousand throats and more there rose a lusty yell; It rumbled through the valley, it rattled in the dell;

It pounded on the mountain and recoiled upon the flat, For Casey, mighty Casey, was advancing to the bat.

There was ease in Casey's manner as he stepped into his place; There was pride in Casey's bearing and a smile lit Casey's face. And when, responding to the cheers, he lightly doffed his hat, No stranger in the crowd could doubt 'twas Casey at the bat.

Ten thousand eyes were on him as he rubbed his hands with dirt. Five thousand tongues applauded when he wiped them on his shirt.

Then while the writhing pitcher ground the ball into his hip, Defiance flashed in Casey's eye, a sneer curled Casey's lip.

And now the leather-covered sphere came hurtling through the air, And Casey stood a-watching it in haughty grandeur there.

Close by the sturdy batsman the ball unheeded sped —

"That ain't my style," said Casey. "Strike one!" the umpire said.

From the benches, black with people, there went up a muffled roar, Like the beating of the storm-waves on a stern and distant shore; "Kill him! Kill the umpire!" shouted someone on the stand;

And it's likely they'd have killed him had not Casey raised his hand.

With a smile of Christian charity great Casey's visage shone; He stilled the rising tumult; he bade the game go on;

He signaled to the pitcher, and once more the dun sphere flew; But Casey still ignored it, and the umpire said "Strike two!"

"Fraud!" cried the maddened thousands, and echo answered "Fraud!" But one scornful look from Casey and the audience was awed.

They saw his face grow stern and cold, they saw his muscles strain, And they knew that Casey wouldn't let that ball go by again.

The sneer has fled from Casey's lip, the teeth are clenched in hate; He pounds with cruel violence his bat upon the plate.

And now the pitcher holds the ball, and now he lets it go, And now the air is shattered by the force of Casey's blow.

Oh, somewhere in this favored land the sun is shining bright, The band is playing somewhere, and somewhere hearts are light, And somewhere men are laughing, and little children shout;

But there is no joy in Mudville — mighty Casey has struck out.

~~~~~~~~~~~~~~~~~~~~~~~~~

May 25, 1963

It's Friday night, and to record the events of today Dr. Hiatt takes an envelope mailed to him from the Contact Lens Co. of America and uses the front of the four-by-ten-inch paper turned on end to write his notes.

I will do my best to decipher the hastily written scrawl.

Underlined on top he writes: *Friday night 25 May.*
Bette drove carload frosh gals and Camille to
Radio Hill, Sundling, and home.
Later I went out, will stay for 's git-box[1] to join
Glendive Tongue Society during a tape of a
Van Hrys Meeting. Then slept on Sundling picnic table and
mattress plus 2 sleeping bags and stocking cap.
Awakened at daylight (0330) by the State's
Spiritually joyous laugh up-cabin. Them birds --
so pulled out "standing up" Pastor Jim Hanson's
hike date because I thought he needed sleep--
Went for long Radio Hill down and for fresh left and over.
Photo-hike-home-shower-shave and to work
til 1400.------ Bette and I drove out next day for
first-scheduled Lutheran amphitheater social,
but raw air overcast must have canceled.
!!!!!!!!!!!!!!!!!!!!!!

<u>P.M. Sunday, 26 May,</u>
36.5 @ 1356 Chamber of Commerce
37.8 @ 2:00 Leave Pavement
39.3 @ 2:03 Cross in view
40.0 @ 2:04 Registration Booth
40.5 @ 2:05 Startup Switchbacks
41.1 @ 2:07 Top
41.9 @ 2:10 Top of Radio Hill
43.9 @ 2:16 Archery Range

Tri-State Archery Tournament
Makoshika Bow-hunters -----
Saw galloping! huge bobcat -----
Inspected, photographed, and took samples from
scoria pair of buttes that Bertha
Sundling ok'd Highway Department manager for
graveling Makoshika roads.
Another long dawn - below photo - hike off Vista Point #1 to N.W.

1. The phrase "git box" is short for the guitar body. The definition is an acoustic guitar. In a 1961 episode of *The Twilight Zone*, a Civil War veteran refers to his git box, so we know the phrase dates back at least to the 1860s.

May 30, 1963

Using custom office letterhead and an ink pen, Dr. Hiatt writes a critical letter of instruction to the company that processes his negatives.

ABC—
Maybe if whoever chops off the wrong "heads" and one side (the S-shaped dead limb on the right) slows down a bit he can re-center and reprint these arrowed prints you sent earlier this week.
You can find negatives for the other three attached prints among the enclosed extra-print orders.
Thanx. RW Hiatt

Encl: $4.00 cash for 35 Jumbo Prints & 3 – 8 x 10 Enlargements.

June 6, 1963

Dr. Hiatt sends a typewritten note and some black-and-white (people-less) photos to State Parks Director Ash Roberts.

Dear Ash,

Doris mentioned last year their department could use some black-and-white of Makoshika. I know publicists think the inclusion of a human being is a cardinal requirement in scenic photography, but Makoshika just might be photographic enough in its own right to be an exception to the rule. At any rate, will you have time to let her browse through these ere your trip east? If she wants a person in one or two of these, we'll so supply her.

Will you also call Soderberg to inquire where he deposited the registration book and the key to the outhouse tissue dispensers? (I wrote asking about the former, but his letter-replying isn't prolific.)

It's been raining cats and dogs here, but at supper time last night, it rained horses and cows! However, I'll get it dried off for you next week.

See you, (when?)

June 12, 1963

Travel editors looking for a quick tour of Makoshika sent a letter to the Glendive Chamber of Commerce with a copy to Dr. Hiatt.

John Lewis, Manager
Glendive Chamber of Commerce
Glendive, Montana

Dear John:

We are in the process of finalizing our PNTA travel editor tour plans and are looking forward to hearing from you and what plans that have been arranged for our stop in Glendive. We plan to arrive in Glendive at approximately 8 P.M. on Sunday, July 14, and will have to leave at 10 A.M. on the 15th.

We hope that you can make arrangements with Dr. Hiatt for a quick tour of Makoshika State Park that morning. The group will be composed of the following editors:

Tim Renken, St. Louis Post Dispatch, St. Louis, Missouri. Dick Otte, the Columbus Dispatch, Columbus, Ohio.

Sid King, Oregon Motorist, Portland, Oregon. Les Barry, Popular Photography, New York City.

There will also be two drivers.

We will look forward to hearing from you soon. Sincerely yours,

ORVIN B. FJARE
Advertising Director

OBF: lb
cc: R. W. Hiatt

June 14, 1963

I just turned 11 years old yesterday, and roughly a month from now I will be standing on the rim of a Makoshika vista point with Dr. Hiatt, a newspaper reporter, and Ed Lewis listening as Ed makes his remarks about a dinosaur bone.

Doris Stalker, Assistant State Advertising Director in Helena, marks her selection of the Makoshika pictures and returns the photos to Dr. Hiatt with a penciled note: *These are just Great! Thanks, but do need two or three with people. Send negs and we'll make prints & return negs immediately.*

On half of the blank back side of a 3 ½-by-6-inch cardboard cutout of a Continuous Vision Lenses advertisement is the penciled note returned to Dr. Hiatt with his photos.

On the other half of the blank side, Dr. Hiatt types up a comment.

Sent negatives of 17 May-63 B&W Makoshika prints to Doris Stalker, Asst State Advertising Director, Helena, selected by her through State Parks Director Ash Roberts.

On a 4-by-18-inch folded two-color brochure, green with brown type, State Highway 20 is featured as a shortcut across Montana. The newly paved highway shown on the map inside the folded brochure starts in Sidney and Glendive and then merges in Circle, on to Jordan, Winnett, Lewistown, Stanford, Armington Wye, Great Falls, Simms, Lincoln, and Missoula. The back of the brochure displays six black-and-white photos of this route's "fine scenic beauty." One is of twin caprocks in Makoshika.

The Glendive Chamber of Commerce "Hungry Joe" reporter easily arrives in the hands of Dr. R. W. Hiatt via a 4-cent postage stamp with an address scribbled out as "1st Natl Bank" and "City."

The 8 ½-by-14-inch newsletter makes into a nice (stapled) trifold mail piece.

The Merchants Committee is sponsoring a Father's Day promotion with a name drawn from each participating business to be entered into a grand drawing with the winner to be announced on KXGN-TV for a free trip to Minneapolis.

Another big event this month is the Little Britches Rodeo. The age limit for contestants is six through fourteen years. There will be an opening-day parade, and anyone wishing to enter a float should contact Gordon Turner, Steve Chouinard, or George Kutzler.

The next subject Dr. Hiatt circles with a red marker.

The information booth Dr. Hiatt previously referred to was opened June 1st. The three attendants this year are Patricia Nellans, Sue Luke, and Carolyn Svenvold. The booth will remain open until school starts on August 26th.

Crazy Days is set for July 19 and 20. Don Erickson is the committee chairman, and the other committee members are Gerry Robbins, Curt Gustafson, Jiggs Allen, Bob Delamater, Dave Bredy, Ray Meissner, John Davis, and Bob Gutcher.

The Chamber's Industrial Development Committee sent out 15-½ × 20-½" oil maps along with information about Glendive to oil service firms across the country.

The state Fish and Game Commission gave the okay for a two paddlefish per day limit. "This is on the honor system, so please don't hook any more than your two fish per day limit."

The Chamber closes out the monthly newsletter with this thought: "If a man stands with his right foot on a hot stove and his left foot in a freezer, some statisticians would assert that, on average, he's comfortable."

June 16, 1963

Luckily, the seven people who were injured when a car went off the road in Makoshika at about 11 in the evening were all released from the hospital. It could have been a lot worse. Deputy Sheriff Howard Hodous and Highway Patrolman Duane Hayward arrived at the scene of the accident to discover three people had been riding in the front seat of the car and seven in the back. The Sheriff's Office is investigating the accident.[2]

Ranger-Review 6/20/1963

June 17, 1963

In wholehearted agreement Dr. Hiatt clips the guest editorial in today's *Great Falls Tribune* written by L. A. Garrison, the Superintendent of Yellowstone National Park.

The title of Garrison's piece says it all: "Let's Preserve Our Scenic Wilds Unexploited by Man."

June 22, 1963

After the train tour, Dr. Hiatt shows Makoshika slides to the Wilkins family reunion at the bank community room at 2 in the afternoon.

June 24, 1963

The correspondence in reply to the Glendive Chamber's arrangement for a tour of Makoshika for the travel editors is copied to Dr. Hiatt.

John D. Lewis
Secretary-Manager
Glendive Chamber of Commerce
P.O. Box 930 G
lendive, Montana

Dear John:

I was pleased to receive your letter of June 21 and the information regarding the PNTA Travel Editor's Tour through Glendive. We are pleased with your arrangements with Doc Hiatt for a tour of Makoshika State Park on Monday morning, July 15.

As stated in previous correspondence, the tour party will arrive in Glendive at approximately 8:00 P.M. on Sunday evening. We note that you have made arrangements for lodging at the Jordan Hotel. I am now wondering if you have been successful in obtaining a host for dinner on arrival. During this dinner, there may be a good time to show the slides of Makoshika as suggested by Doc Hiatt.

Looking forward to a pleasant stop in Glendive with this group of travel editors, I remain

Sincerely yours,

ORVIN B. FJARE
Advertising director

OBF:lb

cc: Dr. R. W. Hiatt

June 25, 1963

A cover letter to go along with the Makoshika negatives is prepared.

Dr. R. W. Hiatt, Optometrist
Box 1086
Glendive, Montana

Dear Dr. Hiatt:

We were certainly pleased to be able to reproduce some of your outstanding Makoshika State Park photos. We were most happy to have such a fine selection of scenes from this area and appreciate the opportunity to enlarge our library.

Makoshika will receive lots of mileage from your photos and we will do our best to publicize it whenever possible.

We enclose your negatives and again we wish to thank you for sending these to us.

Sincerely yours,

DORIS STALKER
Assistant Advertising Director

DS:lb
Enclosures

June 26, 1963

Eighteen negatives of Makoshika Park are returned from the state Advertising Department and received by Dr. Hiatt.

June 27, 1963

Dr. Hiatt mails more slides to Ashley Roberts.

Dear Ash,

Here are 20 duplicate color slides of Makoshika. Send ten each to Doris and the brewery. Each may keep what each feels may be used and return the balance to you.

Some of these duplicates don't quite measure up to the original, so if either, particularly Doris, plans to color-print any of these and wants the original, I'm willing to trade.

Sincerely,
Bob

Encl Signed releases

Dr. Hiatt receives a handwritten thank-you note in the mail:

On behalf of the Ruthrauff Reunion we would like to take this opportunity to give you a special thanks for the showing of your Makoshika Park Slides. We thought it was really nice of you to take the time to do us this favor. Glendive can be proud to have someone like you who shows an interest in their State Park.

The Ruthrauff family

By Dorothy Darak

June 30, 1963

The Sunday *Ranger-Review* publishes four photos taken by Dr. Hiatt with the caption "The Fabulous Formations of Makoshika."

On the same page is an ad for the upcoming "Cody's Pioneer Circus and Grand Ole Opry Show" sponsored by the Moose Lodge, which will be held at the Fairgrounds on July 2nd.

The *Ranger-Review*, priced at ten cents an issue, is the successor of the *Dawson County Review* and the *Glendive Daily Ranger*. Frank J. Burke is the Editor and Publisher.

When flipping over to the front page after viewing the Hiatt photos of Makoshika formations, we find a feature article with the headline "Makoshika Youth Camp Considered." The County Agent Dale Bergland reports to the Dawson County Planning Committee and brings up the possibility of a youth camp in Makoshika. If a youth camp were developed, it would be a valuable asset to Glendive and the park. Discussions of this potential youth camp will continue. Planning board members attending the meeting were: Art Wiedman, Don Erickson, Clarence Wolff, Frank Schultz, George McCone, John Lewis, Perry Peterson, and Dale Bergland.

The top left of the front page shows a group meeting to discuss plans for the State Babe Ruth Tournament to be held in Glendive July 25–27. Twelve years ago the Babe Ruth program started in New Jersey and spread across the country like wildfire. This baseball program was developed for youth between 13 and 15 years of age.[3] The Glendive tournament director is Don Healy and other committee members in the front-page photo are Dick Rigg, F. T. Ewing, Duane Erickson, Jack Thompson, Wiley Taylor, and Earl Young.

3. Babe Ruth League (Web)

I never made it as far as Babe Ruth baseball. My dad was a great baseball player. You could say he was born a baseball player. The catcher's mitt was his tool in the game. My mom thought I ought to follow in his footsteps.

Greg, Age 4, 1956

You could say I was born an explorer. "Mom," I said, "I'm going fishing." She thinks it's okay, have fun. After all, what harm can a four-year-old do going fishing in the backyard? She pays no attention as I wander off down the street. We live in the Heights, on Ames Wye. After about eight blocks I find the creek and slide down the dirt bank. It's easy going down, not so easy trying to climb back up.

I have been missing from home for hours and the whole neighborhood is looking for me. Graveyard Coulee originates in the badlands and meanders past the cemetery and through town. Except when the snow melts or after a rainstorm, the creek is dry except for a few stagnant pools. This is my first encounter with Graveyard Coulee, which in a few years will become my route to the woods and the river.

Unable to make it up the steep bank to the top, I get partway up and slide back down. Now I'm stuck halfway, unable to gain ground but my shoes have a grip and I'm not sliding.

A boy by the name of Pepper White is up on the street playing with a bike tire on a rim. He looks over the top of the bank and gives me a hand up. I'm rescued! Soon I'm back home safe and sound.

Later on that year I get to go fishing with Grandma and Grandpa Hagenston. It turns out to be a cool and windy day and it's difficult to keep an eye on the bobber. The red and white plastic float at the end of the line keeps getting dunked by the waves. I start looking for frogs and soon wander off and find an irrigation ditch. The ditch is dry with good walking conditions and I go a long way exploring. Eventually, I find my way back and can't wait to tell about my adventure. Without getting a word in edgewise to tell my story, I listen to Grandma scold me for running off like that.

By 1957, when I am five years old we have moved to the country and live in a farmhouse on Dry Creek. My older brother and I take up agate hunting, and exploring the creek bottom becomes a favorite pastime of ours. We have a graveled loop for a driveway, and that's where I first learn to ride a bike. Finally, I learn how to stay up on the bike and pedal without wrecking. The problem is, I haven't learned how to steer, and since my route is circular and my skill set is riding in a straight line, the barbed wire fence down one side of the drive and the plumb bush in the center of the loop become my crash sites.

The bicycle is a critically important mode of transportation for me, for an explorer needs a ship, a plane, a dogsled, or a horse to facilitate one's travel; I have my bike.

My first turtle shell, I remember it well, was not fossilized—I found it on Dry Creek in 1957. We had moved from town to the country and I was at a ripe age for exploring. There was the rattlesnake coiled on the road, the gigantic bull snake up in the cottonwood tree, the aluminum snow saucer full of dents because my brother and I didn't put it away before the cows stepped on it. The catfish in the horse trough I fished for with a worm on a safety pin attached to a line and a willow stick. Over and over I catch the fish and put it back in the trough to catch again.

Grandpa Hagenston, for Easter Sunday, used a small spiral notebook to sketch out a treasure map that ended with a few coins under a sagebrush. How exciting!

Dry Creek was not always dry. On one muggy afternoon, I watched as a wall of water tumbles down the creek; the 3-foot-high flash flood was a result of a thunderstorm and downpour up the valley in the surrounding hills. The wading puddle left in the creek bottom after the big storm was like a magnet drawing my brother and me to the pool of water. What a great place to play on a summer day. Next the dog joined us in the water, and soon after to our amazement the cat swam out to join the fun.

The turtle I pick up on the dry creek bed is partially hidden by the sweet clover growing up between the stones. Peering into the turtle shell I look for a retracted head. The shell is as big as a dinner plate and lightweight. No head, no tail, and no legs—the turtle shell is hollow.

I am too young to know what a fossil is, and yet observation tells me the turtle shell is not real old; in fact it looks fresh enough for a turtle to live in.

My mother already suspects I am going to be an explorer, as she is always subject to finding my treasures: in buckets, lying around the house, and in the pockets of pants she inspects before throwing the laundry in the washer. Rocks, agates, bugs, reptiles—and the last two listed she had an aversion to. One day, to keep me occupied, I am given a gallon bucket partially filled with white oil fence paint and a brush. After all, what harm can I do if I spill a little paint on the grass? It looks like miles of boring fence to paint, and after a few strokes with the heavy brush I decide, this is enough. Mom saw what I was up to and dashes out of the farmhouse, but it is too late. I have already poured the contents of the bucket over my head. Oh, the smell of the turpentine cleaning my scalp as I sit in the bathtub. From now on, I am left to my own adventures. No more paint jobs.

Returning many times to explore the gravel bed, always hoping to find another turtle shell I see something blue. I pick it up—a seashell. Holding the conch shell to my ear, I listen. I daydream, I hear the waves. A snail shell, ancient, weathered, pitted, big enough to fit nicely into the palm of an adult hand. The shell is pointed at one end, rounded on the other, and blue in color. It's totally out of place on the prairies of eastern Montana. I add this to my special collection.

By the time I was old enough to enter first grade we have moved back to town. We live in an old two-story house on Slocum Street; my bedroom is up on the second floor. I don't think the house is haunted; however, I swear I hear the sewing machine running, and when I walk up from downstairs, no one is in the sewing room. Explain that one to me. My brother puts a little chalkboard by the window and magically, the next morning, there is a dusty chalk outline of a flying saucer on the slate. I'm hooked: flying saucers are real for sure. There is one event that really gives me goose bumps. I'm in my bed ready to go to sleep and Mom is down the hall in her bedroom. I'm lying on my back with my eyes closed and I sense a presence. I open my eyes and there are at least four ghosts standing by the bed looking down at me. They are wearing white hooded robes. I am scared. They keep peering down at me and I holler for Mom. "Mom! Mom! Mom!" She hurries down the hall to see what's wrong and, right before she comes in the room, they all go over behind the bedroom door. I point for Mom and she looks behind the door—there is nothing there. She tells me everything is okay, to go back to sleep. The ghosts never show themselves to me again, but they were there.

Across the street and past the baseball dugouts there is the outfield, a berm, and over that the woods begin. I am in my element again. Another creek— the same one I explored when I was rescued by Pepper White. Graveyard Coulee, with its stagnant pools of water, is bordered by the woods when you get closer to the gravel banks of the Yellowstone River. Not old enough to tell time, my mother gives me a burlap gunny sack and a kitchen timer wound up to an hour. I can disappear down the creek and into the woods until the timer dings. Then it's time for me to come home, hauling agates, rocks, bugs, and reptiles. One day I ask Mom for the timer so I can go exploring again and she refused. She said go ahead and go, you don't need the timer anymore. This is tough on me—the timer has become my security blanket, my crutch. She has me wear a metal bracelet instead.[4] It looks like a dog tag: name, address, and phone.

4. The bracelet I still possess as a memento.

I love exploring the creek bottom, the woods, and the riverbank. Who is that coming up the creek? After all, this is my territory. We cautiously approach each other and soon Mark Hathaway, a neighbor boy, and I become fast friends. On a certain season of the summer the blue bugs cluster on the young willow shoots. Thousands of the small ladybug-like beetles with deep blue translucent wing shields cling onto the willows. Usually in the willows close to the gravel bank, on an island which becomes a peninsula after the June rise of the river subsides; that's where we find the blue bugs. I hear Mark loudly proclaim "BLUE BUGS!" When either one of us shouts out the word "BLUE BUGS" it is a call to arms. With extreme haste, and no time to waste, both of us grab the nearest driftwood stick and charge headlong into the willows, wildly swing$ng our sticks and batting into the air clouds of the harmless blue beetles. As the bugs swarm around us, nearly obliterating each other from view, we collapse to the ground in uncontrollable, spontaneous laughter.

One day I told my dad about the well hole we discovered in the woods down by the river. He is skeptical and has to investigate. I explain it's right down by the fort we built. Later on, we are disappointed to discover that our trap has been wrecked. The sinkhole was only about three- to four-feet deep and we had covered it over with grass and branches to trap the outlaws that were attacking our fort. It worked, although our intention was not to trap my dad! He said he fell right into it, and from now on, in no uncertain terms, the swallow hole was to remain uncovered. I never did find out why the depression in the ground was there; it appears to be manmade from many years before.

Late summer before school started again, I brought home a painted turtle— probably from the country club pond. On the way home, as I sat quietly in the back seat of the car, my mother asked me why I wasn't saying much. I don't know; after all, I am busy concentrating on the water snake and minnows I have in the vinyl bag. I think I saved us from a serious accident; she found out what I had in the back seat after we were safely parked in the driveway.

I didn't name the turtle; after all, it is a turtle, and you don't have to name turtles. Fall is fast approaching, and I know soon I won't be able to catch minnows and tadpoles to feed it anymore. Grudgingly, on a cloudy and cool fall day I put the turtle in a burlap sack and head down the creek to the river. Standing at the edge of a backwater where the creek meets the river, I carefully release the turtle. It slipped into the brown water and with its short turtle legs gracefully flippered itself away.

The mighty Yellowstone River is not exactly the right habitat for a painted turtle; after all, I've never seen a painted turtle down at the river, and this one came from a pond. The season's cycle continues, and like the ponds that freeze over with a thick layer of ice in the winter, the Yellowstone River does likewise. It's early spring now, a calm sunny day, and with a relaxed gaze across the peaceful expanse of frozen river it seems like time stands still.

The ponds uneventfully lose their frozen cap, while the river ice is pushed up by the rising, snow-melted creek water. Days later the ice groans and pops as the pressure builds, and muddy water flows in rivulets along the edges and over the top of the thick ice. Finally, to the delight of the geese and ducks frolicking in the water bubbling up through the ice holes, the river ice breaks up and goes out. The slush and ice floes jam from the pressure, flooding the lowlands. Small trees and brush are smashed flat; gravel and mud, stuck to the bottom of the ice floes and gouged from the riverbed, find new resting places, forming new sandbars and channels. The ice left behind when the water subsides is up to four feet thick, and when it finally melts there is left behind a thick layer of mud, gravel, and driftwood debris. The baseball field is a mess. Locals drive by slowly, looking at the bent outfield signs and the ice chunks lying all over the infield. It cools off at night: below freezing. It's a Sunday morning before church and I am in my Sunday best, with shoes shined and my suit pants pressed nicely. Such a handsomely dressed young man! But I am just itching to get outside and enjoy the day. The others are all busy getting ready. I'm going to check out the ball field. The dugouts are full of water and have a thin layer of ice on top. I just have to investigate. As I stand on the ice I hear it crack, and before I can get off—down I go, waist deep. Sopping wet with soaked shoes covered in mud, I sheepishly head back home. It is now springtime, my exploring fully resumed. In the creek bottom, limping along is a painted turtle. Having injured itself—I suppose when the ice gouged its way up the creek during breakup—the turtle seems fine other than walking with a limp. Dad notices the pet turtle and asks if it is the same one I released last fall. I said I don't know, I can't tell. The next spring, as the ice melts in the steel turtle tank at home in the backyard, I keep checking to see if the turtle frozen in the bottom of the tank will wake up. I wanted to save it from the river, so I didn't release it last fall. It never woke up.

The helicopter project is short lived. I have a pile of boards, some pieces of metal and pipe, but I could never figure out how to put the darn thing together. Since I can't fly, it would have been nice to be able to ride my helicopter over the woods and creek, but there are other things to concentrate on.

Queenie, my pet rabbit, loves to eat dandelions. Dad must have built me the rabbit cage. I really, really enjoy the pet rabbit. I will go to the grain elevator and ask for rabbit pellets. The man asks, "How much?" "Twenty- five cents worth," I answer. The nice man would give me a small paper bag of rabbit pellets, and then a few weeks later I would be back for another bag. "How much this time?" "Twenty-five cents." I couldn't figure out why for the same price I would get different amounts of rabbit pellets. Sometimes double! Then one night I wake up in the middle of the night; it is dark. I go outside across the backyard to check on Queenie. I feel foolish and don't quite get all the way to the rabbit cage. I go back to bed. The next morning, feeling some anxiety, I go out to check on Queenie and the rabbit is gone. I look all over the neighborhood and find it dead out in front of Brenner's house. A dog had mauled it to death. I go home, get some string, go back to the rabbit, tie the string to a rabbit foot, and drag it back to the house, crying all the way. Dad sees me from the house and comes out to discover what happened. He digs a grave for Queenie and I gently put her to rest.

I always wondered why I got up and went to the backyard that night, worried about Queenie.

Soon I was studying chickens. Somehow, I got my hands on a small egg incubator, probably ordered from a comic book ad. The thought of incubating and hatching a chick seems so exciting. But I need an egg— according to the pamphlet it must be a fertile egg. By now I was adept on a bicycle. Man, I can go anywhere on a bike. So, armed with a paper sack and fifty cents, I mount my bike and head out to a chicken farm. I know where there's one, out toward Circle—probably about five miles from home, just a couple miles out of town. Even though extremely shy, I gathered enough courage to find someone at the farm and ask for a fertile egg. "A what?" Repeating myself several times, I am finally told, no, they don't have any. Dejected, I left the farm and went up the road to the next place, which is a small farm shack. A cowboy answers the door and again I had to repeat myself several times. "Do you have a fertile egg?" He wasn't quite sure why I wanted one, I could tell by the way he is looking at me. Of course, I didn't tell him anything other than I would like to buy one. "Just a minute." He disappeared into the shack and soon came out with two eggs. Then he refused payment. I am ecstatic, hop on my bike, and head for home. Dad investigates my project; I hadn't told him what I was up to, especially since he wouldn't let me order that hand-crank movie projector I saw in a comic book for less than $5. He could hardly believe I went out on my bike to the country to buy an egg. It was made clear I was never to do that again. The only one interested in my project—me. Going through the process, turning the egg regularly, to my amazement one of the eggs began to hatch. My experiment was a success. I will never forget the kind cowboy who gave me a fertile egg.

The country club pond was one of my favorite places to go fishing. Dad liked to go out to the golf course, and I tagged along or just got out there with a ride from Mom. I learned early on to keep an eye on my stringer of fish, because the turtles would eat everything on the stringer but the fish heads if I wasn't careful. Cooking my lunch of fresh fish in my Boy Scout frying pan is a real treat. I first light a paper candy-bar wrapper, and then add little twigs, and then some small branches, and now I have a toasty campfire to cook on.

I have an interesting collection of oddities gathered up from when we lived on Dry Creek and also treasures I have picked up in the creek or out in the hills when we went on family outings in Makoshika. Mom calls Doc Hiatt, and living only four blocks from our house, it doesn't take long for him to get here and inspect my collection. My prized possession is the blue seashell found on Dry Creek. He inspects the shell intently, but doesn't have the answers I am looking for. What, when, where, and why? But now I know who to ask when I have questions about my discoveries.

So, my mother gets me signed up for little league baseball. She wants me to learn the sport, become a little baseball player, and make my dad proud. I soon learned baseball is like swimming lessons, with somebody telling you what to do, how to do it, and when to do it. It's a lot different than exploring, where I call all the shots.

The first order of business at the beginning of the season is for the adults to pick their teams.

The boys lined up remind me of swimming lessons; they are all older and taller than I am. It feels like we are standing before a firing squad of sorts. The coaches start picking their players. One by one the line thins until I am the last one standing. It's clear I'm wanted on a team about as much as I want to play on one.

I am given a baggy, uncomfortable uniform and told when to report for practice.

First of all, I'm supposed to be at practice on a certain day of the week at a certain time. It so happens that's exactly when Rudy, my friend from the neighborhood, and I discover coal in Graveyard Coulee. We take our sample to the Texaco gas station, all the while talking to each other about what it will be like to be rich, now that we made this important discovery. The man at the gas station blew us off, said it was nothing. To top it off, when I get home my mom chews me out for missing baseball practice.

Eventually, we are no longer practicing but actually playing baseball. There is one thing I learn to get good at the few times I am taken off the bench to play right field, and that is to chatter. "Ho, ho, ha, ha, batter's got a rubber arm, hey, hey, you, you, batter's got a rubber arm."

Crack! And it's a pop flyover to right field. When I wasn't chattering I was praying no one would hit the ball my direction, because I have no earthly idea what to do if it comes my way. I freeze and pretend this is not happening to me. People are yelling. As the batter rounds the bases for home, another player picks up the ball that landed directly behind me and says, "Why didn't you pick up the ball?" He doesn't wait for an answer, but I do know one thing. There are 13 tadpoles in the mud puddle not far from the bench, and their marble-sized bodies can really swim good with their single tailfins. They also have tiny frog legs starting to grow out of their fat little bodies. I wish I had something to put them in. If so, I would catch some to bring home.

All of us on our team went down to KXGN and lined up for a live interview. The questions were short as the man with the microphone has a limited amount of time to ask questions to all the kids. All was going well until they got to me, greeted me, asked my name, and then popped the question on me: What is the name of my coach? Thanks, a lot. All I know him by is "Coach." I never asked him his name. He kept pushing the microphone in my face for an answer and I was speechless. He moved on to the next kid and everybody forgot about it, except me.

My dad always said if you want to hit the ball, you have to swing at it. So when I get up to bat I swing at every pitch, no matter how wild it is: over my head, way outside, in the dirt, doesn't matter, I swing at the ball. After all, if you want to hit the ball, you have to swing at it.

My up-to-bat is always quick: strike one, strike two, strike three, you're out! But then, if you want to hit the ball, you have to swing at it. And one time it happens—*Crack!*

I hit the ball. Now, Now, I am Casey at the Bat. Except this time, no matter how many times you hear the poem and wish Casey would hit it out of the park and it never happens, this time it is me, I am Casey, and I hit the baseball. My bat is flung to the side as I burst off the plate towards first base. I'm kicking up dust like the Tasmanian Devil, I fly past first base and on to second base looking like the Roadrunner, and as I round third I slow down to a trot. My chest expands and I feel as gruff and confident as Yosemite Sam. But there is no crowd roar of approval, no slaps on the back and "way to go" as I cross home plate. Only someone telling me I hit a foul ball.

My parents are disappointed, but I am not interested in playing organized baseball. Mother is insistent—she wants me to keep playing—but Dad saves the day. It is short and sweet; he says to Mom, "If he doesn't want to play baseball, he doesn't have to play baseball."

However, I learned to capitalize on the sport regardless. My friend Rudy and I didn't pay much attention to the little league games going on in the ball field across the street, but since we were not going to get rich from our coal find in Graveyard Coulee, we had another idea. Rudy's dad is a carpenter and we talk him into building us a concession stand. Then we talk Mom into taking us out to Warehouse Grocery where we are able to buy candy bars, sunflower seeds, and pop at wholesale prices. Rudy and I pick out our favorites: Hershey bars, Baby Ruths, Butterfingers, Fisher Sunflower seeds, and cans of Coca Cola and 7UP. We help Mom load the cartons of candy bars into the grocery cart after she takes the grease pencil and marks the price on the cartons for the checker to read when we check out. Mom pays for everything; after all, we don't have any seed money to get started. She didn't say anything about a loan; she just paid for the boxes of snacks.

This is great; we are so excited to try out our business. Rudy's dad helps us set up the stand on the corner of our boulevard right across from the little league field. We don't have a sign or anything like that, but as we sit behind the stand the customers stop by in droves. We have to adjust the price on pop as we are getting complaints, but other than that our opening day is a huge success.

Completely wiped out of stock, before games the next day I have to get Mom to take me to Warehouse Grocery again for more inventory. We are making money hand over fist. Soon Dad catches on and insists that we have to learn the business the way it is in real life. From now on we have to buy the candy bars and pop using money from our sales, instead of Mom's money. That greatly cuts into our profits but we still make money.

The next thing that cuts the wind in our sails is the baseball mothers. They see how well we are doing so they decide to set up their own concession stand. That hurts our sales but we don't let the competition get us down. We hired (for a candy bar) a little neighbor boy by the name of Terry to walk through the grandstands with a tray (somebody's mom's cookie sheet) full of candy to sell. Terry is an irresistibly cute and scruffy little guy and wow, did we ever clean house. Sales are fantastic: we run out of everything before the game is over.

It works too well: we are getting all the business and the baseball mothers complain. Our parents shut us down. Boy, oh boy—politics!

I try setting the stand up on the edge of the driveway to catch some customers walking up to the pool during the day. Business is slow but I still made a few sales.

Dad arrives home from work for lunch and takes a look at my operation. He thinks I am crazy and shuts me down again.

Now my friends and I will have to find other things to do to keep us occupied.

To be continued…………..

CHAPTER 9

Cops and Robbers

June 30, 1963

The headlines on the *Ranger-Review* are grim. On one side of the paper are Dr. Hiatt's photos of Makoshika formations. Sandstone stripped of its cloak of soft sand, pinnacles robbed of their caps, the ground vandalized into grotesque gullies; all these crimes against Mother Nature are the natural result of wicked weather. The wind, rain, heat, and cold deliver us the natural beauty of Makoshika. The jury is out and the verdict is not guilty.

Whereas, on the other side of the page we can find the front-page headlines: crimes against humanity. "**Robbery Suspect Warrant Issued**. Police Release Two More Held in Murder Case." An all-points bulletin has been issued and the FBI has been enlisted to aid in obtaining the suspect's arrest.

Another subheading says "**Man Jailed on Felony Check Count**." The defendant was picked up in Baker on a felony warrant. Also in custody is Roger P. Hammond, age 19, who is guilty of the crime of having beer in his possession.

Some criminals deserve their jail sentence, and others just need a wake-up call and help getting steered in the right direction.

Sometimes one's own activities will result in self-corrective action. Take for example a few years back when the notorious Herby and his accomplice Carl were up to no good. These two grade school youngsters have been down at the river prowling around, and they discover a virtual nest of fish congregating below where a flowing pipe is sticking out over the water. We think of fish in schools, but schools of fish move, while these fish act more like baby birds in a nest. They swim around in tight circles with their mouths and pulsating fish lips always pointing up, always calling for more morsels dumping out of the pipe. Herby and Carl can't believe their eyes. These fish are huge, and right below the surface; even in muddy river water they are easy to see. The only time they have been able to catch one is when they are fishing for catfish, and sometimes when they think they have a snag, if the line doesn't break, a big carp is pulled out of the water. But these fish are sitting ducks. It would be like shooting fish in a barrel. They wonder how many they could get with one shot. Wait a minute, and then the incriminating phrase is blurted out: "I've got an idea."

Now, Herby and Carl are not hardened criminals—not yet anyway. Neither one of them would ever think of stealing something from somebody. But the situation they are in now is going to call for some extreme borrowing. They have no money, they have no gun, and they have no ammo. The suspense is killing them; the only way for the boys, blinded by desire and anticipation, to tool up for this caper is going to be schoolboy ingenuity. Carl knows where there is a 410 shotgun he can borrow from a relative, as long as he doesn't ask. Herby has to figure out how to find ammo. He moseys into the Farmers Union store a couple blocks from the river, and even though he wouldn't think of stealing a box of ammo, he borrows one 410 shotgun shell from a box, not thinking of the consequences and stigma of being a shoplifter. Herby knows the difference between right and wrong, and he should know better. To Herby, the scales of justice are tipped by the thought of his finger on the trigger.

A muffled gunshot echoes through town from the riverbank, sounding like the initial blast of Old Faithful Geyser in Yellowstone National Park. And, had there been a witness, the sight would resemble two tourists with their heads looking right into a geyser cone at the precise moment she blows.

One thing we can be sure of: the boys won't pull that stunt again. With heads hanging in defeat and dragging their feet, the sopping wet Carl and Herby keep their hands busy on the way home, picking gunk out of their hair: fish guts, bits of corn, and sewer sludge.[1]

1. Herb Meland's recollection of a grade school prank. Until the sewer lagoons were completed in 1959, the city's raw sewage was piped to the end of Towne Street where the outlet emptied directly into the Yellowstone River.

The Dawson County High School is an Italianate-style building originally built in 1908.[2] In 1938 another section of the school was constructed. This year more new construction is planning to be completed. The new building will be adjacent to the 1938 structure going from Merrill Avenue and wrapping around back to the gymnasium on Kendrick Ave.[3] This new area will be a welcome addition to the school. The older building holds eight junior college classrooms, fifteen high school classrooms, the industrial arts shop, and an auditorium. The auditorium has an old-style design and is quite impressive. Even the steps leading into the theater area are marble slabs.

2. Montana Historical Society

3. *Daily Dispatch* / Western Fire Chief Association / *Ranger-Review*

As is customary during the course of construction, the process involves digging holes and moving dirt. And to grade school boys using their imagination as they play their make-believe war against the Germans, these dirt piles are perfect bomb crater berms.

My friend Rudy is German, and I am German and Norwegian. It doesn't matter: we are Americans fighting the Germans. We dive for cover behind the dirt pile as the tanks rumble past us on the street. Kendrick Avenue must be a major supply road for the enemy. These berms have fairly soft, crumbly soil with clods that make perfect grenades to launch overhand in front of the tanks just in time to explode as the armored vehicle passes over them. As soon as our dirt grenade hits the pavement, we swan-dive behind the loose heaps of excavated earth to protect us from the shrapnel. We have to be careful and make sure our machine-gun nest is not spotted by the soldiers manning the cannon's rotating turret as the enemy tanks pass by.

The *rat-a-tat-tat, phew, phew, phrrrrgh, thhhhhhhh,* and *ssssiiiiizing* sounds produced by our lips, tongue, and vocal cords are synchronized with our dirt-pile ballet and splattering dirt clods. The sounds we produce are as realistic as the explosions and machine-gun fire heard in a John Wayne war movie.

We hear the command: "Rutiger, Uve, Loots!" Oh, that's Rudy's mom calling. It's time for Rudy to round up his younger brothers and go home.

I'm having so much fun I decided to stay and take out a few more enemy vehicles before I shut down the day's military operation. It's a little slow, and then here comes one. The dirt clump splatters the pavement off to the side; I may have only crippled this one. A little while later the same tank comes by again, only slower. This time when I launch, the clump splatters right in front of the vehicle. Perfect shot!

I'm a little late with my dive and roll into the dirt. As I tumble for safety, through the corner of my eye I detect a piercing glare. The vehicle slows, but does not stop and then continues on. There is another lull and something tells me I should call it a day.

Then an official-looking vehicle slowly drives by on the lookout for the pesky soldiers who are causing all the trouble. This is an officer's vehicle and I'm not going to mess with this one. But what fun it is to be lying out flat behind the mound with my chin buried in the dirt and only my forehead, eyelids, and nose peeking over the top to watch as the police car drives slowly past. He keeps going: I'm safe.

Uh-oh! Here he comes again from the other direction. This is not good. Again he passes by. That's it, I'm done for today; gotta get out of here. As soon as the coast is clear I'll hustle across the street and nonchalantly walk home.

It's too late: this time the cop car pulls up in front of the dirt pile and stops. I jump to my feet and run for my life. I make it a ways, all on instinct and adrenalin, and then it happens. A horn honks: I'm sunk.

I freeze in my tracks, legs spread a little with my arms in the air and fingers all splayed out.

The police officer approaches me to ask one simple question. "Why did you run?"

In a quivering voice I answer back, "Because cops give me the jitters."

The policeman tries to keep a straight face as his lips begin to crack a smile. Quickly he composes himself and firmly tells me not to play in these dirt piles. "Yes, sir," I reply, and thankfully he releases me and I go straight home.

The next time we are outside, I tell Rudy we can't play Army in the dirt piles anymore. But right across the street, downstream in Graveyard Coulee, there is an old rock wall set into the bank near the bottom of the creek. It must be rip-rap to keep the water from eroding that side when the creek is running a stream. That's the only reason I can think of for it being there. This low rock wall is probably only three or four feet high. We find some wet clay in the creek bottom that is easily molded by hand into clay grenades. And the perfect hiding place for the wet dirt balls are the gaps between the rocks forming the wall in the creek bottom. The arsenal of ammo is neatly tucked into the rock wall's crevasses for future use.

I don't know Gar very well. He is older than me and lives in the neighborhood so I know what he looks like. I'm down in the creek bottom with my brother, and I notice Gar stalking us as he walks along the top edge of Graveyard Coulee while we're striding along in the creek bottom below. I'm a little nervous, like a deer gets when it senses the danger of a mountain lion readying to pounce. And then *wham!* Out of nowhere I'm hit on my left temple with a huge dirt clod. I see stars—the comic books weren't kidding when they show a character getting conked on the head and a caption bubble with stars. It's true: as my head is recovering from the vibration of a softball-sized dirt ball exploding off the side of my head, my mind's eye is in a scramble with a cluster of little revolving white stars. The stars subside like the sound dwindles after an initial blow to a gong. Too bad he got me with a lucky first shot, because I wasn't too far from my arsenal of hardened clay balls stored in the creek bottom rock wall. I could have counterattacked, and I had plenty of stored ammo to volley his direction.

Even though Gar hit me with a bull's-eye, I believe it was an accident and he was actually aiming at my brother. If he was trophy hunting, Dennis is older and bigger than me, so I think he was shooting for the big buck and missed. Since we were moving he had to aim ahead with his shot, and since I was walking slightly in front of Dennis he over calculated his lead and hit me instead. Harsh words are exchanged between my brother and Gar and that's the end of it. We go our separate ways.

As long as we are on the subject of stars, I'll mention the other three incidents where it was like the shooting stars of a Fourth of July sparkler glittering in my head. Once when I over-dove into the extra bed in the sewing room and hit my head on the radiator. Once when I was doing spectacular backward somersaults on the boulevard grass, and I backwards somersaulted into the trunk of a big Chinese Elm tree. And once when my brother and I both spotted a big flying grasshopper down in the ballpark outfield, and I dove to catch it at the same moment he heaved a big rock to hit the insect. He got me on the head with the stone, and while I was seeing stars the grasshopper got away.

This time I'm determined to make it to my arsenal. Forrest, a neighbor boy a couple years older than me, is in hot pursuit. It wasn't my fault— Dennis is the one that planted the rubber slab of fake puke the size of a dinner plate on the sidewalk in front of the Kartevold house. I witness Dennis getting a scolding from Forrest's mom. He doesn't respond, just hangs his head in shame and takes it as Petee says in her sharp chatter-like tone, "Did you do this? You shouldn't make a mess like this right here on my sidewalk. Now you go get something and clean this up." She storms back into her house. Dennis retrieves the flabby rubber slab, and as soon as we are around the corner and the coast is clear, we laugh hysterically. I think Forrest probably caught a little overflow from the chewing-out, his mom wondering what we boys have been up to.

I skirt through the neighborhood by going down the alley; only one street to cross and then through a backyard and I'm hopping down the steep bank to the rock wall. I decoy him into a perfect trap. Forrest catches up to me and easily counts coup as I desperately go from one rock crevice to another, only to find every stored dirt ball has dried and cracked, crumbling into loose dirt as I remove them from their rock chambers. I lost this battle, and as Forrest glows in victory I show him what I was planning and how I was going to pelt him with dirt clods. Well, my plan didn't work and there is only one thing to blame. Erosion!

CHAPTER 10

Silent Memoria

July 1, 1963

Dr. Hiatt receives a mimeographed form explaining the request for help defending House Bills 313 and 314, which have passed, been signed by the Governor, and go into effect today. The bills provided 1% of gasoline taxes be transferred to the State Park Fund for improvement and maintenance of state parks where motorboating is allowed.

An action has been filed to declare the laws invalid. The highway contractors do not want this gas tax money transferred to parks. And now the Highway Commission is in the uncomfortable position of defending these bills in court even though the Commission opposed these bills during the legislative session.

Dr. Hiatt is very happy with the State Highway Commission Parks Division and his relationship with its director, Ashley Roberts. He senses the conflict between the State Highway Department and its own Parks Division and wonders what this will eventually lead to.

Whichever way the challenge to this new law is decided won't make a hill of beans to Makoshika State Park, since the funding is for parks that allow boating.

Dr. Hiatt files the correspondence and gets back to his photography and color slide correspondence.

July 2, 1963

A letter from Doris Stalker, Assistant Advertising Director, to Dr. Hiatt says the following:

Dear Bob,

Ash just stopped by the office and brought me ten duplicate color slides of Makoshika which you so generously offered this department.

We would like very much to retain the full set; however, we would like to reimburse you for the cost of the duplicate slides. Therefore, if you will send a statement on the cost we will be glad to pay for them in order to add them to our 35mm library.

If we find that we can use one of these slides in a future publication it may be advisable for us to borrow the original but will let you know more about that at a later date.

Again, thanks for supplying us with the new selection of black and white photos and the fine group of color slides.

Best regards,
Doris Stalker

Assistant Advertising Director DS: lb

July 3, 1963

Dr. Hiatt sends a note along with Wing's Studio's last statement. The price is $2.90 if the state prefers to buy the slides.

July 4, 1963

I'm so glad school is out so I am free to go exploring, swimming, and playing with my friends. It still bothers me that one harmless experiment I tried out in school was shut down before I had come to a conclusion. I wanted to see how far I could go writing down numbers in sequence. I had a spiral notebook in my desk that I used exclusively for my consecutive list of numbers. I was up in the thousands with my numbers and no end in sight. When the teacher was lecturing I could keep quietly writing numbers. There was no dillydallying in class with me—I was always busy writing down more numbers. But then after parent-teacher conferences I find the notebook missing from my desk. I'm devastated, but my parents had removed the notebook and refuse to give it back.

Kool-Aid, cookies, ice cream, and candy are the standard summertime treats, but chewing gum is off the menu for me. I had my fill of gum-chewing du$The gum tastes stale by now, with the additional flavor of wet paper that remains stuck to the wad of gum as it is retrieved from a torn section of brown grocery sack I put in my desk to store the gum on. Finally, it is down to just me and one other boy. I was ready to give it up, but I didn't let it show as I enthusiastically retrieve the gum from my desk, with another little bit of paper stuck to it, and resume the chewing of the gum cud. My bluff works, and in disgust the last holdout gives in and makes the journey to the teacher's wastebasket. Just to rub it in to everybody, I kept going for another half a day. At long last I sashay my way up front and, under thunderous applause, bucket the unrecognizable plug.

The bottoms of our feet are like leather from going barefoot all summer long. Mark and I wear shoes if we are exploring Graveyard Coulee or going down to the river; otherwise around the neighborhood and up at the pool we are always barefoot. Rudy never wears shoes, and the soles of his feet are really tough. We are amazed at how he can run around in the woods without something on his feet. Rudy, Mark, and I spend a lot of time at the swimming pool park. Mark has it easy; he only walks across the street to get to the pool. Even though Mark has asthma, it doesn't seem to bother him much and he swims like a fish. Rudy and I walk about two blocks to get to the pool. On hot days we steer clear of the black asphalt in the street, keeping to the cooler cement and grass.

Even Rudy hops fast across hot asphalt. I've only had two mishaps going barefoot this summer—once when I stepped on a thorn from a Russian olive tree, and once when I didn't see the bumblebee on the clover bloom in the grass and was stung on the side of my foot when I stepped on it. Wow, that smarts!

I learned my first nasty poem from a carving on a picnic table at the swimming pool park. Every time I go swimming, I have a habit of walking by that picnic table to take a quick look and see if that nasty poem is still there, and it still is.

My mom has some sisters visiting and they arrive at the pool to watch me demonstrate my swimming skills. They are standing outside the fence at the deep end of the pool. Rudy is a good diver, and Mark can do a cannonball that explodes in a splash that looks like a mini mushroom cloud. I wish I could see how small a splash I make when I do my perfect swan dive off the low diving board. Since I have an audience I am going to show off my high dive. My plan is to bounce extra hard on the end of the high diving board and then while in the air do my toe touch, flatten out, and curve down to penetrate the pool like a straight arrow. I crawl up the ladder, get to the top, and look down the length of the board. It seems a long way up from here. Ten feet above the water will give me plenty of time for my aerial gymnastics prior to plunging headfirst into the pool with my arms extended fully and hands pointed together to quickly slice open the water and minimize my splash. After a brief hesitation and kind of a false start, I gallop to the end of the board and jump extra hard so I will land down on the end of the diving board and really spring nicely into the air. All eyes are on me as I make my jump, and suddenly things happen so fast I have little time to react. When I come down from my jump to hit the end of the board instead of springing into the air, I streak feet first toward the pool as I miss the end of the diving board entirely. And instead of just pointing my toes and hitting the pool feet first, I still attempt to salvage my dive, and just as I spread out perfectly flat to prepare for my pointed nose-dive I hit the pool with a perfect belly flop that knocks the wind right out of me. I just about need the lifeguard but manage to side-swim over to the ledge and crawl out of the pool. My chest and belly are beet red from the slap on the water and it hurts. My aunts wander off. My pride is severely damaged.

Today is one of my favorite days in the summer. I have been to the fireworks stand and picked out my favorites. Black Cat firecrackers are the best. My cousins smuggled in a few cherry bombs from Minnesota but I don't like them—they are too loud. We can't buy them here anyway. This is the worst day of the summer for the dogs in the neighborhood; they hate the sound of firecrackers. We make cannons, we light the firecrackers and throw them in the air, we make cups jump out of the sand, and we float bark in the river and toss the Black Cats at the bark boats just right to explode before the water extinguishes the fuse. We stay away from glass jars: my brother exploded one when we lived out on Dry Creek. Too dangerous! My only mishap is when a whole bag of Black Cats explodes like a machine gun while I am crossing over Graveyard Coulee on the bridge. It hurts my ears and scares the heck out of me. I meet Mark and his brother down in the baseball field, and the worst thing has happened to them. They ran out of punks and asked their dad what to do, so he gave them a lit cigarette to use.

It was about all burned out when I met up with them, but I saved the day by sharing one of my extra camel-dung punks. The one odor that is the most pleasant on the Fourth of July emanates not from the picnic, but from the smoldering dried dung of a punk.

Wait a minute, who says punks are made of dried camel dung? Well, it's common knowledge, don't ya know? It makes sense, and besides, I'm sure that's what my dad told me—or maybe it was my grandpa. At any rate, if someone was burning camel dung, it would smell just like a punk and I'll just leave it there.

July 5, 1963

Doris Stalker replies:

Dear Bob,

Enclosed you will find three $1.00 bills which will help pay for the duplicates which you sent to us of Makoshika.

Again, thank you.

Sincerely,

DORIS STALKER
Assistant Advertising Director

DS:lb Enclosure

Dr. Hiatt turns to the *McCone County News* in Circle, Montana, to plant some seeds for promoting Makoshika State Park. He writes the following:

Greetings:

Congratulations on the new enterprise!

Mark Ferguson wanted a little background on "the Only German Cowboy Band in the World," so I volunteered to send you this *Gazette* clipping of nearly three years ago."

Personnel changes include D.C.H.S. Band Director MIKE ROBERTY, who replaced Dr. Hollis Lefever; JIM JOHNSON, our 11th base player who replaced Bill Buck; and last year I retired after 11 years as leader of the band, being replaced by D.C.H.S. Principal JOHN JOHNSON. (although I still play in it)…..Also this and last summer the band has frequently called on talented teenage ladies to fill temporary vacancies in the clarinet and drum sections.

In your first year or two if you find you can use some "filler" which at the same time would be definitely NEWS to many of your area readers, you may have cuts made of the enclosed prints of MAKOSHIKA STATE PARK here in Glendive's "back yard." Also enclosing an original brochure of a few years back along with a *Ford Times* article on the park for further background of it. If you want more, just ask.

Hope this is some help to you.

Good Luck!
R. W. Hiatt, O.D.

Mr. Bob Prescott is my grade school band director. I play the cornet and have decided to stick with it, since now I'm finally getting the hang of it. After the first few practices I just quit going, so Mr. Prescott kicked me out of band. My mother intervened and talked him into letting me back into band class.

A few weeks ago my friend Mark went down to the dime store and bought me a parakeet for my birthday. We both love animals and vow to someday own a pet store together. I put Pretty Bird in a nice cage and set him in my bedroom by the window. Every morning when I get up, I whistle to the happy bird a "whit whew," "whit whew," and say "pretty bird." I have heard parakeets can talk; so far no response, but if I keep it up maybe he will learn to say it.

July 6, 1963

Freelance writer Margaret Jensen sends a typewritten note to Dr. Hiatt.

Dear Dr. Hiatt,

We would like a print of the map of Makoshika State Park with the data on geology, history and points of interest for use as reference material for another magazine article on the park. Mr. Ashley C. Roberts, State Parks Director, suggested we write to you for a copy of the map. Please bill us for any charges involved.

If you are unable to furnish the map, we would appreciate knowing from whom a copy may be obtained.

Cordially,

Margaret Jensen (Mrs.)

July 9, 1963

Dr. Hiatt replies by writing to her on the Cross card. Dear Margaret,

A partially suntanned copy of Makoshika map-story should reach you in the mail. Do you want to look at some black-and-white prints and/ or color slides?

Sincerely,

R. W. Hiatt, O. D.

Typewritten on the back of another sheet of the Glendive Swimming Pools, Inc., bond application (of which Dr. Hiatt has an ample supply) is a copy of a news release. And below the news, typewritten this time in red, are his notes about this piece.

Above news content to be added to Ranger-Review upcoming travel-editor story this week …Requested by ~~future~~ DCHS English-Journalism instructor CHARLES F. FEMLING, 206 5th St. Highland Park, Glendive (365-4802), summertime reporter, and delivered thereto noon, 9 Jul 63.

In 1956 travel editors writing for the Fort Worth Press, San Jose Mercury- News, Deseret News - Salt Lake Telegram, and the Detroit Free Press ~~toured Makoshika~~ began their coverage of Montana with a tour of Makoshika State Park. None had seen anything quite like it, and they wrote generously about the park in their city newspapers.

Two lady travel editors for the Cleveland Press and Des Moines Register took pictures and copious notes on Makoshika on the first leg of their Montana tour in 1960.

Dr. Hiatt reports just receiving a request for more information about Makoshika from freelance writer Margaret Jensen, whose pictorial feature on Makoshika in the July 1961 *Ford Times* reached a potential readership of 3,500,000 people.

July 10, 1963

As printed on a short news story in the *Billings Gazette*, the travel editors who are on their two-week tour of Montana will be guests of the Billings Chamber of Commerce when they arrive next Monday.

July 13, 1963

A nice two-column story on the front page of the *Ranger-Review* quotes Dr. Hiatt's news release and provides additional details about the Pacific

Northwest Travel Association Editors tour arriving the evening of July 14.

The story is headlined as:
Dr. R. W. Hiatt to Guide July 15 Tour
Travel Editors To Visit Makoshika

Dr. Hiatt cuts this newspaper clipping wide enough to include the four- column photo and caption of the **Send A Boy To Montana** participants. In the photo George Kutzler watches as some of the forty boys ride on horseback. Jim Shirby, who is the program director for SABTM, traveled to Minnesota and appeared with some of the boys in a television interview.

Using his scissors as a silent megaphone Dr. Hiatt clips the contingent news stories, which without the foresight of Cliff Harsh for both the founding of "Maco Sica State Park" and his vision of the "Send A Boy To Montana" program, it's doubtful either would be the successful entities they are now.

The wooden cross on the Amphitheater remains as Dr. Hiatt's personal, silent but visible, standing memorial of Cliff Harsh.

CHAPTER 11

Glendive Boys Find Dinosaur Bone

Roy Chapman Andrews captivates my attention in books—so much so that I write on a page of tablet paper in bold block letters his name followed by "BOOKS I HAVE READ THAT HE MADE." In carefully written cursive, I say he is my favorite author and I sign my name. As an early grade school student I have discovered the exciting world of books, although as far as my writing goes, penmanship and spelling are far from perfected. My first and favorite book listed on the page is "All About Dionosoars[sic]." Two lines below, the next book is "All About Strange Beasts Of The Past." On the rest of the page is written "Periods in the Age of Mammals," and listed below the names of seven periods, the time when each period began and one more column showing how long each period lasted.

July 14, 1963

Acting as a host for the Glendive Chamber of Commerce, Dr. Hiatt shows slides to the writers from the Pacific Northwest Travel Association on this evening of their arrival in Glendive. Tomorrow morning, on the first leg of their statewide tour, the writers will be escorted through Makoshika State Park by Dr. Hiatt. The Chamber of Commerce newsletter reports on the travel tour and comments that the state of Montana has taken notice of the eastern part of the state. The Chamber's goal is to help make Glendive one of the top tourist stops in Montana. Assisting in making a tourist stop in downtown Glendive a pleasant experience, the Lions Club has been providing nickels for expired time on parking meters so the out-of-stater can duck a parking fine.

The welcoming committee of T. A. Vashus, the Rev. James Hanson, and Dr.

R. W. Hiatt will entertain their guests at dinner this evening. In the Sunday *Ranger-Review* the feature article about the travel tour is accompanied by a photo of Dr. Hiatt sporting his bow tie. The black-and-white photo in the newspaper, of course, doesn't show off the red bow tie. However, the guests are sure to notice the color of his bow tie matches the color of his socks.

July 15, 1963

The paper that Ashley Roberts uses to write a friendly note to Dr. Hiatt is standard Highway Commission letterhead. Below the "HIGHWAY COMMISSION" title, "STATE PARKS DIVISION" is typed in.

Well, how convenient is that. There is this undercurrent that the Highway Commission would just as soon be rid of the State Parks Division. Time will tell.

Ashley Roberts' letter says the following:

Dr. Robert W. Hiatt
Optometrist
Glendive, Montana

Dear Bob,

One clipping from the "Ranger-Review" and you come up with more news than the Gt. Falls Tribune.

The Youth Camp idea makes for interesting speculation. Guess we'll just have to stand by and see what comes of it.

The titles you have given the pictures in the paper are good.... But I note one difference in the "Makoshika Big Gun Ready to Defend Herself." Seems to me you had a slightly different title ????

By the way....I had a note from Gordon Platts and he expects to be using your pictures of Makoshika on TV in the very near future. Helps to sell that Great Falls beer.

How are your band concerts going? If you learn to beat a drum with your spare foot you could set yourself up as a "one man band."

Sincerely,
STATE PARKS DIVISION
Ashley C. Roberts
Director

Dr. Hiatt makes copies of his two-page Makoshika write-up for the travel editors. In an authoritative yet layman's format he describes the Geology, Human History, and Uniqueness of Makoshika.

In the Uniqueness category he states the following:

"Whereas the highway takes you BY and THROUGH the North and South Dakota badlands where you get interesting and expansive 'far-off' views, this road leads you intimately INTO the heart of Eastern Montana's badlands where you can feel a part of geologic history and experience the geography.

"Those who find more drama and color in Makoshika scenery than in the North and South Dakota badlands ask why the latter have national recognition. A partial answer might include the historical significance of

U.S. President Teddy Roosevelt's life that he spent there, and the proximity of the South Dakota badlands to the Black Hills, both factors no doubt politically exploited."

For Facilities he lists "26 picnic tables, 16 fireplaces, ~~six toi~~ eight toilets, 1 water well, one baby amphitheater, an archery range, a part-time caretaker."

In the "What To Do" category Dr. Hiatt describes the following activities:

1. Sightseeing.
Three miles from Glendive the switchbacks wind their way to the "top" of Makoshika continuing as the main road for five miles over an interesting and less challenging route. Eleven short side roads take you to an unending variety of panoramic views. Colors are more enthralling at sunrise and sunset.

2. Photography.
Although there are several good "shots" along the high roads, you'll find more "screwball" formations down in the canyons.

3. Picnicking.
Some tables are in the open, some secluded.

4. Hiking and exploring.
It's hard to do one and not the other.

5. Fossil hunting.
They're here, but it usually takes hours, days, weeks, and months with tools to find the spots. Petrified wood and some leaf fossils are quite easy to find, however.

Dr. Hiatt finishes off his paper with a list of twenty-two other state parks and monuments.

Mid-July 1963

It's a pleasant summer day and perfect for a family outing. My parents (Art and Edith) and their friends Don and Phyllis Herron pack up a picnic, load the kids, and head out to Makoshika State Park. It's a great place to turn the youngsters loose to explore. Pulling the vehicles up to a picnic table near Pine on Rock, it doesn't take long for a nine-year-old Steve Herron and myself, who just turned eleven years old mere weeks ago, to take off exploring the badlands. "Pine on Rock" is everybody's favorite picnic spot. A rugged ponderosa pine sits directly on top of a huge sandstone boulder with octopus-like roots enveloping the gritty stone. The majestic pine, at the end of a scenic turnaround which overlooks a large badlands vista, is across the valley from "Red Top"—the tallest badlands peak in the area which has a distinctive red scoria (baked clay) cap. Steve and I, having scampered off as soon as the cars were parked, by now have crossed over the valley floor and are within shouting distance from each other as we explore the hills. The clay mound I traverse is uninteresting. Moving quickly, heading for a rock outcrop that catches my attention, I abruptly stop. A few feet from me protruding from the hill of clay is something unusual. Within seconds I positively know I'm looking at a huge dinosaur bone; even though I've never seen one, I'm sure that's what it is. I'm thrilled, and in an excited voice I holler out, "Steve! Look!"

This day of discovery is a monumental turning point of my youth. From this day on, forever hooked on the mysteries of the Makoshika badlands, my thoughts and dreams revolve around fossils and dinosaurs.

July 17, 1963

A fossil festival for the members of the National Science Foundation held in Allentown, New Jersey, has a picture featured on the front page of the *Billings Gazette* and catches Dr. Hiatt's attention. As he clips out the photo and caption, he makes a mental note of the fossil estimated to be 85 million years old that a nun is waving and hooting about in the close-up.

July 18, 1963

It's Thursday. Dr. Hiatt clips nearly the entire front page of today's *Ranger- Review*. There is a little bit trimmed off both sides of the paper, with only the left-side border on the bottom half cut away and the top border left intact for the three holes neatly punched out for his three-ring binder. Using a bold red marker, he draws three arrows pointing to news stories from a starting point on the Chamber of Commerce article about letter writing help for the general public selling the "product of Glendive" using free brochures from the Chamber, including an example of a pamphlet entitled "Makoshika, The Land of a Million Years Ago."

On the back side of the paper, two more bold red arrows trap an article from the *Ranger-Review*'s "Early Files," one pointing up to the bottom and the other pointing down to the top of a news story from ten years ago.

This edition of the paper hosts ads for Glendive's Crazy Days, which starts tomorrow and runs through Saturday. Other tidbits in the paper include things like fun facts about the four suits in a deck of cards which represent the four orders of society in the Middle Ages. Spades represent the nobility; Hearts depict the clergy; Diamonds, the merchant class; and Clubs signify the peasantry.

A letter to the editor from M. E. Johns scolds the paper for getting the weather report wrong when it said there had been no precipitation between June 22 and July 6. He asks, "isn't Highland Park, Forest Park and West Glendive considered in the Glendive area?" He implies that maybe it was a hallucination that made him turn on the windshield wipers on July 6th. Or maybe the editor has not "lived in Glendive long enough to know that it can rain on one side of town and the sun shines on the other." He ends his letter by asking, "Why not get the facts for the entire area before making such rash statements?"

An advertisement says the new "White Sewing Machine" dealer in Glendive is Farm & Home Furniture. You can stop in the store and register to win one for free.

Another item of interest on the front page announces a new Italian chef was hired by Harry Mehr, who owns the Cedar Grill Cafe and H&M bar.

The front page of the newspaper makes mention of funeral services for Anna Sobotka which were held Tuesday. She and her husband Jake came to Montana from Germany in 1921. Pallbearers were Frank Kreiman, Allen Kreiman, Alvin Fulton, George Zody, Pierce Fatzinger, and Jerome Graber. Koch-Huebl-Silvernale Funeral Home was in charge of arrangements.

Advertising in the *Ranger-Review* works for Chris Siverts. "FOR RENT: Two-bedroom furnished upstairs apartment, washer, dryer, air conditioner furnished." Lacking his name and phone number on the ad, calls flood into the *Ranger-Review* office asking who to contact.

The charismatic Don Erickson from Don's Shoes gives a rundown in the paper for Friday's Crazy Days events, or as Don spells it out, Krazy Daze. Starting off with an employee-employer breakfast at 7 a.m., followed by the employee-employer parade down Merrill Avenue at 8:58 a.m., and then stores open at 9:22 a.m. At 1:22 p.m. the traveling auction begins, and then late in the day at 6:58 p.m. there will be a table tennis ball air-drop for gift certificates. The stores will close at 8:58 p.m.

The headline on the upper left of the paper is regarding a new swimming pool ordinance the Glendive City Council adopted. The new fee for building a private swimming pool will be $1.00, and the regulation provides the authority to inspect and enforce private swimming pools for public safety issues. Our neighbors, the Brenners, have a private swimming pool right past the hedge in the backyard. I'm sure it will meet all the requirements for safety. I've never swum in it, but what they ought to regulate is my sister Audre's inflatable pool she had someone set up in the backyard. It messes up my badminton court, but I was able to move the net and use her pool as the out-of-bounds on the east side of the net, which still leaves plenty of room to maneuver. If the shuttlecock lands in the pool after a serve or a return from the opposite side of the net, it will be considered too far back and out-of-bounds. You know, this was not a good idea, because when I am on the pool side of the net handling the proper return of the birdie, I'm not thinking of stepping over the back boundary, I'm concentrating on my backwards leap while I stretch and backhand a nearly impossible return. It's a beautiful sight, airborne: body fully stretched out, making a perfect save with a bullet like return right over the net, and then suddenly my heel catches on the upper tube of the pool, causing me to lose my balance and land fully spread-eagle on my back in the middle, making a huge splash. Wouldn't you know it, as I recover from the cold wet shock and exit as quickly as I can, hoping nobody saw me, I hear laughter through the hedge. My sister and the neighbor girl watching the ordeal both think this is really funny. As I stand there sopping wet and humiliated I don't think it's funny, I think there ought to be an ordinance.

Starting with the bottom red arrow Dr. Hiatt drew on the front page of the paper to a photo with the travel editors, state officials, and Dr. Hiatt sporting his (red) bow tie (in black-and-white newsprint), there is, besides the detailed caption on the photo, an article covering activities during their stay including the Makoshika Park Tour. After leaving the park the editors stopped at the Ed Lewis residence and viewed some of his fossils, agates, and other relics. Ed was Makoshika State Park caretaker for the first five years of its existence.

The next red arrow on the page points to an article discussing the importance of Makoshika State Park as one of the outstanding scenic attractions in the state of Montana and how the Glendive Chamber of Commerce is working behind the scenes to promote the park. The Chamber expressed its sincere thanks to Dr. R. W. Hiatt, Rev. James Hanson, and Tully Vashus for their valuable assistance in handling the writers' tour.

Doc's third red arrow points horizontally across the page, all the way to a photo of me pointing to a fossilized bone protruding from a gumbo hill. The bold caption reads: "Glendive Boys Find Dinosaur Bone."

The *Glendive Ranger-Review* article recounts how a local do-it-yourself paleontologist and Makoshika Park's first caretaker, Ed Lewis, myself, a local newspaper reporter, and Dr. R. W. Hiatt venture out to Makoshika to investigate the fossil find. While a more elderly Mr. Lewis waits by the vehicles for us to report back, I escort the rest of the party to the bone outcrop. We dig it out a bit, take measurements of the bone, pose for photos, and anxiously hike back with a sample piece for Ed to confirm whether or not this is indeed a dinosaur bone. The reporter, enjoying the excursion and feeling frisky, asks me to watch him display his agility as he tries to navigate up a small hill with the loose clay giving way beneath his feet. It is a pathetic attempt—one try and we move on.

Once we return to the vehicles, the reporter hastily scribbled notes while Ed Lewis offers up his opinion. Doc listens intently while I am in awe. I have never heard of or met Ed before this day, and as he studies our sample and comments in a fairly brief and deliberate manner, not once does he even so much as acknowledge my existence. His slight of my presence not only is of no concern to me, but may even strengthen my admiration for a man who would not waste his time with small talk and instead use those precious moments to let me hear the truth.

Ed identifies the bone, verifying it as a dinosaur. He estimated 150 to 200 million years old. Doubtful it can be moved without crumbling, skeptical of its value without proper excavation expertise by experts, the bone is left to the elements, and as the paper stated, "only to be seen first-hand by the wild animals and the agile of foot."

My brother and I return at a later date, armed with hammers, chisels, and screwdriver to excavate further and shellac the bone surface to try to defend it from erosion. We also built several small earthen dams in some of the veined water creases on the hill to slow down and collect some of the smaller fossils. Gar fish scales, turtle shell and toe bones, small vertebrae, tendon pieces, crocodile and alligator skin and teeth are washing out of the gritty soil when it rains.

This clay, when rained on, becomes what we refer to as "gumbo." Gumbo is so slippery when wet, it's impossible to stay prone if the slightest attempt is made to stride across a soaked patch of the distinctive mud. There is a period after a rain as it dries when it becomes sticky instead of slippery, and any shoe that attempts to take steps at this stage soon becomes a clodhopper. When dried to the sole it takes a chisel to remove part of, but not all of, the rock-hard mud. An easier method to solve the gumboed shoe problem is to find the nearest trash bin. Dried gumbo on the hillsides forms a crumbly surface that takes a knack to learn how to slip and slide across its uneven surface up and down the hills. Like a skier or a skateboarder that has mastered the craft, my self-taught skills of hopping, skipping, and skidding in various bodily positions, whether it be erect, hunched, on haunches, or on my rear end, are as athletically perfected for traversing the badlands as an Olympian instinctively performing a well-rehearsed event.

The newspaper article with a photo of me sitting on the sidehill pointing to the dinosaur bone has a caption that uses the information gleaned from Ed Lewis which states the bone is thought to be 150 to 200 million years old. Even though the age of the fossil is stated incorrectly, the facts are not challenged. The 150- to 200-million-year-old age of the fossil is a statement from Ed that basically says what he thinks the age actually is. He doesn't claim to know for sure, and there is no one else around to challenge his facts since none of the party has the foggiest idea as to the age of dinosaurs. So as far as what Ed says I claim for myself as fact, which I will unhesitatingly use as needed in the future.

Eric, a grade school classmate of mine, referring to the published fossil find, asked if it will make me a millionaire and if I would share some of the money with him. His comment, exaggerated and comical as it is, in a way parallels the one-dimensional thoughts of too many fossil treasure seekers, who view a find only in dollar signs. Whereas the genuine value of a fossil find is not as a financial instrument but as a deposit on overall scientific knowledge. The parts, including the thrill of discovery, the careful preparation, preservation, documentation, and identification all add up to a sum that far exceeds any monetary satisfaction.

The Herron family tones down their excursions to the park after Mr. Herron, in a panic, slips, tumbles, and injures his ribs as he attempts to run and skip down a badlands butte while yelling to warn his son

Steve about the mountain lion stalking him down in the valley below. Don has been up on an overlook watching Steve on a hike, and to his dismay is witness to a mountain lion creeping up on his son. The lion is sneaking along a creek bank above Steve as he moseys along. In the end the lion left well enough alone, but that was enough to cool the hiking trips in Makoshika for the Herron family.[1]

1. From a personal interview with Don Herron.

Dennis and I return to the fossil-find area to do some more exploring, and sure enough on the other side of the hill on about the same level of strata where the big bone was found, we stumble into more fossils. On a level area I notice a cantaloupe-sized vertebra lying on the surface, broken but in pretty good shape. Next to it partially buried, is a huge jawbone. There are no teeth attached, but the washboard-like ribs on the jaw are prominent.

In a few days we return with Dr. Hiatt and are totally geared up for the excavation with a rubberized dishpan[2] to mix the plaster, and strips of burlap to dip in the plaster and wrap the bone. We have to haul in water, plaster, burlap, a mixing pan plus our tools. The jawbone is excavated underneath the middle to form a tunnel under the bone, and after the dirt is scraped and chiseled away from the bone surface and whisked clear, the strips of plaster-soaked burlap are wrapped around the bone, gradually working from the middle to both ends. After the body of the fossil is plaster-wrapped, we gently lift one end at a time and finish capping off the tips with plaster-soaked strips of burlap. Finally, we are able to lift the jawbone onto a stretcher and carry it out.

I still have possession of the dishpan.

Once I have the jawbone at home, I take it down to a bench next to the old steam boiler in the basement. Since my mom and dad are not using this area, I take it over. The wooden shelves which were used for canning jars and old paint cans are cleared off and become my fossil workshop. My mom's red Cosco counter chair/step stool disappears from her kitchen and now becomes my work stool.[3] Many hundreds of hours will be spent cleaning, sorting, and gluing broken pieces in my special fossil workshop in the basement.

I still have the step stool by the workbench in my basement. The red vinyl is worn off the seat, but it is still functional 56 years later.

The jawbone is successfully removed from its plaster cast, and all the sand and clay left adhering to the fossilized jawbone carefully cleared away. Any loose pieces of bone are skillfully fitted and glued in place with Duco cement. The final step is a coat of varnish to seal and highlight the bone to make it ready for display.

Of no concern to me is the fact that my parents have absolutely no interest in my fossil studies. They are busy with work, meetings, golf, and bridge club. Whenever I have spare time you can find me in my fossil workshop in the basement. Sometimes spare time is hard to find. Swimming, fishing, agate hunting, and yard work eat up the days. Dad has me help dig trenches in the yard for an underground sprinkling system. I am given the task of pulling the weeds in our gravel driveway beside our garage and patio at the back of the house. I try to pull the weeds, but when Dad arrives home from work he is not satisfied with my progress and decides to do the job himself.

This is great; I would rather be fishing down at the river. My pals and I have a prime fishing hole right where the river meets the slough. The bank is steep and there is a backwater that makes a perfect place to cast a line. I bait my hook with an angleworm and make a Zebco thumb-controlled cast. Perfect! Now I'll set down the rod while I arrange my tackle box. Oh no, a fish grabs the baited hook and makes a run for it. It happens so fast that all I can do is watch in disbelief as my rod is pulled down the steep bank and disappears into the brown muddy water.

I feel bad for losing my fishing rod and don't know how to explain this to my dad and brother, so I just don't say anything about it. I can hardly believe they are both so blind that neither one notices my fishing rod is gone from the garage. Anxious weeks go by and then we are on our way to go on a fishing trip. All set to go except no one can find my fishing pole. I brace myself, not knowing what to expect as I sheepishly tell them I lost it in the river. No big deal—they laugh and have me use another old pole for now. All that worry for nothing, and from now on I'm going to keep a good grip on the rod.

Dad has some old army side packs which work great for agate hunting. On my nearly daily exploring trips to the woods and the river, I always bring home a bag of agates. Dennis and Mom are into cutting agates. They have an agate saw in the garage set up, and when the cutting starts there is an oily cloud that permeates the air. The oil fog that fills the garage is a concoction of kerosene and oil they use to lubricate the diamond-embedded saw blade when cutting the agates.

The army side packs also work great for hauling my fossil-hunting gear. I found some small purple cloth bags in the house that say "Crown Royal," and they are perfect for bagging small fossils while out in the fossil fields.

Dr. Hiatt's fossil hammer has a wide blade at the end. I prefer a fossil hammer that has a pointed tip, which also can serve as a good grip in the gumbo when climbing. Dad takes me and my hammer to the basement of the hardware store and in a matter of minutes cuts some heavy leather, and using copper rivets makes a hammer holder to fit on my belt. My 16-ounce "Plumb brand" fossil hammer with the leather belt holster is, and always will be, my most prized possession.

Back to the *Ranger-Review* that Dr. Hiatt clipped and saved, on the flip side of the newspaper's "Glendive Boys Find Dinosaur Bone" article are the two red arrows pointing above and below to the "Early Files" from ten years ago.

It's hard to believe it's been ten years since Cliff Harsh, Chairman of the Chamber of Commerce Maco Sica Park Committee, reported the county had given the state a deed to part of the park area and the state was expected to create a state park of the land. Gay Uchytil made some one-by-two-feet signs that have "Maco Sica" lettered on them with one end pointed to direct people in the right direction from the Glendive Chamber of Commerce building to the park. Cliff Harsh posted the signs along with three more points-of-interest signs in the park. They point out the "Devils Tail Trail," "Duck on a Rock," and the lodge. Cliff invites the public to go into the park and name points of interest. Names with descriptions of the area can be given to Cliff.

To me, at age eleven, Makoshika Park has always been there. I don't consider it a new park or an old park. It's just Makoshika, and it's there. Doc Hiatt mentioned it used to be called Maco Sica. That must have been back in the olden days.

I never knew of Cliff Harsh. Never once do I remember Doc mentioning his name. Fifty-five years will pass before I learn who he was and how instrumental he was in the very early stages of our state park.

CHAPTER 12

Hiatt's Park

July 18, 1963

In an attempt to get national attention for Makoshika, Dr. Hiatt writes to Eastman Kodak Company:

To the President
Eastman Kodak Company
Rochester, New York

Dear Sir,

There are no dates in the attached news story. Congratulations on the noteworthy project!

Your crew shouldn't leave Montana without shooting MAKOSHIKA State Park here at Glendive. It is virtually unknown, but that has utterly no bearing on its virtually limitless and photogenic subjects.

Unless the crew's itinerary is rigidly fixed, if they're going to photograph the Black Hills before Yellowstone, Makoshika is scarcely out of the way.

I enclose nine prints as examples and will be happy to lend a batch of color slides, if you think we have something here. (We KNOW we do.)

Sincerely,

R. W. Hiatt, O.D.

July 19, 1963

The Montana Bureau of Mines and Geology and the U.S. Geological Survey put out a news release about a groundwater survey they are conducting in the Baker area. Dr. Hiatt clips the news article from the *Billings Gazette*.

July 23, 1963

A postcard with a return address of L. W. Spencer from Lindsay is addressed to Dr. and Mrs. Hiatt:

Thanks for the wonderful time Sunday. The hike was fun and the dinner was great. Also thanks for the picture. I would have thanked you before but I did not have time to write.

Thanks,

The card is signed by (it looks like) "Steve Le Galla."

Two geologists from Billings working for Shell Oil Company have been mapping Makoshika Park. Lee Garrett is the head geologist, and Gail Bishop is a student of the South Dakota School of Mines. In their opinion Makoshika can be a natural classroom for high school and college students taking tours to help broaden their knowledge of geology. In the eyes of a geologist, Makoshika is a "gold mine" just waiting to be discovered.[1]

1. Column written by Len Carroll

The Texas Employment Service has recruited workers for Holly Sugar this summer. Holly Company pays the workers transportation from southern Texas, and the individual farmer pays the workers' wages. The laborers are guaranteed a minimum of fourteen acres to work for the summer. All the workers are at least fourteen years old. Payment is by the acre worked. The first time over is the most labor intensive with weed pulling by hand and beet thinning along with the usual hoeing. The worker is paid $17.50 an acre for the first trip through, while the second and third time usually don't require the hand work, just the hoeing. The wages for the second time through are $11.00 an acre, and the third trip is $6.00 an acre.

In other news of the day, marketing quotas will not be in effect for the 1964 wheat crop.

From an outsider's view, it appears that more interest in Makoshika Park should be developed among the local people.[2] Locally the farmers and ranchers don't have much interest in what they would consider in their line of work, "a wasteland." Townsfolk are mostly just scratching out a living and not looking at the "big picture."

Glendive is fortunate to have an individual in its midst that sees the beauty in the "wasteland" and has taken the "bull by the horns" to promote Makoshika. Maybe it just takes a local optometrist like Doc Hiatt to see the "big picture."

2. Ibid

The First National Bank of Glendive, "The Bank of Cordial Service," has a marketing piece that says "don't think we didn't notice…" on the front cover of a bi-fold that when opened up reads: "…your recent good news!" In the piece sent to Dr. Hiatt, the clipping attached to the inside says: "If you're still with us, Glendive, start blushing modestly: The place that drew the most raves from visitors thus far was Hiatt's Park—which we understand also goes, from time to time, by the name of Makoshika."

July 26, 1963

The Canyon Ferry Recreation Association sends a mailing to members of the State Parks Advisory Committee with an update on the court case challenging the marine fuel tax bills for financing state parks. It appears the new law is constitutional when compared with eleven other states that passed similar legislation. The defense fund is low and the Association is asking for letters of support and contributions to the defense. The letter is signed by Mrs. John F. Casey (Sylvia).

August 3, 1963

Glendive resident Vern G. Paulson, the Farmers Insurance District Manager, mails a Montana color brochure to Dr. Hiatt with a congratulatory note written on the piece. The heading on the promotional piece says: "'Site' see all of MONTANA … the BIG SKY country." Four color photos of Montana fill the two-page advertisement. The caption at the bottom says: "Everything to do … and Beauty, too!" The Lake Como, Bitterroot Range photo shows off the lake. The Glacier National Park photo shows off a mountain. The Yellowstone National Park photo shows off a waterfall with a mist-enshrouded rainbow. A panoramic photo of Makoshika State Park shows off the badlands. Vern draws a red arrow pointing to the Makoshika photo and writes in red ink: "Doc, This is a hell of a good job. I am proud of the work you have done on this park and want to express my sincere appreciation for your efforts. Vern."

August 29, 1963

In its Thursday edition the *Ranger-Review* announces the Frontier Gateway Museum in Glendive will officially open its doors this weekend with an open house Saturday, Sunday, and Monday. Coffee will be served. The new museum is open 1 to 5 daily and is located on Highway 10 just south of the airport.

August 31, 1963

The Glendive Rock and Hobby Club, better known as the Glendive ROC- HOB Club sends out a newsletter to its members. Reverend Lenz is the president of the club, and a copy goes to Dr. Hiatt with a personalized note written on the page. It says:

Dear Dr. Hiatt,

I hope you haven't forgotten your promise to speak to our club next Sunday evening.

See you then!

The ROC-HOB Club is located in Glendive, "Montana's Agate Haven." The newsletter announces the following:

ATTENTION! ALL ROC-HOB MEMBERS!

PICNIC - - - The Yellowstone Agate Club of Miles City has invited our Rock and Hobby Club to join them on a picnic and tour of the Makoshika Park. They also hope some of our members can guide them to a good rock hunting area. Members who wish to participate in the picnic bring their own lunch. Meet at the N.P. Depot, Sunday, September 8th at about 11:00 a.m.

MEETING - - - In turn our Roc-Hob Club has invited the Miles City Club to a special program Sunday evening, Sept. 8th at 7:30 in the Courthouse Assembly Room. This will be our regular monthly meeting for September.

PROGRAM - - - Dr. Hiatt of Glendive will show unusual slides and present an informal talk on our local Makoshika Park. This feature alone should bring everyone out.

DISPLAYS - - - Please bring samples of your prized hobbies, rock or finished gems, fossils, unusual collections of any type and etc. to show Miles City our creative and artistic abilities.

REFRESHMENTS - - - Please bring one dozen cookies per family. The kitchen committee will take care of the coffee and etc.

Since the Rock and Hobby Club is playing host to the Yellowstone Agate Club every member should make a special effort to attend this program. By having a 100% attendance we can impress our Miles City guests that we are strong and active.

DO NOT FORGET!

SUNDAY, SEPTEMBER 8 7:30 p.m. Courthouse Assembly Room
BRING ONE DOZEN COOKIES
SHOW YOUR HOBBIES, ROCKS, FOSSILS, COLLECTIONS ETC.
Don't Throw This Away! Read it Again! This message is addressed to you! Your President has spoken!

———— ❧ ————

Sept 2, 1963

Labor Day.

Dr. Hiatt sends a reply to Vern:

Dear Vern, (G. Paulson)

Thanx for the recognition. You, too, are entitled to several bows for the time you've dedicated to young baseball.

It wouldn't surprise me if Glendive is more on the ball per capita than any community in Montana.

You may even see Makoshika on Great Falls Beer's TV ad in the near future!

Thanx again, sir,

———— ❧ ————

September 8, 1963

After the program and meeting of the Roc-Hob Club, Dr. Hiatt takes his bold red marker to the invite letter and announcement. He semicircles the program and writes a note to himself below in black fountain pen: *After all this the president himself didn't show!*

———— ❧ ————

September 9, 1963

The day before today, Dr. Hiatt mailed photos to Pat Gudmundson, the Society Editor for the *Miles City Star*. She types up a note to him on her "Chit Chat from Pat" customized letterhead.

Dear Dr. Hiatt - -

Such service - - I think your pictures got home before I did. We had a blowout on our brand new Rambler and then the jack wouldn't work, so it was well after midnight before we got home.

Your pictures are excellent and I so thoroughly enjoyed the slides last night that I'm really impressed with Makoshika. I'm writing an article to be in our Miles City paper Sunday and this one for the Billings Gazette will be later on. With so many nice pictures I wanted to use as many as I could!

We had a very pleasant day in Glendive with our visit to the park, fossil hunting and the meeting. Didn't even get to the museum as we intended, and after your slides we want to see more of the park, so think we'll have to come back.

Thanks so much for the quick service. I couldn't believe it when I found an envelope on my desk at 8:30 this morning - - about 11 hours after I asked you.

Sincerely, Pat G

———— ∽o𝒞⁄∾०∽ ————

The *Glendive Ranger-Review* announces Governor Tim Babcock will be the featured speaker at the dedication of the new Dawson County High School. The program for this event will have an invocation by Rev. James Hanson, and the Dawson County High School Band will play. Introductions by the principal, Ed Sommerfeld, and a performance by the DCHS Choir will be included in the program. Following the Governor's speech there will be an invitation to an Open House by A. C. Hagenston, Chairman of the Board. Other announcements by John Johnson, the assistant principal, will be followed with a benediction by James Hanson.

———— ∽o𝒞⁄∾०∽ ————

Nearly as many visitors as last year stopped at the Glendive Chamber of Commerce tourist information booth this season. Last year thousands of tourists passed through this area on their way to the Seattle World's Fair. Many of the tourists, representing every state in the union, toured Makoshika State Park as a direct result of their stop at the booth. The young ladies who can take credit for a job well done working the booth and introducing Glendive and Makoshika Park to the 2,435 tourist cars that stopped by are Patricia Nellans, Carolyn Svenvold, Debbie Toppins, and Sue Luke.

The 1962 Seattle World's Fair last year was close enough to Glendive for a Herron and Hagenston family vacation. It will take a few days of driving to get there. Space Needle, here we come! I don't remember if we went to the family cabin in Silver Gate first. I do remember when we made it all the way to Washington State and pulled over to a roadside motel for the night. Three events from the 1962 vacation to the World's Fair stick out in my mind and this is one of them. What I remember about the motel was its proximity to the woods. It is late afternoon when we arrive at the motel, and the first thing I want to do is explore. After we settled in my parents left to go on a trip to town, and said they would be back by dark. That was fine with me; it seems we are out in the middle of nowhere, but evidently there is a town down the road a ways. I head out behind the motel and am fascinated with the forest I enter. The trees and vegetation are all different from what we have on the river bottom in Glendive. Ferns everywhere and mosses hanging off branches, dampness, towering trees, different bugs, and bird songs take me into a fairy-tale world. I wander aimlessly for an hour or so and finally realize I don't know where I am in relation to the motel. I've never been lost in the woods before. At home I emerge into a clearing or to a riverbank and can easily find my bearings. It's not dusk yet, but will be soon. I don't know which way to go so I walk and walk and walk through the forest and finally break out into a meadow. And there in front of me is a road to follow, but I don't know whether to turn left or right. I turn right and start walking. Fortunately, I guess correctly and just before dark the motel comes into view. Soon after I get there my parents pull up in the car. My mom asks if I had fun while they were gone. Oh, I sure did, but I don't tell her how I was lost in the woods and by pure luck found my way back.

The World's Fair has a lot to offer. My brother claims the Wild Mouse Roller Coaster is the scariest ride there is. He goes to never-never land eating the best treat ever: a Belgian waffle covered in whipped cream and strawberries. The Space Needle was a memorable experience for both of us, and discovering ski ball, to me, is unforgettable. I could get a rack of balls for ten cents. I am hooked on the game. I go through a whole roll of dimes and then Dennis, my older brother, tells me it's time to go. Just one more game, please! No, it's time to go. If only I had time to play one more game. Life is the pits. If I ever play ski ball again, I know one thing: just one more game.

September 11, 1963

On Dr. Hiatt's letterhead with a Makoshika photo on the upper left, Doc types up a letter to Ashley Roberts. The photo chosen to customize his correspondence shows two caprocks in the Makoshika badlands with the skyline in between silhouetting the cross on the Amphitheater.

11 Sep 63

Dear Ash,

Attached is some yottety-yottety to prove that Makoshika in its antiquity can still excite even Eastern Montanans.

The guy who was to spearhead the Makoshika Youth Camp study is taking a year's leave of absence from his County Agent position which probably reclassified the idea as "fragile."

A lease-happy stockman is contemplating grazing 100 head in Makoshika soon, but Bertha Sundling won't lease her water, bless her.

Coming east before Christmas? Sincerely, Bob.

Please return two enclosures.

September 13, 1963

Dr. Hiatt scours the newspapers every day for articles on state and national parks, tourism, and any news related to Makoshika.

Yellowtail Dam began construction in 1961 and is not projected to be finished until 1967. William Barnett, President of Yellowtail Development, Inc., wants to donate 40 acres along its shore for a state park. The corporation offers to build a boat ramp, and once the reservoir fills, the box canyon will become a sheltered bay. The state has neither accepted nor declined the offer as of yet.[3]

3. The *Billings Gazette*

Crowds have thinned in Yellowstone National Park, and even though people generally believe the season ends with Labor Day, fishing is open through October 31 and roads are kept open until the snow forces closure. The entrance stations are no longer manned after the end of October, but the route from Gardiner to Cooke City remains open throughout the year.

September 14, 1963

Hold it, says the Bureau of Reclamation! The 40 acres that Yellowtail Development wants to donate to the state for a park is within the Bureau's "taking line." The Bureau of Reclamation doesn't permit any private ownership of land within the boundary. The Bureau will purchase or condemn the land and won't permit any transfer of ownership.[4]

4. Ibid

September 15, 1963

The *Miles City Star* on page 12 publishes 5 photographs of Makoshika formations, courtesy of Dr. R. W. Hiatt, accompanied by a write-up by Pat Gudmundson.

In her article, Pat introduces Makoshika State Park, which is now 10 years old, to Miles City residents, the majority of whom have never been there. She explains how Makoshika got its name, that the actual land included in the park is 784 acres, but the badlands stretch out for many miles beyond. She talks about how versatile and multi-user Makoshika is for the camera bugs, rock hounds, fossil hunters, hikers, campers, and picnickers. She mentions the deer, bluebirds, and a herd of wild horses. She says someone recently found the head of a Texas longhorn steer in a cave in the park. She invites the readers to make a visit to Glendive and Makoshika, but first pack a camera, a lunch, and wear your walking shoes.

"While you're there, don't miss Glendive's new Gateway Museum, located east of Glendive near the airport. The museum opened just about two weeks ago in a new building, and visitors there report it is well lighted and a good start to a fine museum. The museum is open from 1 to 5 p.m. daily except Monday."

The State Board of Health reports three cases of sleeping sickness in Montana. A number of other cases have been reported in Canada and North Dakota in both horses and humans. A 15-year-old Belgrade girl died of encephalitis on July 29th. This serious disease, believed to be transmitted by insects, has symptoms marked by fever, tremors, lethargy, weakness, and wasting.

Visiting hours at the hospital in Miles City are 2 p.m. to 8:30 p.m. A small notice in the paper lists the names of the patients admitted and the ones dismissed.

The Associated Press puts out a photo of a student protest at Woodlawn High School in Birmingham, Alabama. The *Miles City Star* publishes the demonstration of white students protesting the integration of schools. A student is shown standing on a brick Woodlawn High School sign near the entrance of the school waving a Confederate flag.

Some years back in Sunday school at the Methodist church, we were taught to sing a song that rattles off all the colors of people and how we are all God's children and we are to all love one another and no matter if somebody is (and then the colors get rattled off again), and we accept everyone and we treat everybody with respect.

I always wondered why we were singing that song because of course it doesn't matter what color of skin some kid has. We don't need to be told that. Kids play, no matter what nationality they are.

My friends and I don't have a racist bone in our bodies. We don't even know what prejudice is. We are so naive that sometimes we don't know the difference between right and wrong in what we say. A popular television show that I sometimes watched was *Amos 'n' Andy*, but it's not on TV anymore. We only watched that program in black and white; color TV had not come out yet. I thought it was a funny show and didn't know it was racially offensive. It makes me wonder how the Native Americans felt about the one-sided Cowboy-and-Indian shows on TV. We usually stopped at "Lil Black Sambo's" restaurant when in Billings and I really liked their pancakes. The walls in the eatery were decorated with scenes associated with "The Story of Little Black Sambo." Again I never gave a thought that the term "Sambo" could be viewed as a pejorative towards African- Americans.

It wasn't until a bunch of us kids, including some cousins, are playing in the front yard that I first find out that even though "sticks and stones will break my bones," there are words that are also hurtful. In my case I am using a racist slur that I don't know is a bad word. There must have been a wedding that caused some of my cousins and other kids to get together, or maybe it was a funeral. The adults are all dressed up and they are in the house visiting. As far as the kids go, the boys are dressed in school clothes and the girls in dresses. In our front yard we have a Russian olive hedge bordering one side and several small trees parted by the cement sidewalk leading from the street to the front steps. Normally I play in the backyard, which is a lot bigger and only has a couple of hazards, like my sister's wading pool and the occasional dog pile, which I have a keen eye to dodge when I'm playing football with my friends. The dog has a kennel to do his duty in, but you know, he is one of the team when we play in the backyard, and if he gets overexcited, well, nature calls. Mark's little brother Pete claims I tackled him just so he would roll in it. I don't agree that I tackled him right there on purpose, but then again I do know where the dog piles are and he doesn't. Maybe I shouldn't have laughed so hard, because Pete doesn't play with us anymore, and his dad Joe "read me the Riot Act."

So even though there are a lot of kids and cousins here, and they are all dressed up, it's safer to play in the front yard. Especially since we are not barefoot so we don't have to worry about those nasty Russian olive thorns. A bunch of us join hands around the trunk of a small ash tree, and one of my cousins who is wearing a pretty dress leads us in:

Ring-a-round the rosy,
A pocket full of posies,
Ashes! Ashes!
We all fall down.

After a while we change to:
London Bridge is falling down
Falling down, falling down
London Bridge is falling down *My fair lady.*

Well, now since we are going to play tag, I think it is my turn to take the lead. So as we merry-go-round holding hands, I start out with a rhyme to decide who is "it."

Eeny, meena, mina, mo,
Catch a nigger by the toe;
If he hollers make him pay,
Fifty dollars every day.

My mother told me to choose the very best one,
Oh - you - tease - him,
Out - goes - HE!

My cousin with the pretty dress dashes up the front steps into the house.

As we dance around in a circle, I keep leading the group in a sing-along of the rhyme.

Let's try it again.

Eeny, meena, mina, mo,

My cousin's mother, who is also wearing a pretty dress, comes out of the house, trots down the front steps, and joins our song circle.

Catch a nigger by the toe;

"NO!" she says. "You DON'T say that word."

Quickly, as she continues to lead the dancing circle, the lyrics change back to "London Bridge is falling down."

I'm sure glad somebody told me not to use that word. I didn't know that. I won't use it anymore.

Humpty Dumpty sate[sic] on a wall,
Humpti Dumpti[sic] had a great fall;

Threescore men and threescore more,

Cannot place Humpty dumpty as he was before.[5]

5. "Humpty Dumpty": first printed version of the original lyrics. In the 17th century the term "humpty dumpty" was a slang term to describe a dull person.

Dr. Hiatt makes note of a new Glendive arrow-shaped sign posted at the Amphitheater turnoff to keep returnees on main road.

Highly impressed, Dr. Hiatt types up a quick congratulatory note to Pat Gudmundson for her article in the *Miles City Star*.

Dear Pat,

S u p e r b !!!

My only complaint is that you sent me but one copy. Can you snip off five back pages and mail same to me on Monday?

Thanx,

Dr. Hiatt

(Encl'd 5 dimes for 15c paper! - rwh)

———— ⟡ ————

September 16, 1963

Five Makoshika story clippings are sent to Dr. Hiatt along with a "Chit Chat from Pat" that says the following.

Dr. Hiatt - -
Glad you liked it. So did a lot of people - - on account of your pictures. I don't think the Gazette article will appear until next spring. We are planning on a "See Montana First" series, and will include it in that.

Sincerely, Pat G
Pat Gudmundson
Society Editor
Miles City (Mont.) Star

———— ⟡ ————

September 17, 1963

On Dr. Hiatt's seven-by-six-inch professional notepaper with the upper left- hand photo featuring two caprocks of Makoshika silhouetting the cross on top of the Amphitheater, a note is scribbled out and sent to Ashley Roberts along with a clipping of the Makoshika story in the *Miles City Star*.

Ash,

Isn't this a goodie? Its author says it went over big in Miles City. Congratulations on making the Billings Gazette headline story last week! (!)

Feels autumnish here,
Bob

September 20, 1963

Another note from Pat Gudmundson says:

Dear Dr. Hiatt - -

Your latest pictures are even more fascinating than the others.

We made engravings of four of them and will use some day when we need something to fill up a little space. It's a little soon to use them right away, so thought we'd just make the engravings and save them. I'll send you some papers when we use them.

Hope your pictures are luring Miles Citians to Glendive and Makoshika. They make me want to go back again!

Pat

October 10, 1963

The manager of the Eastman Kodak Company Photographic Illustrations Division from Rochester, New York, sends an official reply to Dr. Hiatt.

Dear Dr. Hiatt:

We appreciate your interest in our assignment to obtain pictures for use in the Kodak building at the 1964-65 World's Fair. Should we need help in producing pictures in Montana, we will get in touch with you.

Thank you for your interest and cooperation. I am returning your pictures herewith. We appreciate your letting us see them.

Sincerely, P J Braal

October 26, 1963

Dr. Hiatt immerses himself in a study of local geology. At the Glendive Public Library he discovers a U.S. Department of Interior paper, "Geological Survey Professional Paper 189-1." The title of this paper says, "Fossil plants from the Colgate Member of the Fox Hills Sandstone and adjacent strata." The author of this paper was Roland W. Brown. He died last year and Ed received a notification card from the administrator of his estate.

Hiatt's page of geology notes are voraciously recorded with a pencil and describe in detail the geologic formations such as the Colgate member, which is the uppermost unit of Fox Hills Sandstone and has yielded 19 species of well-preserved fossil plants (out of 37 now known) that lived in the warm temperate environment.

He notes the composition of the 35-foot-thick white formation that consists of a band of silicate and clay, angular quartz, and feldspar grains with scattered flakes of mica that emerges 1 ½ miles southwest of Glendive, rising gently westward to the crest of the Cedar Creek Anticline 11 ½ miles southwest of Glendive, beyond which it dips steeply and disappears into the west flank of the Cedar Creek Anticline.

He describes the formations layering the Iron Bluff 8 miles southwest of Glendive made up of Pierre Shale, Fox Hills Sandstone, and the Hell Creek formations. Six of nineteen species of flora in Fox Hills survived into the Hell Creek Formation. The "Hell Creek" name is derived from a Missouri River tributary located 20 miles north of Jordan.

His page of notes end with a discussion of the Hell Creek Formation (Lance), which is the stratum immediately overlying Fox Hills Sandstone. He describes the appearance of a few thin coal seams and his pencil runs off the page talking about Triceratops bones, primitive mammals, and abundant, though not well-preserved, flora.

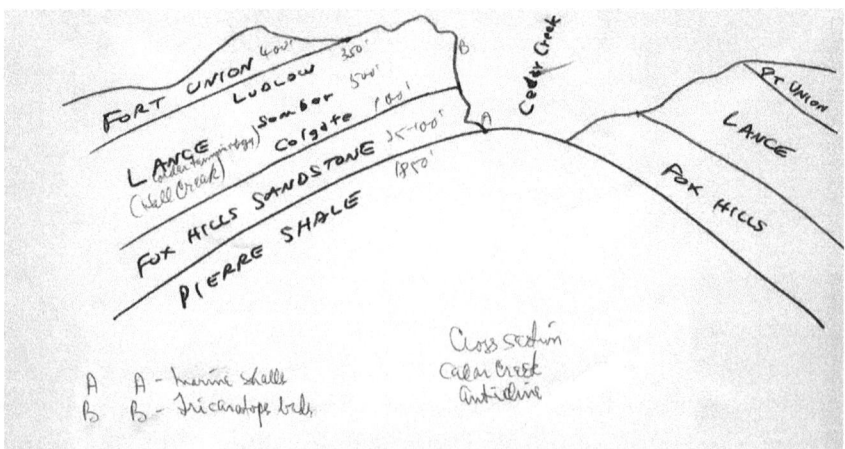

October 29, 1963

In an attempt to spark a new idea to life, Dr. Hiatt types up a memo to John D. Lewis, Secretary-Manager of the Glendive Chamber of Commerce. Dear John, At this week's Glendive Lions Club meeting an enthusiastic audience watched my four-magazine color-slide story of Makoshika.

One of the better idea men of Glendive came up with one of the best ideas for promoting Makoshika that I've heard in a long time.

A morning and an afternoon tour of the park by horse-drawn carriage is the idea.

If the tourist promotion committee did no more than actuate this one idea during the '64 season (June through August), its existence, achievement, and contribution will be commendable.

No doubt a cooperative enterprise between said committee and the Maco Sica Riders would be the logical approach.

November 5, 1963

Dr. Hiatt types up two more letters today—one to the Frontier Gateway Museum and one to the *Ranger-Review*.

Mrs. W. D. Murphy

Frontier Gateway Museum

405 N. Meade

Glendive

Dear Mrs. Murphy,

Enclosed are five photographs of the Colgate member of the Fox Hills sandstone formation, each with its negative in a separate envelope … … . . It's the whitest stratum and at ground level… … These were all taken 4 miles S.W. of Glendive and can be viewed from a distance where the Marsh Road crosses the N.P. mainline tracks... ... . In one week I'll have a color slide or two of the same feature, if that will be of value... Sincerely,

R. W. Hiatt

———— ⊸o⦶o⊶ ————

The Ranger-Review

Glendive, Montana

Dear Editor,

With all the excitement and change going on in Glendive I was happy to read in Sunday's issue about the tea in honor of Mrs. A. J. McCarty along with a resume of her outstanding career.

On behalf of State Parks Director Ashley Roberts and thousands of local and tourist users of Makoshika State Park over the past decade I take this means to publicly and enthusiastically thank Mr. and Mrs. A. J. McCarty for:

(1) deeding a parcel of their land to the State of Montana that Makoshika might become a state park,

(2) letting us -- the public -- have access to their private water well, and

(3) permitting construction of the Makoshika amphitheater practically in their cabin's backyard.

May God bless them,

Dr. Robert W. Hiatt

———— ⊸o⦶o⊶ ————

November 7, 1963

Dr. Hiatt's letter to the editor honoring both the McCartys for their contribution to Makoshika is published in the *Ranger-Review*.

The newspaper features a photo of Mrs. Catharine McCarty seated by her husband "Mac" as she opens a gift presented to her by Mrs. John Kubesh in recognition of her years of community service. The honorary plaque has inscribed in gold "50 Years."

The open-house community tea at the assembly room of the courthouse in honor of Mrs. McCarty was attended by about 150 persons. Signa Kubesh was in charge of the guest book. Sandwiches, cookies, candy, nuts, coffee, and tea were served during the afternoon. Pouring coffee and tea were Ila Scharff, Edith Schepens, Louise Erickson, and Mae Popham.

Mildred Thompson and Irene Kizer were in charge of decorating. The kitchen committee was headed by Aloha Brane and assisted by Dora McDonough, Lena Jones, and Margaret Temple.

The bouquets of flowers were contributed by First National Bank and the American Legion. The tables were decorated by the Legion Auxiliary.

Mrs. Esther O'Neil presented Mrs. McCarty with a red rose corsage.

A neatly typed and folded thank-you card that measures 3 by 4 inches is sent to Dr. Hiatt.

Dear Dr. Haitt[sic]:

Mac and I were surprised to read your nice letter in the Ranger-Review. It is wonderful of you to think of us, and we assure you that we are very proud of the work you have done and your interest in the park. What you, with a few others, gave realized its magnificent setting.

We remember when we first looked upon its beauty—we walked to see it, and it was breathtaking. When we had the opportunity to acquire it, through the kindness of Mr. Hustad, we wanted the people of Glendive and visitors to share it with us. We took the county commissioners out there and through their interest the WPA built our first road.

Through your interest, hundreds of people are now enjoying it. As one couple told us it was equal or surpassed anything they had seen in Egypt. I miss our wild horses and deer which used to make our place their range.

Thank you for your nice letter, and remember you always have friends in the McCartys if there is anything we can do to help keep Makoshika one of the primitive parts of our great state.

Cordially yours,

Catharine McCarty

The front page of today's paper announces a grand opening of the new Professional Building in downtown Glendive, which will be held Saturday afternoon from 1 to 4 with fresh cigars for the men and flowers for the ladies. The old locker plant at 115 West Valentine was completely renovated in an artistic and modern design. The owner, Henry H. Dion, stated, "this is just one more step forward in Progress of Glendive."

The headline of the paper announces a curfew on minors in West Glendive that was adopted by the County Commission at their meeting on Tuesday. Kids under the age of 18 have to be off the streets by 10 p.m. during the week and 12:30 a.m. Friday and Saturday.

Wow, it's a $100 fine. At least it only applies to the kids across the river in West Glendive. It wouldn't affect my friends and me anyway, since we don't prowl the streets at night. We don't have to. We can see everything we need to at night from our backyard or from the garage roof. We gather up nuts during the day from the chestnut trees up by the swimming pool park. Late in the summer after they have ripened just right, when the shells polish up nicely by rubbing them with your thumb, that's the best time to gather the nuts. We don't crack them open, and no, we don't roast them by an open fire—we have other uses. Competition for the chestnuts is nil; people consider them a nuisance and there are no squirrels. Glendive doesn't have squirrels. It's a shame. We don't have acorn trees like they do in Minnesota. Maybe that's why we don't have squirrels. When I visited cousins in Rochester, Minnesota, I was fascinated with the squirrels and the acorn trees. There are squirrels up in the mountains of Montana; they must like the pine nuts. My brother Dennis and I set up a squirrel trap when we were at the cabin in Silvergate, Montana. When Dennis pulled the string to jerk the stick propping up the weighted wooden box, the box came down and conked the squirrel right on the head; knocked him out cold. Somehow we smuggled squirrels to Glendive and released them in Lloyd Square Park up by the swimming pool. Those squirrels were in hog heaven, with all those unclaimed chestnuts lying around.

We place the chestnuts sparingly in the street and hightail it to the backyard. Soon enough a car approaches, and if we are lucky, and placed it just right, when the tire runs over the chestnut it cracks with what sounds like a gunshot.

We liked to get a blanket and set up a pup tent in the backyard. Dad shows up and comments in good jest, "What the Sam Hill is that?" Later, Mark asks me if my dad said "Hell." "No, I think he said 'Hill,'" I replied. Around dusk Dad sees us scampering around the backyard, like we are preparing for something. "What the Sam Hill," he says. Now I'm getting embarrassed; it did sound like "hell," but I defend my dad and disagree with my friend, who might tell his dad that my dad is going around cussing in front of us. Mark's family is Catholic and I guess Catholic families don't cuss. Already they don't approve of Mark playing with me, especially after the dog-doo incident, and his parents think I taught Mark some of those new cusswords that he taught me. Now, I break into a cold sweat when Dad shows up with a smile on his face, and I dart off, worried he might say it: "What the Sam Hill?"

The good thing is we are anonymous when we pull our pranks from the backyard. The problem is, most everybody who drives by knows whose house this stuff is coming from, so my dad hears about it at work from his irritated customers. 216 Slocum is getting a bad reputation. We buy some balloons at the dime store and fill them with water. Some are round and some are elongated. The round ones we use for hand-launching, and the long ones when filled up look like giant legless caterpillars. Now, you've got to admit, these water balloons are harmless. Friday nights are great. The high school kids are out driving around, and some girls get out of their car to inspect the strange alien object crossing the road. One of them touches the green balloon and it jiggles. The girls all scream, jump back in their car, and roar off to safety. Soon more cars show up to inspect and the guys just laugh. They drive over it—*squish*—and that's the end of it: just a wet spot. If we place the balloons just right we can get the cars to dodge them when passing by and explode one of our strategically placed chestnuts. *CRACK!*

The goal is to hit the car driving by right in the middle of the windshield with a hand-launched water balloon. And of course this has to be carried out from behind a bush, tree, or fence so as to not be seen. Sometimes we put the water balloon into a brown paper sack before we heave it, just for extra effect.

Since we live in a neighborhood, and most of the cars we see traveling at night are neighbors from the area either going to or returning home from somewhere, they know whose yard this is coming from, and after my unsuspecting dad gets bombarded with complaints it trickles down to me and I have to put a stop to the operation.

I didn't know who was driving which car, so this is equal opportunity bombardment. If I had known Dr. Hiatt was in one of the vehicles driving by, I certainly would have let that one pass. Especially since, nearly fifty years later, during our final reminiscence, I was reminded of the time he drove by our house one evening and a bag of water hit his windshield.

Other than an "Oh," I am left speechless.

CHAPTER 13

Seven Years a Fossil Hunter

November 9, 1963

Dr. Hiatt receives an invoice from Lyons Company. The Culver City, California, company billed $2.80 for two dozen pairs of LYONS GRIPS- ALL, soft flesh temple covers. Typed on the bottom of the invoice is a note to Dr. Hiatt:

THANK YOU DOCTOR HIATT
Like your envelope showing Makoshika State Park -- very nice.
I'm going to get over in that park of beautiful Montana one of these days. Best of Good Wishes. Lyons

———⋙⋘———

November 20, 1963

The fall meeting of the State Parks Advisory Committee is being held today at 1:15 p.m. in the auditorium at the State Highway Department building in Helena.

Due to the inclement weather, only a few members of the committee are able to attend.

Activities from this past summer plus a few ideas for next year are reported on.

Makoshika State Park gets a brief mention in the four-page report. Some new picnic tables, fireplaces, and sanitary facilities were added along with some road improvements. There was above-normal use of the park this summer.

The next meeting is scheduled for some time in April.

Earlier in the month the State Parks Division Director, Ashley Roberts, prepares a letter to Dr. Hiatt.

Dear Dr. Bob:

I liked your letter in "red."

It can't compare with all the activity that goes on in Hardin but I think I prefer the Glendive "red letter" activities.

Congratulations … . . You have now reached the "fat and forty" stage of life. I have already completed this era and found that it was quite interesting. Hope you find it the same.

Your use of my name in your letter to the editor was quite alright. I don't think that I ever met Mrs. McCarty but am glad that you extended our best wishes.

Not long ago we finished putting in some new facilities at Makoshika. I hope we got them in the right places. Maybe I can get down that way yet this fall and see how they look.

Thanks again for your "newsy" letter.

Sincerely,
STATE PARKS DIVISION
Ashley C. Roberts
Director

November 27, 1963

Now that the "hands on" season for hiking in and studying the badlands has come to a chilly conclusion, Dr. Hiatt dives into a geologic study in the library.

His carefully handwritten outline is legibly scrawled in such profuseness as to not only cover the local geology of Makoshika, but details the geologic time eras of Precambrian, Paleozoic, Mesozoic, and Cenozoic with important information relating to physical events and organic events in each period of each era.

Dr. Hiatt's notes are written on plain unlined paper with such fervor that a page of his script, inked with black fountain pen, blue and black ballpoint pen, and with asterisked red ink notations, takes on an artistry that if framed in a gallery would make a geologist viewing such a masterpiece faint at heart.

After his written record completely details geologic time, he expands on the October research about geologic formations and then studies ancient plants. His script weaves into scientific names and details on phyla commonly known as ammonoids, snails, clams, and crinoids, and then he gets into describing the insects. After the cockroaches and scorpions, he inserts notes on the chief natural cementing substances (mineral matter) in groundwater. Finally, the first vertebrates, which were armored fish, lead him to the MESOZOIC ERA ("age of reptiles"). He writes that the cold-blooded, egg- laying vertebrates that ruled over land, sea, and air are referred to as <u>Dinosaurs</u>, which means "terrible lizard."

Dinosaurs, crocodiles, and turtles followed by early mammals round out his research, and a side note on the lower left of a page describes the 1923 American Museum of Natural History Mongolian Gobi Desert expedition led by Roy Chapman Andrews, who discovered a nest of seven-inch-long dinosaur eggs.

Buried in his notes are four bullet points highlighting Dinosaur National Monument:

1. Extreme NW corner of Colorado and NE Corner of Utah.

2. Incredibly majestic canyons of the Green and Yampa Rivers and they meet in the middle of area in the heart of Uinta Mountains > 3,000 feet deep.

3. From 1909 to 1922 Carnegie Museum quarried 700,000 lbs of dinosaur bones to Pittsburgh.

4. National Park Service enclosed unique museum where paleontologists expose skeletons to tourist view.

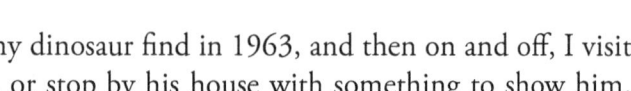

Beginning after my dinosaur find in 1963, and then on and off, I visit Doc at his office, or stop by his house with something to show him. Just a simple question; and I always get a good answer. His reply is drawn out, winding around each inquiry, and since I'm a good listener and Doc an avid storyteller, we make a great pair.

It all starts about the time Doc Hiatt sets up shop in Glendive. His optometry practice is a way to make a living, and although a gifted optometrist, his passion revolves around the scenic beauty surrounding Glendive. He studies the Medora badlands and South Dakota Badlands and comes to the conclusion that the Makoshika badlands are more interesting in many ways. They have more diverse plant life, more interesting formations, and more fossils. Medora can claim Teddy Roosevelt; however, it is suspected that Teddy visited Glendive as documented in a photo of a man that appears to be Roosevelt looking over the plants in the Glendive Greenhouse.

(Photo Courtesy of Swanson's Glendive Greenhouse)

We know from the Theodore Roosevelt Timeline put out by the National Park Service that he delivered a speech in Medora, North Dakota, in 1910/1911 and also made a 1918 train stop in Medora. If that was him, surely he took notice of the eastern Montana badlands.

Teddy said of the Medora badlands, "It was here that the romance of my life began."

A little farther west in the 1950s, the badlands first known as Maco Sica serenade Doc Hiatt.

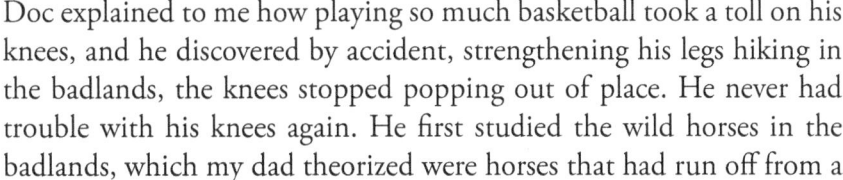

Doc explained to me how playing so much basketball took a toll on his knees, and he discovered by accident, strengthening his legs hiking in the badlands, the knees stopped popping out of place. He never had trouble with his knees again. He first studied the wild horses in the badlands, which my dad theorized were horses that had run off from a local rancher's herd.

One day, driving on a dirt road through a cut in the badlands, Dr. Hiatt looks out the window and sees what appears to be three large spools stuck in a sidehill. His curiosity demands a look, and from here forward the discovery of these three vertebrae has him hooked.[1] His garage soon becomes a mini museum, with his finds scattered about and organized on shelves. The study in his house is full of correspondence, little white and green boxes from his optometry practice now recycled to house fossils labeled up with black marker—"Tullock anthill #2 Oct - Nov 65 Estes (Richard Estes, Boston University)." At least nine professors/researchers from places such as Yale, Boston University, Princeton, American Museum of Natural History, etc., are the recipients of and cooperate with Doc Hiatt in examining and identifying fossil specimens from Makoshika. He studies, becomes familiar with, and teaches others about the geology and paleontology in Makoshika. A few years after he starts his fossil studies, he does a comprehensive study of the flowers observed in Makoshika, publishing a booklet describing the common and scientific names of the plants, along with the color of the flower, whether it was an annual, biennial, or perennial, and the month and day he first observes a bloom.[2]

1. Conversation with Dr. Hiatt

2. 1972 Dr. R. W. Hiatt & The Glendive Woman's Club 9-page booklet titled *Makoshika Park*.

Sometimes Doc and I will go out on a fossil hunt together, usually to show each other a new "spot"; however, both of us are totally content as loners, enjoying the solitude, deep in thought, scouring the hills. I develop a few close friends as fossil-hunting buddies. Mike McCrate, who moved to Oklahoma in 1968, and John Harmala are two friends that have a strong interest in the badlands, and we are out hiking every chance we have. P. A. Norton is another classmate that had adventures with me hiking and camping in Makoshika; however, he did not develop an interest in fossils.

"Mizz Dotta"—that's how Mike McCrate, with his southern accent, sounds as he addresses the lady that has the little rock and fossil shop at the corner before turning off on the gravel road to Makoshika Park. We make a point to stop in and see her on our way to the park. She has some small trays of crocodile and alligator teeth for sale. Her collection also includes garfish scales, fish vertebrae, dinosaur bone chips, triceratops teeth, hadrosaur teeth, turtle shell sections, and turtle toe bones. Even though suffering from emphysema, always in good spirits, her signature comment is "well fo' land sakes." Not old enough to drive, our main mode of transportation is bicycle. Biking over the cattle guard is too hazardous on the gravel road heading out to Makoshika Park, so we dismount and walk our bikes over the steel pipes. It is scary. Greeting us at the crossing is a mean-looking, barking German shepherd dog that doesn't want us to pass.

Regardless of the weather, we mount our bicycles and make it across town to the park. Today it drizzles, but we go anyway. The road base in Makoshika is dirt and clay, and soon the bike tires look like balloon tires, all caked with sticky mud. Sometimes Mom is kind enough to allow me to load my bike in the car and then drives the bike and me to Makoshika. It saves a lot of travel time, which leaves more time for fossil hunting. Into the badlands I go. It's kind of like the burlap bag and the kitchen timer; she trusts me to return home. Eventually as teenage years advance, my bicycle mode of transportation is replaced by a red Willys Jeep, a blue VW Bug, or a salmon pink Rambler station wagon. I have fond memories of the Jeep and Bug. The Rambler is okay, but it is stuck in the snow or mud too many times and the dust boils in through the rear window seal.

The choking dust every time a car passes my bike on the road nearly obliterates the view. A horse-drawn tourist carriage sounds romantic, but unless something is done about the road dust I'm afraid our visitors riding in an open-air stagecoach would riot.

To keep our drinking water cool when we drive out to our destinations, we hang a canvas water bag on a side rearview mirror and let it sweat. Warm canteen water is unappealing and we much prefer a cool drink from the water bag, despite the taste of canvas. Water in a corked earthenware jar is my Grandpa Knauff's method of toting water while out in the pasture or fields. He surrounds his jug with newspapers or burlap to protect it from cracking while he is bouncing around on the tractor or truck. His water has the distinctive odor of chewing tobacco.

Greg drinking from the water bag.

One summer, a boy we befriended was living in Glendive, his dad employed as a beekeeper. He just loved to hike in Makoshika. At the time, I didn't realize his family was extremely poor and that's why he didn't have any shoes. My friends and I were amazed at how tough his feet were. We all ran around the neighborhood barefoot, and to the swimming pool park, but not when hiking down at the river or out in the badlands. The soles of his feet were like leather. Even though barefoot, he never complained about his feet. After one afternoon of hiking in the badlands, he met up with us at the base of the hills and told us about a crocodile jawbone with teeth he saw in the side of a hill. We came back to that range of hills several times and searched in what seemed like every square inch of where he could have been. He seemed to want us to move on, but my friends and I were determined. To no avail, we were never able to find the jawbone.

Thirty years later I receive a call from Florida. The phone line doesn't have the best reception, and the caller is talking fast. He is excited to be speaking to me. To my amazement it is the boy with no shoes. Now a curator at a museum in Florida, he tells me about the well-preserved ancient human remains they find in the peat bogs. He couldn't remember my name but called around Glendive asking if anybody might know the boy whose daddy used to run a hardware store. Because of his time in Glendive fossil hunting in the badlands, he wanted to let me know it was the influence from that summer long ago that steered him to what he loves to do as a museum curator. I asked him if he remembers the crocodile jaw. He does not.[3]

3. Conversation with Mark Hathaway about the boy with no shoes.

One of the early finds in Makoshika is an ancient sheep skull, which found the way to display itself on the top of Dan Norton's garage roof. Pat wasn't a fossil hunter, but the old skull with the curved horns he found in Makoshika would make a nice ornament on his dad's garage. No longer protected from the elements by the clay that encased it, the Audubon sheep skull began to deteriorate. I don't recall when Pat first told me about his find, but it was many years later, after the Makoshika visitors' center had been built, that I vaguely recalled Pat mentioning his sheep skull. When he informed me it was on his dad's garage roof, I was aghast. It wasn't long before I crawled on top of Dan Norton's garage and rescued the skull, taking it out to the visitors' center for safekeeping as a donation from Pat Norton.

Although Dan had exhibited no interest in the sheep skull, he did have the foresight to preserve some old letters handed down through his family since before the Civil War. One day as he was getting his affairs in order, he took the letters out to Frontier Gateway Museum. One of the letters was written to Dr. James Hackelman by his affectionate son Wm. Hackelman from Jefferson Barracks, St. Louis, Missouri, October 7, 1846. Stating he was well after a tedious thirteen-day journey on the steamboat *Colorado* from Newport Landing in Cincinnati, Ohio, he goes on in the letter to tell about his experiences on the journey. Jefferson Barracks served as a major military post during the Mexican-

American War (1846–1848) and was a rest and supply station for most U.S. troops deploying to Mexico. The United States Regiment of Dragoons was formed and stationed at Jefferson Barracks. They were the first unit of permanent cavalry in the United States Army, trained to fight mounted or dismounted, and were later called the 1st

U.S. Dragoons.[4] Wm. had second thoughts about volunteering for the service and wrote, "If was set at liberty I would not enlist again, but as it is I shall not murmur, for it was my own fault. But I keep my spirits up, all I regret is my liberty, but why should I grumble, for there is somebody that has got to serve the country, and why not me as well as anybody." Wm. tells in the letter about while on the Ohio River "a little Dutch boy fell through the floor of the steamboat into the water and drowned. The mother of the boy fainted some two or three times and it was hard work to bring her too."[5] The nameless little Dutch boy, who didn't survive to grow up and write of his adventures, whose short life should be a long-forgotten speck in the dustbin of history, whose mother's anguish is universal and only understood by a mother who has lost a child, is no longer forgotten. The little boy's memory from the fall of 1846 was kept alive by a few pencil strokes written on a letter by a soldier, passed on from family to family, and brought to a final resting place in a drawer, at the Frontier Gateway Museum in Glendive. The suffering of the little Dutch boy's mother is reflected in a bronze statue in Our Park on Merrill Avenue in Glendive. Pamela Harr, a local artist, renowned for her artistry, placed a bronze monument in the park depicting the agony of a mother embracing a dead child. Though it's not a sculpture of the little Dutch child, the mother's anguish is universal. I can't help but think somehow, the spirit of the little Dutch boy and his mother guided the creative energy of Pamela Harr to place this masterpiece of eternity in the town of their last destination.

4. Wikipedia

5. Letter handed down in the Norton family and donated to the Frontier Gateway Museum in Glendive.

On a return flight from Florida shortly after researching the Norton family letters housed at the museum in Glendive, I had an interesting encounter. While waiting for the flight I remember slouching on the chair, half asleep, my head hanging down, and I notice a lady standing close by. All I saw of her were her legs and shoes with heels. There was a flight delay and a change of planes and somehow my wife Evelyn and I ended up in First Class, however not seated together. The lady with the heels, seated next to me, offered to give up her seat to Evelyn, but we were content staying seated where assigned. She traveled a lot for a law firm and seemed quite comfortable in First Class; when offered a complimentary beverage she ordered a Bloody Mary. The lady was quite chatty, and during some trivial conversation I inquired where she was from. She said "Cincinnati." "Oh," I said, "on the Ohio River?" "Yes," she replied. I asked, "Have you ever heard of Newport Landing?" She said she could see it from her house. Cincinnati's official riverboat cruises sail from Newport Landing on the banks of the Ohio River. Soon I was telling her about the letter from 1846 and the drowned little Dutch boy. Her daughter is an up-and-coming artist, was still in school, and does very nice work, judging by the pictures she shared with me. I had in the back of my mind a sculpture of the Dutch mother Vand child, and it came to be, sort of.

Doc Hiatt and I were simultaneously making fossil discoveries, and by 1970 Doc had discovered the fossilized skull of a new species of turtle, which led Doc to a co-authored paper with Dr. Gaffney for the *American Museum of Natural History Journal*. During the same time period, John Harmala and I put out a report for Mr. Palin's advanced biology class titled "Glendive Area Fossil-Hunting." My big find out on Sand Creek was a tarsometatarsus of a bird from the Late Cretaceous period of time. I first sent the bird bone and a sample of the dirt where I found it to a paleontologist at Texas Tech University who was doing a paper on birds from the time of the dinosaurs—fossils of which are extremely rare. Later the bone and a cast of it were returned to me, and I have since donated the bone (I kept the cast) to the Museum of the Rockies in Montana. I must mention I saw a similar tarsometatarsus fossil on display at the Dinosaur Museum in Dickinson, North Dakota. It looked exactly like the one I found, so it was interesting to see another one from the same geographic area.

John and I worked together putting together an outline, and then John typed up our "GLENDIVE AREA FOSSIL-HUNTING" report for Mr. Palin's class. The report is dated April 3, 1970. Together we presented our report to the class, and after Mr. Palin read through and graded the report he returned it to us with this note:

John and Greg - excellent reports both in class and in the paper. Hope you both continue your avid hunting! Maybe you could write this up slightly differently and send it to Senior Science for publication and donate this to the museum.

A for quarter

John Harmala and Greg Hagenston

GLENDIVE AREA FOSSIL-HUNTING

Advanced Biology

Mr. H. R. Palin

April 3, 1970

A summary of our report follows below.

On the bottom of the PREFACE page of our report, we have a photo attached that John snapped of me as I was overlooking the badlands and planning our route across the canyon.

"PREFACE"

"Here we will show what dinosaurs roamed around Glendive in the Late Cretaceous period, approximately 60 to 80 million years ago. We will show in what areas different types of dinosaurs roamed by utilizing information we have obtained from extensive fossil hunting. We also will give a brief history of how our fossil hunting was started and what we have accomplished through seven years of fossil hunting."

Late spring near amphitheater.

Our first page of script is headed with "BASIC NATURE OF FOSSIL-BEARING STRATA NEAR GLENDIVE." This page is a description of our fossil-hunting area around Glendive and the fossil layer in relation to the strata.

The following thirteen pages are numbered. Page 1.

"EARLY HISTORY OF GLENDIVE AREA FOSSIL HUNTING"

Starting off by recounting the "GLENDIVE BOYS FIND DINOSAUR BONE" event in 1963, the report continues on to say the following: "Geologists from Billings came to Glendive two weeks later and also examined the find. Although the fossil was in no shape to be excavated, it was the first large dinosaur bone ever found in the Makoshika area of the Hell Creek formation. Other smaller fossils had been found previous to this, but this was the find that really opened and published the area to more extensive fossil hunting."

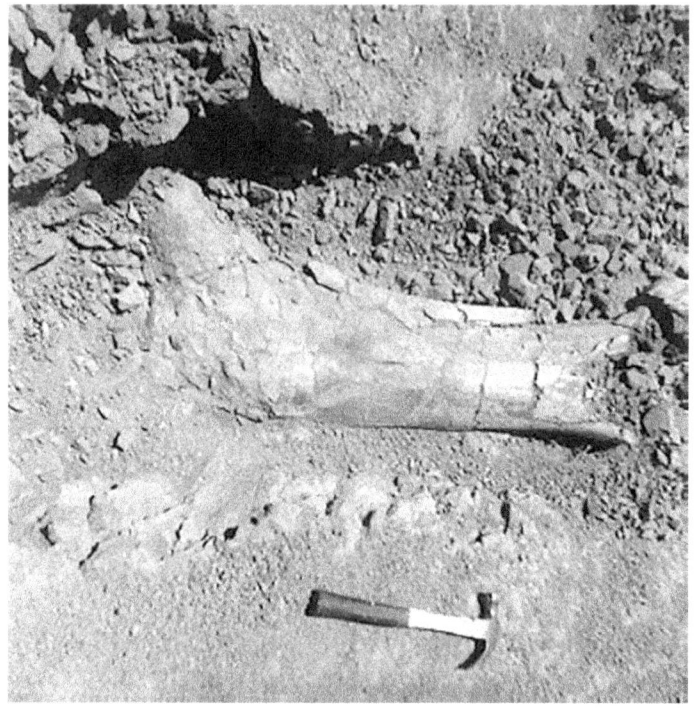

"Our first trips to the fig hill area (more details later), which produced numerous finds of figs, various small bones, and various small vertebrae, were made in 1966 and 1967. Another early find was a hadrosaur jawbone (minus the teeth) that was excavated in June of 1966 by Dr. R. W. Hiatt and Dennis and Greg Hagenston."

Page 2.

"The earlier finds of any consequence were without exception found in the area in the immediate vicinity of the amphitheater; we did very little early hunting below the switchbacks. John Harmala did not move to Glendive until 1964, and thus was not able to participate in the discovery of the hip. On our first hunt of 1967, in early April in the amphitheater area, we attempted to excavate a large bone using the burlap and plaster method. This attempt did not turn out at all and the bone was a total loss. We never used that method again, but instead utilized a totally new concept of wrapping the bone with masking tape. We totally mummified the bone and thus it forms an excellent cast surrounding it. This method has met with great success and we have not lost a bone yet with it."

[This bone was in perfect shape and not exposed until it was discovered by digging with a pick around another bone. While chopping out a pathway with the pointed end of the pickaxe, the pick hit the lower left of this arm bone as seen in the lower left under the tube of glue. After hearing the crunch when the pick connected with the fossil, we carefully excavated the bone.]

⊸∘ᴄ⁄◯∘⊷

"This brings to a close the earlier history of our fossil hunting. Later events will be discussed in the following pages."

Page 3.

"Our naming system for the various fossil-hunting areas around Glendive is purely arbitrary, and is meant to be a fairly accurate description of those areas. For example, the area "Left side of the road to the Switchbacks" includes all ranges in the immediate vicinity of the road from the cattle- guard to the switchbacks. As you can see, it is logical and self-explanatory."

"LEFT SIDE OF THE ROAD TO THE SWITCHBACKS"

"This area has proven to be quite productive, and one of its main attractions is the "fig hill." This first picture shows the hill and the surrounding area. This hill is the only one in the park that has been abundant in its production of figs. Geologists have literally removed bucketfuls of the figs from this hill and yet they can still be found on the hill. There has been some controversy over what these figs really are—they could be a fruit that grows on a mahogany tree, parts from segmented plants, or most likely, figs."

Page 4.

"Small bones from dinosaurs and other assorted reptiles seem to be the most common findings. Larger bones have been found in this place but not as frequently as in other areas. John found our first hadrosaur jawbone with teeth still in it on this side of the road. It was broken in four places but the breaks were clean and it glued together perfectly.

This was the first hadrosaur jawbone ever found with teeth in it in the park."

[It is in view of the "Cross of the Badlands," before you get to the switchbacks in Makoshika, on the left-hand side of the road about halfway up the hill, that John hollers out. He catches my attention; I'm on the same sidehill a ways away, and my first thought is rattlesnake. It was that kind of yell. Or maybe he broke an ankle; with haste I scramble over that way. John is holding something up, pumping his arm up and down. I can see the mud on the object, and the wet bentonite clay over his hand. I stand beside John as he smears the clay off of a small hadrosaur jawbone. He wipes more off to reveal the teeth. This is a fantastic find. I jest to John, "This is preserved so well it looks like roadkill."[6]]

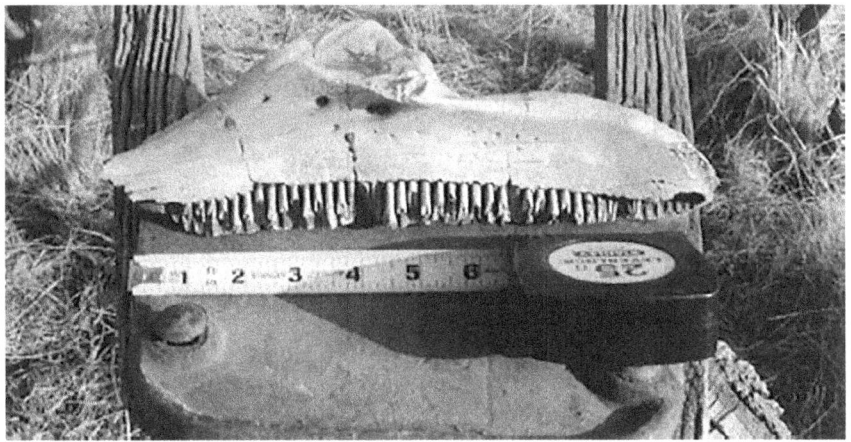

6. The small hadrosaur jawbone was donated and has been on display at Makoshika State Park's visitors' center.

"Another major find was sections of a crocodile jaw. This next picture shows the way back into the place where it was found. This jaw was also found in a number of pieces and had to be soaked in water so that the dirt could be scraped away. Approximately forty teeth were found with thirty of them still intact in the jaws."

Rear entry to place where crocodile jaws were found.

"A pile of assorted vertebrae and other small bones of a champsosaurus were also found in the vicinity, over the last range of hills in the picture shown below, which was taken from on top of the switchbacks. This partial spine included sixteen vertebrae which came from the neck, back and tail of the reptile. This finding was significant in that it helped us to identify more positively vertebrae we had found that resembled those of the champsosaurus."

Page 5.

"We found a lot of garfish bones, scales and vertebrae in this area along with a good small fish jaw that still contained the teeth. We took our first, last, and only whole turtle from the area, with Greg receiving the honors of putting the puzzle back together. We found beyond all doubt what was a turtle's vertebrae inside the shell. This next picture is of Wesley Aardahl excavating a 125-pound hip section. It was discovered in late fall and was taken out in midwinter. It had to be uncovered and the frozen dirt chipped away. After it was taped up and tied on a toboggan, it was hauled out by Wes Aardahl's father, John, and Greg. Needless to say, it was a long, cold, grueling hike."

Wes Aardahl excavating hip section.

⟶⟵

[Wes had a favorite fossil-hunting hill and had invited me along to hike out to "the spot" and check it out. His recollection of the T-Rex hipbone discovery is best delivered in Wes's own words: "I was indeed part of the excavation crew! You and I had been hunting fossils on my favorite hill earlier before the snowfall and we were making our way out via a gulch directly below that hill. I put my hand on a big "rock" to steady myself and noticed that it looked like marrow, to which you responded with something like "Holy Cow! That's a bone!" I think that we scraped away some of the gumbo or somehow tried to mark the spot so that we could find it when we returned. It was close to a little cave. When we did return, joined by Harmala, we had to scrape away snow and hunt awhile to find it. As I recall, the ground had gotten cold enough by then that digging it out was quite an ordeal. You brought loads of masking tape. I have a picture in my head of my dad showing up with the toboggan, but I think that you or John or I must have brought the toboggan. I think that Dad came later, followed our tracks, and that we were surprised to see him. I distinctly remember Harmala's amazement. He said that if it had been his dad he'd have had a heart attack a hundred yards in!"

[Wes continues, "I remember when Dr. Hiatt came to my house to see the bone. He said it was the biggest bone to come out of Makoshika. He was mystified by it, but had a book with him that he began paging through. On one of the pages was a photo of a T-Rex skeleton and it was from that photo that he identified the bone as the "ilium to the pelvic girdle."

[An update on Wes Aardahl's Tyrannosaurus hip bone: Eventually, Wes and his dad donated the bone to Frontier Gateway Museum. After many years of neglect and exposure to the elements in the back of a wagon out at the museum, Wes rescued or as he says "re-possessed" the fossil, and it has been in his safekeeping until he can be assured it can be safely displayed and studied. Wes has named his pelvic fossil "Illy." I have invited "Illy" back home and promised inside seating.]

Page 6.

"AREA ON THE RIGHT SIDE OF THE ROAD TO THE SWITCHBACKS"

"This area has been productive in both larger bones and smaller material. We have picked out several spots where the fossil deposits are better than average, and these are the places we return to most often. The largest Tyrannosaurus rex tooth ever found in the Glendive area was taken from this place. The tooth measures six inches long and was found in fairly decent shape. A mammal tooth, which is a very rare find, was discovered with a small piece of jaw still intact and clinging to it. This tooth is in the best condition of all the mammal teeth found in the park, although it is not of the rarest type. On our first trip to this area we netted a large assortment of fossils. We took out a femur, tibia, a large chunk of triceratops frill, and a large assortment of teeth and smaller vertebrae."

Greg with fossil assortment

<<>>

[Update on the T-Rex tooth and the mammal tooth: Dr. Hiatt had gained valuable knowledge on early mammals and was able to identify our mammal tooth as one of the more common types found in the park. The first mammal teeth he found were by sifting the sand from an anthill. He tells of sending them back East to a paleontologist for identification and was pleased with the information he received about the teeth and was then dismayed when the scientist thanked him for the samples. Dr. Hiatt was very frustrated about not having his mammal teeth returned to him. My luck with the one and only mammal tooth I ever found was no better. I sent it with my son to a grade school show-and-tell, taped to a small cardboard display along with a sequoia cone, and samples of turtle shell, small vertebra, garfish scales, and other assorted small fossils. When Stanley returned home with the display after school, the mammal tooth was missing. The cardboard display had been passed from desk to desk for the kids to look at, and who knows what happened to the tooth. The fate of the T-Rex tooth is worse yet! I remember the day I discovered the big tooth. It was already exposed to the weather, just lying on its side with the enamel in place but cracked. I didn't dare move it in its present condition, so I coated the exposed side with Duco cement and let the glue dry before I safely extracted the tooth.

[A pack of Boy Scouts stopped by my house one afternoon and asked to look at fossils. I passed around my prized specimens and then was distracted by a young scout asking about another bone on display in the old glass cabinet in the living room. The glass display case was originally from the hardware store and had been stored in the warehouse since the new fixtures were installed in the store sometime in the 1950s. It made the perfect fossil display case. When the coast had cleared and the scouts had all left, I carefully placed the fossils back into the glass display. To my dismay the six-inch Tyrannosaurus rex tooth was missing along with a smaller tooth that had great enamel with perfect serrations on the edges. Needless to say I was very disappointed with the scouts. One of the boys came up to me at a church dinner a year or so later and said he knew who had the big tooth. Several of the boys were hanging around together, but as soon as I was informed, they all scattered. It was sometime later I discovered several sections of crocodile jaw with teeth turned up missing. The scouts were not responsible for this loss. My problem was not having a lock on my display case. The fossils were just too tempting.]

"On March 10, 1968 we excavated another large femur from the same general area, which you can see in the accompanying picture."

"In the first picture on the next page you can see the bone with its toe ends partially taped. The aluminum foil was put around the bone before the tape so that the fragile surface would not stick to the tape. The second picture on the next page shows the bone as it is ready to be carried home on a stretcher. The streaks in the picture are snow, as it was quite cold on the day of the excavation."

Page 7.

March 10, 1968

⸺∘◦⟨⟩◦∘⸺

[This is the only fossil my parents came out to look at during excavation. They hiked up the hill far enough to view the partially uncovered bone in the sidehill. As far as they were concerned I was just digging out a rock. They had no interest, no questions; they just tolerated my goofy hobby. At the time, John and I had not yet brought out the stretcher for our careful removal of the prepared fossil. Had my dad seen it he would have probably asked about where I got the rug to cradle the bones on the stretcher. Well, from the warehouse of course. I always scoured through things stored away at the warehouse to find what I needed. Nobody else was ever going to use that excess stuff once it found its way to the warehouse. This Persian rug is from Grandma and Grandpa Hagenston's stuff. Grandpa had died and Grandma is never going to use it anyway. The bigger rolled-up Persian rug, I have my eye on for future use. Surprisingly, years later my dad did ask me about what happened to the big antique rug. It was too late by then: Roger, Pat, and I had already used it for the deck of our four-barrel raft we floated up at Fort Peck. The raft named *"G R P Cantippi"* is another story, or at least another chapter.]

⸺∘◦⟨⟩◦∘⸺

"The excavation of a large fragile fossil such as this is just the first part of the long process of getting it ready for display. After it is home and safely resting on a workbench or table, the tape has to be carefully removed. When removing the tape, it is best to start at one end and completely unravel that end, and then continue the process down the length of the bone to the other end. As this is done all loose pieces must be glued to the surface of the bone. This particular bone sucked up some fifteen large tubes of Duco cement. It was successfully reconstructed and looks just as it did in the hill, but it cannot be moved because of its extreme fragility. In this same vicinity Greg successfully took out the largest triceratops femur yet found in Makoshika. This bone is complete and weighs approximately ninety pounds. Quite a large assortment of triceratops and hadrosaur teeth have been found in this area along with small vertebrae from various ancient reptiles."

[The large triceratops femur disguised itself as a bone chip on the narrow trail. I walked past it several times as I was going back and forth across the hillside surveying for fossils. When in a fossil area, miscellaneous bone chips can be a common occurrence. Once a fossil has become exposed from natural erosion, the hairline cracks in the bone expand and the fossil naturally breaks apart. Sometimes if a bone is on a level area the pieces can be recovered and fitted back together; however, in most cases the breakup happens on a hillside and the fragments become impossibly scattered. The bleached fossil I keep walking over is only three or four inches long and slightly imbedded in the sand and clay. There are no other bone chips or fossils in the immediate vicinity so I have little interest in this indistinguishable lump of bone—just barely enough to give it a kick off the trail as I walk past. Oops, it didn't move when I kicked it, so I dig along the edge with the sole of my shoes and nudge it again. It still doesn't move. I get down on my knees and dig beside it with the tip of my fossil hammer and then get out the screwdriver to scrape along the edge as I follow the contour of the bone below the surface of the ground. By now I'm thinking maybe this is the edge of a vertebrae I'm scraping around. I continue to scrape and dig, scrape and dig and brush with the whisk broom and paintbrush. I am oblivious to my surroundings as I carefully carve clay and dig away, now into the hillside. The dinosaur ribs I saw sticking out below a seam of hard sandstone around the hill a ways will have to wait. I have to see what I'm digging out. Three hours go by and I have a small cave carved into the hillside with no end of the bone in sight. It's time for me to go, so I pack up and head home. Several days later I have time to get back up and around the hill to my project, now determined to dig to the end of the bone. Finally, after another three hours of chipping away with my rock hammer and screwdriver, I carved away the hard clay around the end of the femur. This thing is at least three feet long and very well preserved: just one break through the middle. After more hours of tedious work, I get both pieces of bone taped up for transport.

["Hey, Greg," I hear. It's Pat—he saw my vehicle parked along the road and he hiked up to see if he could find me. "Pat, you got any water? I'm parched." Gazing across the horizon towards the Yellowstone River, he replies, "No, but I know where there is some." We know each other well enough that nothing else needs to be said. Together we momentarily look off in the direction of the river, and then in tandem we're off. It's about two miles to the Yellowstone River, as the crow flies. Down the clay butte we climb, then across a broad grassy valley and then up and over another range of badlands, and this time across a narrower grass valley. One more range of badlands to cross and I hesitate. It's hard to be going over new territory without taking time to prospect for fossils. To keep up with Pat, I have to keep moving. My eyes lock on fragments of a large vertebrae, just lying on the surface. Sixty-five million years of protection encased in the clay, only to be eroded to sand and dust in the blink of a geologic eye. The bone calls to me but I keep going—we are on a mission. Down off this range of clay buttes, we get to the Marsh Road and cross it. Through the woods and we finally arrive at our destination. We wade out into the current, but it is too swift and too deep for us to make it all the way to the island. Standing parallel in the current thirty yards apart, in nearly waist-deep water with firm footing on the gravel river bottom, we both bend at the waist, and like livestock, suck into our bellies a cool, clear, hearty drink of Yellowstone River water. Now with our thirst quenched, we stand there in the water, feeling the current working at our feet and legs. Underwater below the waist, and dripping wet from the waist up, the two of us stay where we are for moments, just taking it all in. We don't want this to end: *this is the life!*

[Grudgingly, we snap to reality and turn back to the riverbank to begin our trek to the fossil femur. Back through the woods, over the badlands, across the small valley, over the badlands again and back across the big valley, up three-quarters of the last range of badlands and we are there. Pat and I each take a section of bone, and while cradling the beast in our arms we hike around the hill and back down to where we are parked on the Makoshika road. Even though we are on the Makoshika road, the land we were prospecting on belongs to Mr. Dowson, and he couldn't care less about anybody hiking in his badlands. Once back home I found a steel bar, and with the help of multiple tubes of Duco cement I used the bar to pin the two sections of femur together, which fit perfectly. After cleaning off the surface and applying a couple coats of varnish, the huge femur is prepared for display.]

Page 8.

"AMPHITHEATER COUNTRY"

"The amphitheater country which includes everything from the switchbacks to the transmitter roads and the second set of switchbacks, has proven to be more productive in large bones than in smaller fossils. The first hadrosaur jaw to be taken out of Makoshika was found in this vicinity. This picture shows Greg and his brother in the final stage of the plaster process, which is the method that most authorities recommend for amateur paleontologists. This process involves placing a plaster cast around the fossil so that it can be taken out without breakage. Equipment for this process includes pre-cut burlap strips, newspapers for wrapping the bone, shellac or varnish, water, plaster, plastic gloves, and a large plastic mixing bowl. This process is not always successful due to the fact that the plaster can easily be mixed wrong. We have found that wide masking tape does the job better and is much less weight to carry to the site of excavation. This method has been much more successful with all of our bones so far."

Page 9.

"This is a picture (immediately below) of Dr. Hiatt and Greg fossil hunting in the amphitheater country."

The back of Dr. Hiatt's bald head is in the foreground.

"In the next picture (lower right corner) John is posing with a large section of a triceratops brow horn."

"Close to the amphitheater itself, the longest line of vertebrae from one dinosaur is found. A positive fifteen vertebrae were uncovered by the removal of the sandstone in which they were encased. Only two of these fragile pyrite vertebrae were successfully taken out. Along with the vertebrae, ribs and some of the tendons were also preserved. A section of tendon was removed that was eleven inches long. We believe that the rest of the dinosaur follows the sandstone shelf and disappears into the hill. But the steepness of the hill and the hard sandstone covering will prevent us from making any further attempts at unearthing this dinosaur."

[We have been hiking in the badlands heat for hours. Earlier John and I headed off in different directions to cover more ground. After a while I start back toward John to see how his prospecting is going. I haven't found any fossils; maybe my pal is having better luck. I round the corner of a hill and I see John sitting on a rock ledge. His head is hanging in exhaustion. I approach, asking, "How's the fossil hunting? "Nothing," John says. "It's a bad area." I get closer and to put it mildly, I'm stunned. This is one of the most exciting moments of our fossil hunting together, unbeknownst to John. He is so weary he is not aware of the dinosaur rib bones protruding out of the dirt beneath and around his feet. The rock ledge John is sitting on encases the backbone of a dinosaur. Quickly recovering from our fatigue, we carefully peel back a chunk of the hard sandstone ledge and discover two vertebrae. With a lot of meticulous work over a period of time, we unearthed fifteen fused vertebrae. With it being impossible to recover soft bone encased in hard sandstone, we preserved the first two vertebrae with a lot of Duco cement and tender loving care and took some photos of the rest.

[I consider this John's find, since he was the first human to sit on this dinosaur backbone. He took the fused two-vertebrae home and did an excellent professional job of restoration. Later when John was heading off to college he brought the bones to me for safekeeping.

[A decade and a half passes, and daughter Angie and I attend one of Doc Hiatt's Makoshika field trips. Cradling my young daughter in one arm and with fossil hammer in the other for balance, we skip and hop down the canyon to catch up with the group of Hiatt's adult students. He proudly shows the group his discovery of a row of vertebrae leading into the hill. It was quite the discovery, and I am glad he shared our earlier find with his students.]

Page 10.

"This picture (below) shows an interesting red scoria-topped hill. It is the highest point in that area of the park and the scoria marks the start of the Fort Union formation."

"Big Red"

[Mike, John, and I, now old enough to drive, head out on a warm summer day to camp out in Makoshika at our favorite spot, Pine-on-Rock vista point. After hastily setting up camp we take one look at the red top butte across the valley and we're off like jackrabbits down the canyon and over to the base of the butte. The heat of the day and lack of better judgment to bring our water bag or canteen doesn't stop us from our goal of surmounting the peak. By the time we reach the base of "Big Red," we are sunbaked. However, to turn back now would be to admit defeat, so we all make it to the top. Now, severely dehydrated, we trudge back. John was really done in—he barely made it to camp. Of course hindsight is 20-20, but we regret we didn't take our water bag along on the hike.

[It's fun sitting out at night around the campfire looking at the stars. Mike is startled! Zigzagging completely across the sky is a UFO. Spooked, we all crawl in our sleeping bags for the night. Mike is up in the dark of the night to visit the bushes and is greeted by the frightful sound of a rattlesnake in front of his feet. It's one of those unforgettable nights.[7]]

7. Recollections of Mike McCrate

"The amphitheater country is known to us as the only area in Makoshika with a hill of sequoia cones. In one trip to the area we found 55 of these fossil plant cones, along with numerous seedlike fossils, which at this time are unidentified.

"All through the park petrified wood can be found, but the amphitheater area is known for the largest chunks, which appear to be huge parts of upper root sections of ancient trees."

Page 11.

"RADIO ROAD COUNTRY"

"This area, past the second set of switchbacks, is known chiefly for larger bones. It is a difficult area to hunt because one must drop down to the bottom of the canyon from the switchbacks to get to the fossil layers. Below is a picture of what the country is generally like."

"GRAVEYARD CANYON"

"This area which is in the vicinity of the local sanitary landfill is a favorite spot for earth science field hikers. It is productive in a wide variety of small fossils. Two pachycephalosaurus head ornaments have been found in the area, in addition to three large vertebrae fused together. It is interesting to note that when vertebrae are found fused together, this means the dinosaur's particular vertebrae were fused in life."

Page 12.

"SAND CREEK"

"Sand Creek, which is a relatively new area, has produced an assortment of larger fossils. The largest conglomeration of bones from one dinosaur found in this part of the Hell Creek formation turned up in this area. It included four hadrosaur jaws with teeth, a hadrosaur humerus (upper arm bone), a hadrosaur shoulder blade, along with several vertebrae and rib sections. Other bones and probably the remainder of the skull are still in the hill but have not been excavated as yet. Several hadrosaur jaws—some with teeth and some without—have been found in other parts of the Sand Creek area. A basioccipital bone and a shoulder blade of a triceratops were also found in the vicinity. Some strange hollow-birdlike toe bones, probably from ornithomimus, were also found in the Sand Creek area."

[John and I had driven "the yellow pickup" out to Sand Creek. The two- wheel-drive Chevrolet pickup is the delivery pickup for Sam Kuntz, the appliance repairman at Hagenston Hardware. When not in service at the store, I used the truck for my personal transportation. About eleven miles out on the Sand Creek road there is a trail off of the main road that leads to a windmill. We plan to drive off the main road and follow the service road to get us a lot closer to the badland breaks. After we bounce the pickup off the main road and slowly jostle our way across a dry sandy creek and over the trail to the windmill, we park the pickup and take off to the badlands to do some prospecting. This new area is easy to hunt in since the layer that contains fossils is relatively close to ground level. We didn't have to hike down in a deep canyon or way up near the top of the hills to be in the right layer of strata. After several hours of prospecting we turn back to the pickup, disappointed with the dearth of fossils in this area. Dusk is right around the corner, so it's time to call it a day. And then right before I climb down off of the last gumbo knob to get to the pasture, I spot a cluster of bones. They blend in so well with the surface gravel—the stains on the bones take on the same color as the iron pyrite gravel on the surface of the gumbo—that one has to have a well-trained eye to spot the fossils. Most people would walk right across this boneyard without ever knowing it was there. Upon inspection of the broken small bones I can see they are hollow, and there are numerous toe bones lying on the surface. Of those that have fractured I also confirm the toe bones are hollow. This is the largest conglomeration of ornithomimus bones I have ever seen in one location. It would take a lot of tedious work to excavate this ostrich-like dinosaur. I consider this a significant find, but it's now time to get back to the pickup and head for home—it will be dark soon. John and I toss our packs in the truck, fire it up, and work our way back to the main road. Heading to the sandy creek bottom, I take it slow off the short drop to the creek bed. And as I drive across the sand I notice we are not moving. This sand is deceiving, for right underneath the dry surface is greasy mud that quickly becomes quicksand as the tires spin and I rock the truck back and forth. John and I get out to inspect and it's hopeless: we are stuck. We grab a flashlight from the truck; I have my fossil hammer in its holster on my hip, and other than that, since we don't have any water left, it's going to be a long dry hike home. Of course there is no traffic and the air is cool, which helps. We trudge down the road, first in the dusk and soon in the dark of night. Pitch-black you might say, when you can't see your hand in front of your face. I use the flashlight sparingly to save the already weak batteries. After hours of stumbling down the road we are finally getting closer to the Marsh Road, which will bring us to about four miles from home. We are probably still a mile or more from the Marsh Road and I am in the lead; John has fallen back a hundred yards or more, but still making way. And now I spot taillights on a parked vehicle up ahead. I get within shouting distance, turn on the flashlight, and holler out to the vehicle. I get closer; it looks like a little red car but I can't really make out the color very well in the dark. I shout out, "Hey, hello!" The engine fires up and it lurches ahead, then starts to drive off. I start jogging behind the vehicle, waving my flashlight and hollering, "Wait! Stop! Help!" It slowly pulls ahead, leaving me and my flashlight that no longer shines, only glows, back in the dust. The flashlight batteries are dead. John and I feel about the same way. We finally make our way to the Marsh Road and turn towards town. It's two o'clock in the morning when we get close to a small farmhouse. My parents are out of town, so our plan is to call John's dad to come and give us a ride home. John is too chicken to knock on the door and ask to use a phone at this time of night, so I do it. I pound on the door. Nothing. Maybe I should try the back door. As I head around the house I glance through the picture window and notice someone sleeping on a couch. I rap on the window and the person gets up and staggers into another room; looks like he is sleepwalking. I give up. It's on to the next farmhouse. It's now about three o'clock in the morning, and after a brief argument I prevail and it's John's turn. I stay out by a corral and John walks up to the house. Jess Engle's dogs start barking up a fit, and after a while John returns with good news. His dad is on his way to pick us up. His folks had been worried sick when we didn't return home by dark. Let's put it this way: they were glad and mad at the same time. As Cliff Harmala gives us a ride home, my thoughts drift back to the sight of Jess stumbling out of his house wearing a bathrobe or a trench coat flapping in the breeze, to see what in the world the dogs are having such a fit about. Cliff dropped me off at home; my parents have made it back from their trip and are in bed sleeping. Somehow I have to explain to Dad what happened to the store pickup, so I wrote him a note, put it on the kitchen table, and then I went up to bed.

DAD

I got the Pickup Stuck out on Sand Creek. It's on the road in a creek with wet sand.

It's about 10 miles out. We walked back to a phone and John's dad came and picked us up. I think a winch will pull it out because it isn't stuck too bad. Greg[8]

[In the morning, Dad of course was not happy. He asked if I wanted to try and pull it out with the Jeep. Then I had to tell him about the Jeep. I was hoping he had not noticed it was missing. I had been out cutting up some of Grandpa Knauff's cedar fence posts for firewood and I had it stuck with all four tires buried in the mud out by Grandpa's old grain shed behind Mastvelton's house. Kent Dion and I were planning to go out and jack up the tires, put boards under them, and then drive quickly back to the road. I was hoping to have that done before Dad noticed the Jeep was not at home.

[So the pickup was my problem. I called Hilger Chevrolet and the service manager, Bruce Bartholomew, said he could pull it out for either $32.00 or $38.00. I can't remember which was the exact figure, but in either case it was a small fortune to me, but I had to do it. To my surprise, Bruce was the one that drove me out in the winch truck to pull it out. I think he enjoyed getting out of the shop for an afternoon.

8. My mother saved the note.

[The ornithomimus remains in its resting place; it's been there for sixty-five million years and I doubt anyone will ever find it. I could if I went back, but I don't plan to; I've got the feeling that it wants to be left alone.]

"In the following final pages we will show pictures of various fossils, excavations, and general scenery of the Sand Creek fossil area."

Good fossil country

Notice our stretcher upper right, under the ridge of sandstone rocks.

[Up there somewhere is Cliff Harmala's pick we borrowed. John said his dad wanted it back. Many years later the remnants of the rotted-out stretcher were still visible. Eventually, I recovered the pick and carried it out. The handle is rotten and the pick head just falls off. Unfortunately, Cliff Harmala died years ago so I can't give it back. John doesn't live here anymore, so I keep the old rusty pick head with the rotten handle under a window in "The Buffalo Room," which is also my man cave, fossil room, and extra bedroom. So far, neither my wife, nor our kids when they come home to visit, have asked me why I keep an old rusty pick in the "Buffalo Room." Besides the buffalo head mount and a big wall display case full of fossils, the pick just kind of blends in with the other oddities in my room. If they ever do ask me why the pick is there, the answer is: *Never mind, it's special.*]

Large vertebra

Hadrosaur shoulder blade and jawbones

[I trot up the office steps to Dr. Hiatt's office, excited to tell him the latest. The hadrosaur jawbone I had been working on in the field was encased in hard sandstone. Unlike fossils uncovered in sandy clay, the sandstone won't chip off around this bone. I will have to carry out the fossil jawbone encased in its sandstone sheath. It's a good thing I am in shape, because this thing is heavy. I cradle it in my arms like I am holding a baby, and step by step climb up to the top of the hill. I have to get across the top and then it's quite a climb downhill to my vehicle—but at least it's downhill. Going down is an old game trail to follow, and John and I have the route pretty well memorized. We could walk it with our eyes closed. On the hike up that trail, we were never able to make it all the way without stopping for a breather before we get to the top. Across the dome should be easygoing, except I can't see where I'm stepping with this big fossil in my arms blocking my view. It's rough ground with sagebrush clumps and sinkholes.

When I'm packing only my fossil bag across my shoulder, plus sometimes a water bag and carrying my fossil hammer out of its sheath when the going is rough, I normally have no problem hopping and skipping across the pitfalls, sinkholes, and sagebrush clumps. But now I'm blindly stumbling along trying to feel my footing as I go. My mouth is agape as I gulp air to keep my lungs up to par with my exertions. And then suddenly down I go, flat on my face. Like a mother holding a child, my only concern is what I have in my arms. There is not much time to react when falling flat down, except to keep my arms under the cluster of rock and fossil to make the landing as soft as possible. After the dust clears I struggle to get myself in position to inspect the damage, and to my delight there is none. The fossil is totally unharmed thanks to my skinned-up forearms that protected its fall. And then I see the blood. Right on an exposed row of hadrosaur teeth there is a blotch of red. When I fell, my face smashed down on top of the jawbone, splitting my lip.

[Like a champion prizefighter proud of his fat lip, I exclaim to Doc, "I am the only person I know of that's ever been bitten by a hadrosaur!" We both have a hearty laugh.]

Page 13. "CONCLUSIONS"
"We are able to predict with a reasonable amount of certainty, based on our own fossil-hunting experiences, what might be found in certain areas around Glendive. But since all the fossils were deposited and preserved over such a long period of time and over such a wide area, it is impossible to be able to tell <u>exact</u>ly what will be found."

Old Duke posing with dinosaur bone.

John Harmala in front of Dr. Hiatt's house with a triceratops
shoulder blade.

Fossils are not the only discoveries we make. The badlands are so interesting in many ways. Whole hillsides will crack and slowly over the years slide away, leaving a lopsided prairie that was once part of a flat plateau now growing on a slope. One such area we hike across has deep cracks all around, and peering in we can see the wet clay. There is a complete bleached white horse skeleton laid out below some sagebrush. It's been there awhile; there are no signs of skin or hide, just the bones. It is unusual to see a complete skeleton in this condition, without having been disassembled and dragged away by the predators. However what shocks us most is the size of the sagebrush on this slope. The angle of the sun, the moisture on the roots deep in the crevasse, and the juices from the dead horse are the perfect combination to create a giant sage. Standing there in the shadow of this plant, we feel like little men in the land of Lilliput. The moment is enchanting.

The sandstone formations that make these badlands so unique sometimes seem to be designed by an architect. John calls my attention to a rock wall. We are on a high ridge below a big plateau overlooking a green valley—a valley that will soon take on a golden cast as the prairie grasses dry out in the summer heat. This is not an easy location to get to, there are no trails, it's quite a ways from a road and a difficult climb. This rock wall, however, was not designed by nature. The stones had been placed in a semicircle overlooking the valley. It is puzzling; we drop our side packs and take a much-needed break. It's such a nice view, I step back and snap a photo of John sitting on the stacked stones. After a bit we gather our gear and head back to a fossil layer in the strata. As we are leaving I have to holler to the dog. "Come on, Duke, let's go." Duke is frantically digging with his front paws—he is on to something. The dirt is flying and the dog won't listen to me as I call again, "Duke, Duuuke!" He lifts his head out of the pawed earth behind the semicircle of stones, shaking the dirt off of a white bone. "Come on, dog, let's go." I grab the flat white bone from the dog's jaws and give it a toss. Looked like a shoulder blade but I didn't take one second to look at it before I propelled it off the bluff with a flick of my wrist. John inquires and I tell him about the bone. "Must be from a deer."

We visit the site a couple more times—it's one of our special spots. One of the last times I saw John before he went off to college, he told me he had been back to the rock wall and he seemed quite irritated. I asked him what's wrong and he said, "You know." I said, "Know what?" He asks me, "Why'd you kick it down?" Well, I didn't kick it down, and I'm not sure if John really believes me. It is puzzling. We have never seen any footprints up there, other than ours. I investigated the wall at a later date and was as dismayed as John. The top layers had been knocked off, so I found some of the sandstone blocks and crudely placed them back in position, however not as good as the original placement.

Over the years I occasionally would run across the photo of John sitting on the rock wall, and in rethinking the events that took place I now wonder if the semicircle of stones was a burial site and if the bones could have been human.

On July 25, 2009, with the help of a photocopied picture, daughter Sarah and I rediscovered what was left of the tumbled down rock wall. It took some effort to be sure we were in the correct location. It was the layers in the badlands behind John in the photo that we were able to match up by looking across the gorge and comparing to the picture. While on our hike we observed several large outcrops of dinosaur bones. Again, to the untrained eye, most people would simply walk by, not noticing the bones have taken on the stained colors of the surrounding rocks. Sarah set her fossil hammer down someplace, probably when we were taking photos, and it too will eventually take on the stained color of the surrounding rocks, probably never to be discovered. To our amazement, a monarch butterfly, out of nowhere, flew up and landed on Sarah's shirt. After a brief rest, it lit off again to continue its journey. What a delight! Interestingly, Sarah discovered a 1967 Roosevelt dime at the rock wall. It's amazing she spotted the dime, since the silver had tarnished itself black and it too blended in with the surface stones. The day became quite hot and with our water bottles drained dry, the last leg of our hike across the top stratum was just about too much for me and my old dog Maude. The younger Sarah fared much better and at the last quarter mile hiked ahead for more water, which saved the day.

It's not just the fossils or the spectacular landscape of Makoshika that can stir a person to appreciate natural beauty, as relayed in a short anecdote shared with me by Dr. Hiatt. He tells of fossil hunting deep in a Makoshika canyon on a stifling hot summer day. Later in the afternoon before dusk when the sun is low in the sky, on the hike back up to where his car is parked, he says, "I was so dry I couldn't even spit." He tells of nearing the top of the ridge and looking up to see an unbelievable sight. As he is telling this story to me, his voice changes and becomes rich and booming. He exclaims, "I looked up and saw the MOST SPECTACULAR sky I've ever seen! The deep vibrant colors— it's hard to explain—just the sight made me feel close to God."

Avis Anderson explains it best in her writings. She describes "the thin spaces" as: "there are times in our lives when the veil between heaven and earth is very thin, when God is closer than we realize."

I too will experience this phenomenon of "thin spaces" in a dramatic event that I must say was the most profound moment of my life, but it needs to be told in the proper sequence. I'll have to share that experience with you in PART II of *Greg and Doc*.

It is June of 1971; we graduated from high school last year and Pat and I have decided to take a trip. Patrick Allen Norton likes to be referred to as P.

A. Norton, but to me he is Pat. His nickname is Claw, mine is Hogason, and we are going to drive to Texas to see Richard Rawl. Richard graduated with us, has moved to Texas to go to college, and is currently working for Texas Instruments back in the warehouse. Richard is a Baptist, and when called on to preach, can give a good sermon. His nickname is Brother Rawl. We also plan to swing by Tulsa, Oklahoma, to see Mike McCrate and his wife Wanda. Mike's nickname is Muckrow.

We embark on our trip, driving my Ford Pinto. I can tell you a couple things about that car: It had a black vinyl interior with no air-conditioning. The seats in the Pinto are very uncomfortable, causing great misery and the constant shifting of one's seating position.

On the way to Wyoming, driving at night we get into a construction area. There are no workers; the site is completely shut down and the signage is terrible. We are detouring the way we think we are supposed to and drive up onto new asphalt. As I speed down the nice smooth road that will soon become new highway, I realize there is no other traffic, no shoulder, no stripes, no reflectors. It finally dawns on me that we are not supposed to be driving on this unfinished highway. Stressed, we find our way back to the right road.

Denver traffic was not something we are accustomed to, and panic sets in when we get to an intersection with four lanes coming from all directions. Who knows what the signal indicated as we did what comes naturally in a crisis situation like this. We stomped on it, winced, gritted our teeth, and somehow made it through without a scratch. We are glad to get out of the Big City.

Camping is easy for us: we find a spot to pull over and flop out our sleeping bags. We are used to sleeping on hard ground—so much so we prefer it. The sleeping bags have a lot of little burned holes in them from sleeping a little too close to a campfire. Cottonwood fuel was never a problem, but if we had a piece of cedar in the fire it will pop and spit, and that's where the sparks come from that burn the pinholes in the sleeping bags.

On the way to Oklahoma it got up to 110 degrees in Kansas, and with no air-conditioning in the Pinto with a black interior it is unbearable.

We pull into a Kansas gas station and purchase a bag of ice. When we get to Enid, Oklahoma, we have a nice visit with Mike and Wanda. Mike is working for the New Holland dealership and was moving equipment when we found him. Tongue in cheek, I ask Mike to show me the "Dust Bowl." We stayed overnight in their bungalow and the next day headed for Texas.

By the time we get to Dallas, due to our lack of personal hygiene, we are getting a little ripe. Our daily cleanup consists of brushing our teeth once a day with the canteen water. We are ready for a bath. The first exit to Dallas pulls us down a ramp to some magnificent fountains colored by spotlights right in front of a Hyatt Hotel. It looks good to us. We are overwhelmed at how fancy this place is, and the price for a room is outrageous, but we have hardly spent any money so far on our trip, so what the heck. There is no place to heat up our pork and beans in the room—we usually have a campfire—so I guess we'll just eat them cold.

After we get cleaned up and refreshed it's time to call Richard Rawl. Using the hotel phone and a phone book, we look up the number to the college he is attending and I make a call. "Hello, is Richard there?" "Who?" "Richard, Richard Rawl." "Don't know um." *Click*. Well, that's the pits. We don't know how to get ahold of Richard; I guess tomorrow we will pack it up and head for Colorado.

I don't know how we found the road, but Pikes Peak here we come. It's now nightfall and we drive up and up and up the mountain, as far as you can go. We didn't see any scenery—it was pitch-black out—but we drove up and back down Pikes Peak that night.

After lots of sweat and long hours of driving, we discovered the Green River Canyon. We drove down into the canyon and camped by the river. I remember seeing some rafters go by. What a magnificent canyon!

Not far from Vernal, Utah, we visit the Dinosaur National Monument. Again, it's been numerous hot, sweaty days with smoky evening campfires and no bath. We never even thought about washing our clothes on the trip. People keep a wide berth as we stand in amazement watching the paleontologists working on carefully exposing the dinosaur bones on the sidehill in the Exhibit Hall Quarry. Having not shaved for days, we look scruffy. As we watch the scientists working away, I mention to Pat I'm thinking about going into paleontology. He suggests I talk to somebody here; after all, I'm in the right place. I feel my scratchy face, look at my dirty clothes, and notice the people going by us nearly holding their noses. Pat wanders off, giving me time to think. I watch the paleontologists intently, and I start thinking about what it's going to take to get into this field of study. I recall conversations with some of the paleontologists that have come to Glendive to see Dr. Hiatt. Every one of them said they loved the fieldwork the best, but seldom had the pleasure. Most of their work and study is done in the lab. I track down Pat; let's go, time to head for Cooke City and do a little trout fishing. Pat asks me if I talked to the paleontologists. "No, I decided not to."

Little did I know that in 1963, the year I became a fossil hunter, Dr. Hiatt made notes about Dinosaur National Monument, the place I'm now standing at. Even though this is the time and place I make my decision not to pursue study in the field of paleontology, I know that during the seven years I spent as a fossil hunter, I was in my element, doing what I love to do, surrounded by badlands.

Adventures and discoveries in the badlands were a large part of our lives, and more excitement is yet to come in part II of *Greg and Doc*.

References

Newspapers:

Billings Gazette

Glendive Ranger-Review

Wibaux Pioneer Gazette

Corpus Christi Caller-Times

National Geographic Magazine

Montana Historical Society

Books:

Crazy Horse and Chief Red Cloud
2004 by Ed McGaa, J.D.

Our Times Our Lives
Dawson County Montana 1889-1989
Artcraft Printers, Billings, Montana. 1989

Land of NAKODA
By James L Long
2004, Riverbend Publishing

An Uncommon Journey
2009, By H. Norman Hyatt

A Hard Won Life
2014, By H. Norman Hyatt

As I Remember, Volume I
Stories of Eastern Montana Pioneers
2006, Gladys Kauffman

As I Remember, Volume II
Stories of Eastern Montana's Pioneers
2006, Gladys Kauffman

Buffalo Nation
2007 by the Board of Regents
Of the University of Nebraska
Ken Zontek

To The Gates of Richmond
The Peninsula Campaign
1992, Stephen W. Sears

Encounters at the Heart
Of the World
A history of the Mandan people
2014, Elizabeth A.Fenn

Journal of an Expedition to the
Mauvaises Terres and the
Upper Missouri in 1850
2015, Forgotten Books
Thaddeus Culbertson

Sioux Code Talkers
Of World War II
2917, Andrea M. Page

www.ingramcontent.com/pod-product-compliance
Lightning Source LLC
Chambersburg PA
CBHW051133120626
46547CB00012B/781